Mesopotamia 1914-15
Extracts from a Regimental
Officer's Diary

Fatigue Parties building 'Dams to hold up Floods at Mazera, February 1915.

Mesopotamia 1914-15 Extracts from a Regimental Officer's Diary

With the Oxfordshire & Buckinghamshire Light Infantry during the First World War

ILLUSTRATED

H. Birch Reynardson

Mesopotamia 1914-15
Extracts from a Regimental Officer's Diary
With the Oxfordshire & Buckinghamshire Light Infantry during the First World War
by H. Birch Reynardson

ILLUSTRATED

First published under the title
Mesopotamia 1914-15

Leonaur is an imprint of Oakpast Ltd
Copyright in this form © 2019 Oakpast Ltd

ISBN: 978-1-78282-808-2 (hardcover)
ISBN: 978-1-78282-809-9 (softcover)

http://www.leonaur.com

Publisher's Notes

The views expressed in this book are not necessarily those of the publisher.

Contents

Acknowledgements and Preface	7
The Beginning of Things	15
November 1914	23
December 1914	39
Basra	54
17th Brigade Move to Mazera	63
January 1915	80
February 1915	87
Transport Difficulties	99
March 1915	110
April 1915	121
April and May 1915	136
May-June 1915	150
Enemy Movement on the Tigris	163
July and August 1915	180
September 1915	199
Kut and Its Conquerors	210
On the March	223
The Battlefield	234

First Sight of the Arch	239
The End of the Year	248
Lionel Muirhead's Letter to Henry Birch Reynardson & Book Reviews at Time of Original Publication	271

Acknowledgements and Preface

When the present publishers discovered this book, written by Henry Birch Reynardson within a comprehensive bibliography of the allied campaign in Mesopotamia during the First World War, they were impressed by the high praise it had received as an account of the war the British experienced during the first phase of the conflict in what is today, Iraq.

Further examination of the actual text revealed that this book was, indeed, very well written. Of course, since the author was a captain in the 1st Battalion The Oxfordshire and Buckinghamshire Light Infantry, the book provided a detailed and intimate insight into the campaign as it was prosecuted by the British Army against its Ottoman Turkish enemy from the perspective of a British infantry battalion engaged in the sharpest end of the war.

Perhaps more uniquely, it transpired that H. Birch Reynardson was a sufficiently talented writer that he could not only also describe the landscape and peoples of Mesopotamia for his readers in interesting and entertaining detail, but that he was able to evocatively portray a sense of what it was to live through that time, in that place. It is not unknown that all of these attributes have appeared together within one book of military personal recollections, but it is rare enough (and this publisher has read many such accounts) as to be particularly noteworthy.

Although he might possibly not have been aware of the significance of his decision for posterity at the time, Henry Birch Reynardson took a camera to war with him. His photographs of the British campaign in Mesopotamia (particularly portraying the '1st Ox and Bucks') which appear in his book have also appeared in other publications and are essential and rare source images of the activities of the infantry particularly in marshland and other inundated areas which required the troops to move on water. This new edition has given us the opportunity to enlarge and enhance those photographs to best effect.

The catalogue of books published concerning the Mesopotamian Campaign is not a particularly large one, though interest in the conflict abides among aficionados of the history of the First World War. This fact, of course, only serves to underline the importance of Henry Birch Reynardson's book and the imperative to ensure it does not disappear into obscurity in the near future.

The so called 'side-show theatres' of the war hold particular interest for historians because, unlike the, often static, warfare of the Western Front with its miles of trenches and barbed-wire separated by the mud of No Man's Land, these often mobile campaigns were fought in often exotic settings, over challenging terrain, employing local forces or the colourful troops of the empires of the protagonists. The aspect of the campaign in Mesopotamia described in this book, fought between the rivers Tigris and Euphrates, was no exception.

This book has not been available in print since its first publication in 1919, not so long after the last bullet of the war had been fired. Henry Birch Reynardson survived the war and lived a long life and so if there was to be a modern edition published by this publisher permission would necessarily be required from his present-day family for the work to proceed. This publisher must extend its grateful thanks, therefore, to the author's grandson, Thomas Birch Reynardson for giving permission for his grandfather's book to be represented to a contemporary readership. Further thanks must be extended to H. Birch Reynardson's granddaughter, Clare Hopkinson for providing access to her copy of the original book together with its accompanying ephemera.

Finally, this publisher must extend its ongoing thanks to Charles Radford, former commanding officer of the 16th/5th The Queen's Royal Lancers and the Parachute Squadron, RAC, who qualifies as the most stalwart supporter of this publisher's efforts in the field of military history. To do justice to do the contributions that this gentleman has made in the creation of several Leonaur titles would require a catalogue of freely given support, encouragement and generous collaborative efforts on his part.

As regards this book particularly, it must be acknowledged that this edition would not have been published without the assistance of Charles Radford who liaised with the Birch Reynardson family on the publisher's behalf from the outset to bring the book into being. We are additionally indebted to his talents employed on our behalf as a rostrum cameraman (which have been developed as he has worked on his principal focus which is the creation and expansion of an enduring archive for the 16th/5th The Queen's Royal Lancers at Stoke-on-Trent) which on this occasion enabled us to employ quality digital images of H. Birch Reynardson's photographs and other relevant items.

Readers attention is drawn to the fact that this edition is not identical to the original one and these differences have served to make this book somewhat longer. Firstly, all the maps in that edition were sketches made by H. Birch Reynardson and were of the 'fold-out' variety which enabled them to be larger than the normal size of the bound book. Indeed, a large map of the Mesopotamia theatre of operations appeared in a rear pocket. The combination of a necessary reduction in size of these maps for our production model combined with the potentially difficult to read fine lines and handwritten captions of the HBR maps has persuaded the present publisher to include them, but to augment them by the inclusion of formally produced maps for the sake of clarity for the contemporary reader.

The photographs which appeared in the original edition likewise all appear in the book you are holding, but additional images have also been included to illuminate the text. Finally, upon examination of the book in Clare Hopkinson's possession it was discovered—since we may assume it was once Henry Birch Reynardson's own copy—a letter written to him by his friend, Lionel Muirhead together with some reviews of the book which appeared at the time of first publication. These have been included in this edition for readers interest. Curiously, the original edition began with a double page of organisational tables and these have been moved to the rear of the book in this edition.

The republication of 'Mesopotamia 1914-15, Extracts from a Regimental Officer's Diary' in this new and expanded edition has given this important book a new and extended lease of life for those who study its subject today and for those who may wish to study it in the future. This is surely no inconsequential conclusion for there are many books of this kind which are in imminent danger of becoming lost to general readership as the passage of time leaves them in its wake.

****

A SHORT ACCOUNT OF THE 1ST BATTALION OXFORDSHIRE & BUCKINGHAMSHIRE LIGHT INFANTRY IN THE MESOPOTAMIA CAMPAIGN OF THE FIRST WORLD WAR

The 1st Battalion of this famous light infantry regiment can trace its history to its formation to the 18th century in 1741 when it was raised as the 54th (Fowkes) Regiment of Foot, though it was re-designated the 43rd regiment in 1748. The regiment subsequently served in the Mediterranean, during The French and Indian War in which it fought in the battle for Quebec, during the American War of Independence and in the West Indies.

In 1782 the regiment was given the territorial title of 'Monmouthshire', but perhaps the most significant milestone in the regiment's history came about in 1803, during Britain's long wars with Napoleonic France, when it became a light infantry regiment—only the second British regiment to be permanently so converted.

For students of the Peninsular War in Spain, Portugal and the South of France during the first years of the 19th century the achievements of the 43rd are well known, for it was an active part of the famous 'Light Division' under Wellington. In keeping with several regiments of the 'old Peninsular Army that could go anywhere and do anything' it missed taking part in the Battle of Waterloo, which defeated the First Empire of the French in 1815, because it was dispatched, once again, across the Atlantic Ocean to fight in the War of 1812 against the United States of America. Whilst Canada was saved, the war ended ignominiously for the British and the 43rd at the Battle of New Orleans in 1815 which was a pointless engagement since peace terms had already been agreed between the opposing nations in Europe weeks before the battle was fought.

With the exception of inevitable periods of garrison duty in Ireland, the regiment spent much of the remainder of the 19th century during the colonial and Victorian era campaigning across the globe as the British Empire inexorably 'turned the map red'.

Eight years' service in Canada until 1830 was followed by bush fighting in South Africa in the 8th Kaffir War. Ten years spent in India ensured the 43rd would be swept up in the brutal Indian Mutiny of 1857 and by 1863 it was in New Zealand engaged in difficult conflict with the formidable Maoris of Waikato. Further service in India and Burma followed.

In 1881 the new system of linked battalions was introduced so that one battalion would serve at home whilst the other served abroad. The amalgamation was a perfect one for the 43rd merged with its old and faithful comrades from the Light Division of the Peninsular—the 52nd (Oxfordshire) Light Infantry.

Thus, the regiment became the first and second battalions of the Oxfordshire Light Infantry and as such the battalions served again in India and during the Second Anglo-Boer War in South Africa. In the early years of the 20th century another regimental title change occurred. In 1908 'Buckinghamshire' was added to the existing regimental title.

In 1914 as the First World War broke out, the 1st Battalion The Oxfordshire and Buckinghamshire Light Infantry was serving in India as part of the 17th Infantry Brigade of the 6th (Poona) Division. The 2nd battalion of the regiment had been sent to France in August 1914. Half of the strength of the 2nd battalion was made up of reservists, whereas the 1st battalion was comprised of regular soldiers some of whom wore Boer War ribbons on their uniforms.

The Ottoman Turkish Empire formed an alliance with Germany and came into the war in November, 1914. H. Birch Reynardson's book deals with this early period of the war so there is little value in repeating what will be related later in considerable detail about the 1st battalion's activities. It remains sufficient to note that this development meant that the British had to look to their interests in the Middle East which embraced the Persian Gulf and Mesopotamia. Of primary concern was the protection of British oilfields on the Karun River.

On the 2nd September, 1915 the Poona Division moved up the Tigris successfully assaulting the Turks in entrenched positions at the Battle of Es Sinn (Kut). The objective was the capture of Baghdad to be achieved by marching up the Tigris bank. At the end of the first week of October the battalion was engaged in the hard-fought Battle of Ctesiphon which lies about 20 miles from Baghdad and 80 miles from Kut and suffered severely. Despite initial successes victory for the British was denied to them by a Turkish counter-attack of numerical superiority. Of a British force of 11,000 men over 4,000 had become casualties. The 'Ox and Bucks' casualties constituted almost half their engaged strength and it is at this point that the Birch Reynardson narrative concludes as he was one of the seriously wounded.

The retreating British fell back on Kut where it arrived in early December. There was little hope of immediate relief or reinforcement and so Kut (which is situated in a bow of the River Tigris which serves as a defensive barrier to the south-east and south-west) was made ready for a siege. Command fell to Major-General Charles Townshend which initially augured well since he had come to notice for his successful defence of the fort at Chitral on the Indian North-West Frontier. Initially the Turks attacked the town aggressively determined to take it and on Christmas Eve and Christmas Day the 'Ox and Bucks' were fighting off a heavy attack by the Turks in which it was estimated approaching 700 of the enemy fell.

By mid-January of 1916, however, the Turks were aware that relief was not imminently expected by the Kut garrison and they decided to play a waiting game, keep the British and Indian garrison confined to their lines and starve them into submission. The siege dragged on for four months until further defence became untenable and, on the 29th April, 1916, the Kut garrison capitulated. The 'Ox and Bucks' battalion within Kut was by this point reduced to 9 officers and about 300 other ranks.

Following the surrender, the officers were permanently separated from their men. There then followed one of the most notorious incidences of atrocity against prisoners of war of the entire conflict. The officers of the battalion were sent on to Baghdad in transport, but the other ranks were subjected to a forced march of hundreds of miles. Such was the inhumane treatment the men of the 'Ox and Bucks' were forced to suffer on this march that of the 253 of them who began it, only 76 survived.

The battalion in name was not, however, entirely out of the fight since some of its strength were not besieged in Kut and so avoided the surrender and its aftermath. A provisional battalion of 100 'Ox and Bucks' men reinforced by a further 300 men who had recently come out to Basra from Britain was formed in early January, 1916. It was, of course, eager to relieve its comrades who at this time were still holding out in Kut. This small unit, known as '2/43rd', comprised two rifle companies and formed part of the 28th Infantry Brigade, 7th Division.

The Kut relief force reach Sanniyat (just 12 miles from its objective) after a hard-contested advance on April 5th, 1916, but the attempt to break through resulted in total disaster. Of the 13 officers and 266 other ranks of the battalion who went into action at Sanniyat, 10 officers and 235 men became casualties. Despite these terrible losses it suffered the unit retained its identity as it was placed on the divisional reserve. This remnant was gradually reinforced to become once again the official 1st Battalion, Oxfordshire and Buckinghamshire Light Infantry on the 30th April, 1916. Unfortunately, the object of all the battalion's efforts and sacrifice—the Kut garrison—had been finally forced to capitulate on the previous day.

There followed a long period of rest and reorganisation which endured to the end of the year. In February 1917 the Turks withdrew from their Sanniyat positions, evacuated Kut and pursued by the British and Indian armies retreated to and beyond Baghdad. The British entered Baghdad on the 11th March, 1917. The battalion had, however, been employed for most of 1917 to this point protecting lines of communication, particularly essential railway traffic destined to troops at the front.

By October, 1917, the battalion had been transferred to the 50th Brigade, 15th Division, at Fullaja on the Euphrates. Up to strength again, it now comprised approaching 1000 officers and men. The Turkish Army's effectiveness was now failing and in March 1918, the 'Ox and Bucks' took part in the capture of Hit. The pursuit of the retiring Turks was relentless and on the night of March 25th a reconnaissance including a company of the 'Ox and Bucks' attacked Turkish advance trenches taking several prisoners. By the following morning the British attack was general with armoured cars and cavalry positioned to cut the enemy line of retreat. The battalion led the infantry assault towards Wadi Hauran. The victory achieved was overwhelming with over 5000 of the enemy surrendering to become prisoners of war.

Turkish resistance in Mesopotamia was, by this point, all but over, though the battalion remained in the Middle East for almost a further year. The First World War came to an end on November 11th and initial demobilisation began in the battalion during December 1918 though the final 5 officers and 46 other ranks of did not return to barracks in Aldershot until April, 1919.

As it transpired the 'Ox and Bucks' had not done with soldiering in this period for the battalion was nominated to join the allied expedition to Archangel to assist the White Russian forces in their ill-fated attempt to stem the tide of Bolshevism. The men who took part in that campaign would not come home until October, 1919.

****

Although the 1st Battalion Oxfordshire and Buckinghamshire Light Infantry had not seen action on the Western Front with their comrades of the 2nd battalion, theirs had been a hard-fought war which exacted a very high price in the number of those who lost their lives in action, from disease or as a consequence of criminal abuse at the hands of their captors. The number of lives altered forever by wounds was higher yet. In effect, the battalion had all but been annihilated twice in a campaign that has been largely forgotten in the context of the wider conflict which has focussed on the conflict in Europe.

At the time of the publication of this new edition of Henry Birch Reynardson's book one hundred years has elapsed since the end of the Great War which was optimistically proclaimed as 'the war to end all wars'. It was not to be, for in a little over 20 years after it was concluded Britain was again at war and the new men of The Oxfordshire and Buckinghamshire Light Infantry and, indeed, the men of the Birch Reynardson family were marching away from their homes in defence of their nation and its way of life.

Many of those who will read this book, this writer among their number, have been blessed never to know war with all its horrors. For that we all owe a debt to these men and many others like them that can never be repaid—except in one simple regard.

LEST WE FORGET.

John Lewis
Leonaur, January 2019

Chapter 1

The Beginning of Things

Looking back on it now, one realises with a sense of surprise—and with some feeling of shame, too—how slightly the shock of war disturbed the backwaters of our world: in particular, the backwaters of the East.

In Europe there was an explosion. As History considers Time it may appear instantaneous. Almost in one night, war came upon Europe, so that it awoke to watch incredulously the threatened dissolution of civilization, the wreck of commerce, the confusion of established boundaries; and—touching the heart of Europe more nearly than all else—the breakup of Home and Peace and Security.

But the explosion was in Europe and the full shock was felt there: nearby, the world shook and men looked up and wondered—wondered for some time until finally they understood. And farther off, thousands of miles from Europe, in the backwaters of the East? *There* our world did not shake, and even for a little while we wondered what all the noise had been about: there was no sudden paralysis of business—no rush on the banks—no panic—no fear of imminent starvation—no roar of troop-trains through the night. There was nothing to "stab our spirits wide awake": and though indeed the newspapers said war, war was still a word—perhaps a fact, a very exciting and stimulating state of affairs; but not The Explosion.

In our particular, and rather private, backwater, an upcountry station in Southern India, the Great War had come upon us rather gradually, but it had found us ready: there was nothing much more to be done after the first spasm of excitement and a few days of orderly preparation when all went smoothly as if by clockwork, except to wait and wonder when and where we should be invited to join in. And in the meanwhile, the war, for most of us, resolved itself into an exciting and stimulating state of affairs, from which we knew ourselves tantalisingly distant, and felt ourselves strangely and shamefully aloof. And, to look at the other side of the picture, there were the casualty lists, in which dear and familiar names seemed a reproach—distance indeed could not make the parting easier, nor remove the consciousness of such unequal sacrifice.

We had our more critical moments of excitement, it is true—when the wire announcing the declaration of war arrived; when at last, after what seemed an eternity of waiting, the order to mobilise came; when the *Emden* shelled Madras; and then a false alarm—"Be prepared to move at eight hours' notice": but almost immediately a cancelling wire dashed our hopes to the ground.

And gradually our outer life in its lighter aspects again assumed the ways and customs of Peace—hounds met as of old, "at 5.30 a.m., at the fourth milestone on Khanbagh road," and we chased the grey Deccan foxes among their stony hills; on the polo-ground again sounded the click of stick and ball and the thunder of the little ponies' hooves. At the club in the evening were the same faces, the same jokes, the same drinks—the faces a little changed perhaps by that first spasm, the jokes a little forced—but on the whole we of the Backwaters remained as before.

So much for the lighter side of life. Professionally of course there was a change which dated from the arrival of that first wire early in August. Long route marches, long field days, tactical exercises, lectures, were the order by day and by night: inspections even "to the last gaiter-button," made sure and doubly sure that our preparations were complete. By degrees as week after week went by the somewhat easier life of former days was forgotten and the new order lost all novelty: inspections came as a matter of course, night operations were a habit, and our identity discs were no longer "curios."

It was a cool evening at the beginning of November: in the club garden the little tables had been moved from under the trees into the open, and round them now were congregating the usual *habitués*, to discuss the one subject and ask the one question, "When are we going?" From the billiard-room came the monotonous click of the balls, and, beyond, a crowd of congenial spirits propped up the bar, where over cocktails and long drinks the latest "gup"—rumours and facts and fancies—was being exchanged. It was all very much as usual, and this evening was as other evenings had been: the Club full of light and talk and laughter—outside the night still and breathless, and the white moonlit road running through its dark tunnel of mango trees; beyond, a stretch of *maidan* loud with the croak of frogs and chirp of crickets; beyond the *maidan* the massive walls and battlements of the old Mahratta fort silhouetted against the stars.

It was all so exactly as it had been before and no doubt would be again, that when from the distance came the sound of a motorcycle going "all out" no one paid any attention. The rider was evidently in a hurry, and with furious toots of the horn came tearing down the moonlit road, stopped in front of the club with a screech of brakes, and almost threw his machine into the arms of a gaping *syce*.

So far nothing very unusual. From the billiard-room came the first signs that something was up, and there the balls ceased their clicking suddenly and a buzz of conversation came through the lighted windows. Then a certain animation appeared among the little tables in the garden—here and there figures got up and went across to other tables—the doctor's wife, a charming representative of our Allies, gave her well-known *staccato pianissimo* scream; and then from under the big tamarind the band struck up "Tipperary."

Our friend of the motor-bicycle with a long whisky and soda in his hand confirmed the news—this time it was official, absolutely certain sure, and without a shadow of doubt; the brigade would "proceed on active service" next Friday, our reliefs would arrive on Wednesday—and this was Tuesday evening!

So, at last we had been invited to play with the others.

In earlier days there had been much speculation as to where our orders would finally land us. In the early days of August, we had been for France, then had come an ominous hint from Olympus that we should be provided with spine-pads, mosquito nets, and glare-glasses, and consequently we decided that we shouldn't go farther west than Egypt. Again, the rumour was whispered that we were bound for Akaba, the whereabouts of which no one knew very exactly, beyond that it was a gulf and very hot, and in some way hazily connected with the wandering of the Children of Israel.

But lately we had had little doubt that our goal was Mesopotamia, and by the evening that our orders arrived we had known for some days that the rest of our division—that is to say, the other two brigades and some divisional troops—had already preceded us: now we were to follow. Matters seemed sufficiently settled and our orders really decided and official; and yet for some incomprehensible reason uncertainty still dogged us, and in the end our short notice was made even shorter.

By 7 p.m. on Wednesday evening there was still no sign of our relief—a Territorial Battalion newly arrived from England—and as the process of "handing over" the station could not be done in five minutes, the problem was becoming acute, and it looked very much as if we shouldn't get off on Friday—in fact the rumour went round that we should not start till the next week. However, sometime in the small hours of Thursday morning the luckless Territorials were dumped down at the railway station and we were all pleasantly surprised later to hear that they had arrived while we were asleep: they must also have been rather surprised at their unceremonious reception. In the meantime, a wire had come from Headquarters suggesting that we should stand by and await further orders, which we naturally interpreted as meaning that the Authorities considered it impossible to get us off by the next day; but no chances were taken in this direction, as even a start on Monday meant many crowded hours of glorious life and a good deal of hard work.

Still on Friday morning time was found for one last route march, and at 8.30 a.m. a regiment might have been seen plodding its way down the white dusty road—four hours foot-slogging to Khanbagh and back was just to put the finishing touch. We will leave this regiment, then, tramping its way along the scorching road to the accompaniment of shrill and varied renderings of "Tipperary," sung, whistled, and mouth-organed, and take a look at what is happening nearer home. There all is Peace—an air of satisfaction broods over the deserted barrack—satisfaction at having completed the heavy task and having three whole days in which to look round and do the few small odd jobs that remain. The quartermaster sits in his office leaning back in his chair—everything had been served out, all the necessaries were packed and lists completed: the orderly room Q.M.S. goes leisurely about his business and decides not to pack the typewriter yet awhile—and one or two other things could wait.

Over the way, in a bungalow near the mess, a subaltern is conferring with the bearded *salutri* (native vet.) over a lame pony, with which, its lameness at least temporarily disposed of, the owner hopes to tempt one of the innocent newcomers: the subaltern's kit is not yet packed—but three days is heaps of time!

It is now two hours since the regiment left on its route march, the time being 10.30 and at this moment the Practical Joke Department (if I may borrow the title from a great chronicle) got busy. Its method was sharp and to the point—it intimated that the brigade would entrain for Bombay that afternoon, and that the regiment in question, at present enjoying a route march somewhere on the Khanbagh road, was due to leave at 5 p.m.

Recollections of the next few hours are hazy: it is sufficient to say that, arriving in barracks soon after twelve and expecting the best part of three days before we were torn from our happy homes, we found that that painful operation had to be performed within the next three hours. Punctually at 3.30 p.m. the regiment marched off the parade-ground, and as it swung out on to the road to the railway station the band struck up the regimental march: it was the last time we were to hear it for—how long?

Our departure was certainly not impressive: there were no flagged streets, nor enthusiastic crowds—an omission easily forgiven—only a few natives watched us quietly and dispassionately from a distance. But this was no *tamàsha*; quite unmoved and uninterested they returned to their business, deaf to the martial strains of "Tipperary": as yet the Great War had not shaken them up.

But quiet as our leave-taking was, one cannot help feeling that the few of us who still remain will not easily forget it. Our station was not a popular one and we had often bewailed our lot—and yet that afternoon it seemed not altogether undesirable, and one realised a sense of regret as barracks and bungalows and mess and polo-ground, full of memories of good times, faded out of sight. We marched past the Club and reflected that it really wasn't half a bad little place; and past the old Mahratta fort, its black stones shining ruddily in the afternoon light; and past the tree under which Wellington had breakfasted on the morning of its capture more than a century ago; and then on down the dusty road with the native city on the left, for some strange reason looking almost beautiful for the first time in its history. But perhaps "goodbyes" are never very pleasant!

Arrived at the station, hot and dusty and in a state of pleasurable excitement, we were doomed to devastating disappointment. Another regiment of the brigade, acting, we presumed, on the maximum that "*all is fair in love and war*," had annexed our train, and instead of starting in half an hour we should have to wait two hours for the next train; so, we waited disconsolately outside the station, vowing vengeance upon our friends when next we should meet them. Then at 7 p.m. a wire arrived to say that our train had unfortunately broken down, that another engine was being sent for from the junction 50 miles down the line and that we might expect the train at 11 p.m.—about. Thereupon some authority (I shrewdly suspect the Practical Joke Department again) decreed that we should be allowed to retire behind the station, where there was some open grass ground, and bivouac by companies: the men were given wood and were to be allowed to cook.

We accordingly proceeded to do as directed and were beginning to make arrangements for cooking and bivouacs, etc., when it was noticed that there was a mysterious and overpowering smell coming from all directions at once. We decided to move a few hundred yards; but it was just as bad there—no one could bear it, and no one could make out what it was. Light was at last shed upon the situation by an officer of an inquiring frame of mind falling into a cess-pit; it was then discovered that the Authority concerned had selected as our resting-place the town refuse-ground, in fact the sewage-farm—though there is not much farm about it in the East! However, we had to make the best of it, and there we waited till 1.30 a.m., when the train came in and we got safely on board and were at last really on our way to Bombay.

The journey to Bombay, beyond the picturesque climb up and down the Ghats, held nothing particularly worthy of notice, except that we did the twenty-four hours' journey on remarkably short commons: though arrangements were supposed to have been made for breakfast and tiffin at stations *en route*, there was precious little to show for it when we reached those stations.

As far as I remember, no one minded very much at the time, because, I suppose, we were far too pleased with life in general to find room for a "grouse"; but, by the light of after-events, in the jumble and muddle of the start may perhaps be traced that lack of foresight which was later to prove so disastrous.

Reaching Bombay late at night, after so many stops, backings, and shuntings in the last few miles that we thought we never should arrive, we detrained and bivouacked for the night on the platforms. I walked round about 2 a.m.—under the flickering glare of the arc-lights, surrounded by the bangs and clatters of a noisy station, on their hard beds of concrete it was extraordinary how soundly the men seemed to be sleeping—like long lines of swathed mummies all down the platform, with the glittering piles of arms between them, guarded by statuesque sentries; it is a picture, one of many, that remains.

We had orders to march to the docks at 8 a.m., where the regiment was to be embarked at once, and by six everyone was astir and breakfast served out; at the last moment a slight hitch occurred, as those concerned had omitted to provide us with any transport, but a resourceful officer scouring the streets of Bombay returned with many *bhil*-carts—slow but sure—which served the purpose. We were soon at the Alexandra Docks and alongside our transport, which we found to be the B.I. ship *Tongwa*, a cargo boat with a limited accommodation for passengers, now turned into a transport, but by the fortune of war still on the same run as formerly, for she had been engaged in the Gulf trade. This, as it proved, was fortunate for us, for most of the ship's officers were familiar with the climatic eccentricities of that part of the world, and it was from them that we first heard that Mesopotamia was not always a burning fiery furnace; very soon we were to experience this for ourselves, and to wonder why the powers that be had seen fit to conceal it from us.

Whatever shortcomings we had found in organisation and "*bund-o-bast*" up till now, were certainly not present in the arrangements made for our embarkation; everything went smoothly, and though it was very hot work between decks, everyone was stowed away by 11.30 a.m. Furthermore, we knew exactly the particular places where we were to lie, sit, stand, eat, wash, and smoke, which operations it appeared must at sea be performed in different parts of our floating home, and in no way confused!

An infantry battalion is a big thing when it comes to tucking it away between the decks of a small transport, especially when that transport is an improvised one; and to add to our difficulties we had a detachment of Imperial Service Transport with their complement of squealing, kicking, country-bred ponies and equally obstreperous mules, as our travelling companions. But things went smoothly, and as the ship was not due to sail till next morning, leave ashore was available; there was plenty to be done, and not too much time to do it in.

The shops must have been taxed to their uttermost with crowds of officers all making last purchases, and all asking for very much the same things—camel-hair blankets, large tins of Keating's, carbolic soap, air-pillows, mosquito-nets were, I think, the chief articles in requisition—and very soon none of them were to be had. Cox's Agency presented a curious and somewhat humorous spectacle: crowds of natives of all sorts, shapes, and sizes were being interviewed by distracted mess presidents and others who were struggling to secure at the last minute cooks and waiters for their messes, bearers for themselves, and probably for a dozen or so friends; because at the last minute the prospect of crossing Kala Pani had proved too much for our dusky henchmen, and with one accord they had disappeared and could not be found.

A bath and lunch at the "Taj" was a pleasant change from the hot work on board the transport. If one goes into the "Taj" with the firm conviction that it is the last time one will enjoy civilization for many a long day, one can do oneself very well indeed—and I may say none of us forgot his imminent fate.

The day passed quickly enough, and ended with dinner at the Yacht Club, where, from the smooth lawns of the terraces overlooking the moonlit bay, we bade a final farewell to the comforts of peace and the charms of milk punch and returned to our several ships ready for an early start.

It was not till we got aboard that night that we learnt the true story of a most unfortunate affair—though rumours had been flying about all the evening. Luckily the truth, though tragic enough, was not so bad as the rumour, which had reported wholesale mutiny and murder in one of the native regiments of the brigade. There was absolutely no question of mutiny or unwillingness to fight the Turk, but, owing to some imagined grievance, a Mahsud *sepoy* had stabbed a British officer of his regiment as the latter was walking up the gangway of a transport, and killed him.

However, it was plain that there was trouble of sorts in the regiment concerned, and it was thought advisable, even at the last minute, to remove the regiment from the brigade, though there was no other available in its place at the moment. Finally, another regiment which had already sailed for France was recalled by wireless when nearing Aden and diverted to Mesopotamia, where it joined, and completed, our brigade.

CHAPTER 2

November 1914

One voyage being very much like another, I will waste little time in chronicling our five days' journey up the Gulf.

Warm weather was very soon left astern, and 7.30 physical drill on the upper deck became quite popular before we were half-way on our journey—that is, until it was found that our energetic and concerted efforts were extremely likely to jerk the old ship to bits; after that we had to indulge by half companies at a time.

Unfortunately, we had no ports of call, and so no chances of exploring the mysteries of the "Pirate Coast" and other points of interest in which the Gulf littoral abounds. Pasni and Gwadur, where Alexander's army halted on its march to the Karun; Hormuz, once the island-city of fabulous wealth; Bahrein, the pearl-island, whence, some say, came the earliest navigators of the earth, precursors and forefathers of the Phoenicians—all now deserted, and their glory departed, but still full of history full of romance to the twentieth century.

But perhaps it was just as well, as, however romantic, the spots are not health resorts; most of them for eight months of the year are flaming hells of heat and glare, thirst and fever and flies, and having once seen them one can only wonder how it is possible for men to live there all the year round. The work done by the servants of the Eastern Telegraph Company, or rather the appalling conditions of climate and loneliness under which it is done, are, of course, never realised by the world outside—it is hard to express the admiration one feels for these exiles.

Bunder Abbas we saw from the distance, a low smudge of yellow above a grey sea, and H.M.S. *Ocean* lying off in the open roads. There was extraordinarily little shipping about, which was surprising considering that we were on the direct line of an overseas expedition, and

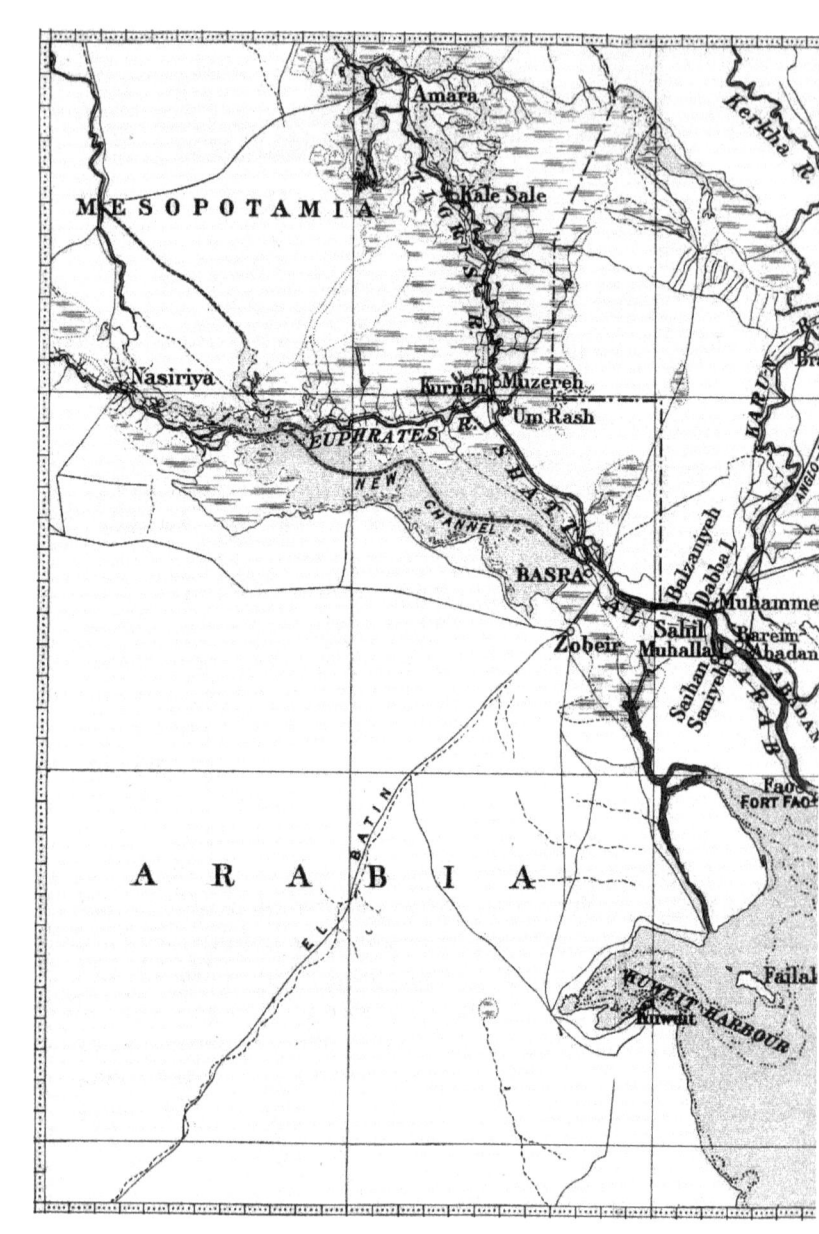

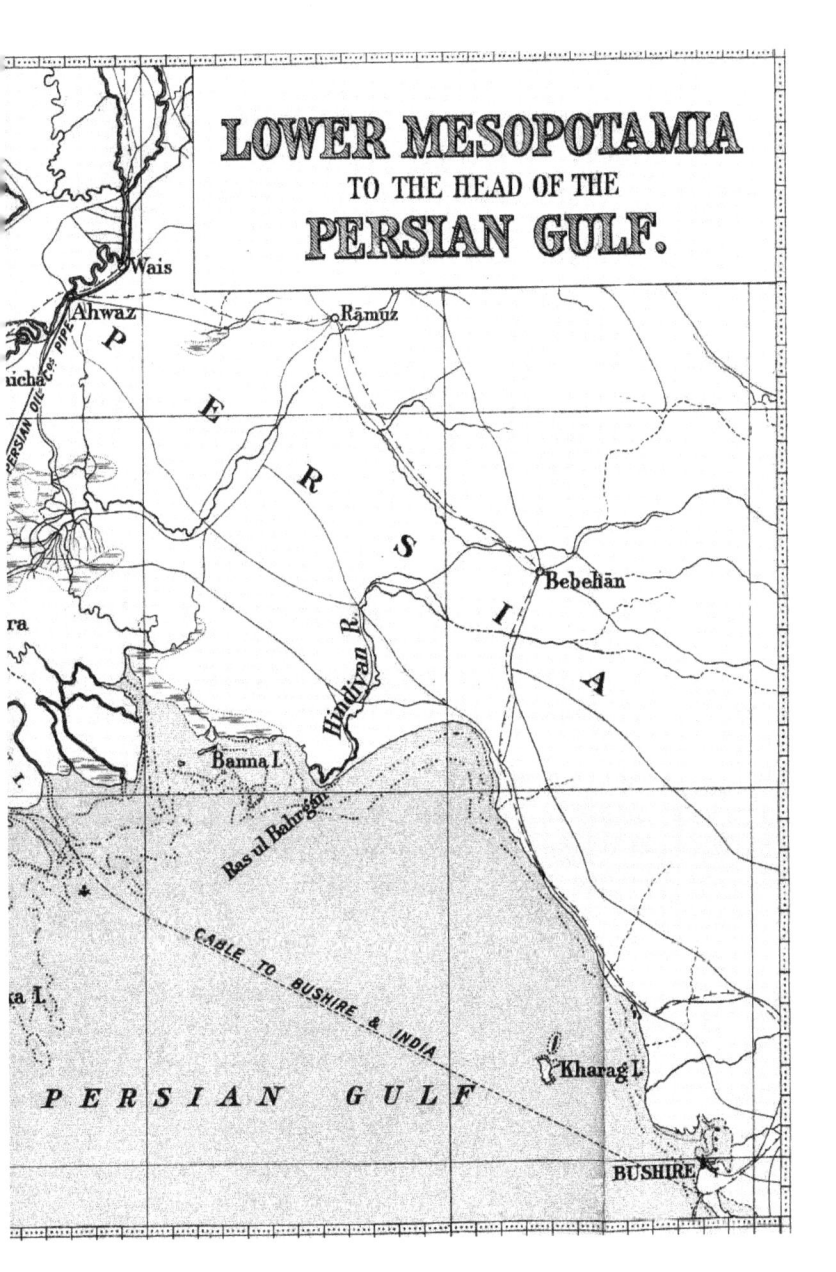

it served to increase our forebodings that we had been relegated to a side-show, and a very small one at that.

However, there was soon, a change for the better. By 24th November the end of our voyage was approaching, and that evening we expected to be in sight of Fao Lightship; as it turned out we weren't quite up to time, but next morning we awoke to find ourselves one of quite a crowd of ships lying some distance off the mouth of the Shatt-el-Arab, with the palms of Fao in the distance. So far so good. But unfortunately, we weren't the first comers, and there being a difficult bar across the river-mouth, we had to wait our turn till earlier arrivals had been passed over in safety and disappeared up the mouth of the river—into what was then to us very much the Unknown.

Breakfast that morning was enlivened by many arguments and much prophecy, all of which turned out woefully wide of the mark, which was hardly surprising, considering that we were totally ignorant of the country and conditions and had only very hazy ideas as to what exactly we were intended to do. But our plans for an immediate landing and march to Basra were brought to a sudden close by the news that we were just crossing the bar, so a move was made to the deck, to see what might be seen. All round us the sea was a tawny yellow, stained by the mud of the bar we were churning up; from the dark patch of which we were the centre stretched a long pale-yellow stain away into the distance, finally disappearing among the palms which marked the shore.

After much bumping and churning of the screws, we wriggled ourselves over the bar and headed up the yellow stream—the outflowing waters of the Shatt-el-Arab—towards the distant palms. As we gradually drew nearer a rough jetty at the river-mouth came into sight, and against the blue sky and over the dull green of the palm tops, a splash of colour: The Union Jack, the first sign of those who had gone before us. Then on the opposite bank appeared the much-battered remains of Fao fort, a miserable collection of old mud walls, apparently exceedingly obsolete, and a telegraph station guarded by a double company of native infantry; we imagined, with an optimism that was to be soon withered, that our voyage was ended.

The first sight of a new country, even when one is engaged on the peaceful-tourist stunt, is full of excitement and interesting surprises, or the expectation of them. But there is more in it than this when one is among thousands equally curious, when the country is in truth something of a *terra incognita* to each and all, the air full of strange rumours, and last, but not least, when one is engaged, not in peaceful touring, but, as the Boche would no doubt say, in the business of blood and iron. Over and above these considerations, although to the unelect definite military information was lacking, there was a wealth of legend, rumour, and history attached to this unknown country, sufficient to light a spark in the most unpromising imagination. Who could possibly resist some whisper of romance at the thought that we were heading towards the homeport of Sinbad the Sailor, and that beyond lay the ruins of great Babylon, Ur of the Chaldees, Nineveh of the Assyrians; a land crowded with great and terrible ghosts, full of strange history and mysterious legends?

So much for the imaginative side—what actually met our interested gaze was rather a damper. On either side of the river, up which we were now steaming, was a thick belt of date palms stretching out into the distance, about three miles wide, close and impenetrable, and shutting out all views of the country beyond with their level, cabbage-like tops. It may seem rude to describe the date palm as cabbage-like—no doubt when picturesquely arranged by nature, or the artist, in graceful twos and threes against a desert sunset they are very beautiful; but when grown for business, crowded closely together, carefully pruned, bolt upright, they are an intensely Prussianised form of tree, and not pleasing to look at. This scenery continued for several miles as we headed up the river, and there was very little of interest to be seen; here and there picturesque creeks broke the wall of monotonous tree-trunks, and Arabs in *bellums* and *mashoofs* whirled by, managing their craft extraordinarily cleverly in the rapid stream, which here was moving about six knots. As no account of Mesopotamia can get on without the *bellum* and the *mashoof*, two forms of local boat, a short description of them must be suffered.

The *bellum* is a canoe-shaped boat of teak, from 20 to 30 feet long and about 4 feet beam amidships: prow and stern are of the same shape and decorated with curling, carved beaks, often covered with brass. The *bellumchis* (the boatmen) will never use paddles if they can help it but prefer to dodge along the banks out of the stream using long bamboo or reed punt-poles, which they handle very cleverly. The *mashoof* is generally much smaller than the *bellum*, built either of reeds or thin laths, covered over entirely with a thick coating of bitumen, which makes it very heavy, though at the same time it is a wonderfully wobbly craft which requires great skill, and several baths, to punt properly. On the higher reaches of the river and in the marshland all

Ashar Creek, Basra.—"Bellums" for Hire.

round Kurna *mashoofs* are the usual means of progression, and the *bellum* is not common much above Basra, except near towns such as Amara, Kut, and Baghdad. The *mashoof* with its high black hornlike prow looks exactly like some uncouth water-beetle; it would be rather interesting to know the origin of these high prows, for they make the boats quite unmanageable in the high winds which so often blow on the rivers.

Presently the view opened out a little and we came into sight of Abadan, an island on the Persian shore of the river, and saw a crowd of buildings and chimneys—the refining works of the Anglo-Persian Oil Company—about which we had heard a good deal of talk. The safeguarding of our oil supplies was not the chief and only reason that an Expeditionary Force was sent to Mesopotamia; but it was one of the reasons and, at a casual glance, one of the most obvious and intelligible, and at the time we regarded that group of buildings and the clustering chimneys, the tanks and wharves, as the cause of our arrival.

There is little doubt that one of the enemy's pet schemes was to make a surprise move against the oil depot here, cut the pipe-line and generally break things up before we had smelt a rat—probably, indeed, before war was declared. As a considerable quantity of oil fuel for the navy was, and is, derived from this source, matters would have been rather serious if they had succeeded. But luckily, we were not caught napping and, by the movement of a brigade to Bahrein Island, so as to be on the spot in case war broke out, the situation was saved. General Delamain's force (the 16th Brigade of VIth Poona Division) was too near to allow of any monkey tricks, and as soon as war *was* declared, this brigade soon disposed of Fao fort, effected an entrance to the river, and together with the 18th Brigade fought two actions, in both of which the Turks were heavily defeated, and on 23rd November captured Basra, so disposing of any immediate menace of an attack in force on Abadan.

The matter of guarding the pipe-line, however, was far more difficult, as the oil is brought down from Maidan-i-Naphtun, N.E. of Ahwaz, to Abadan, a distance of 150 miles through country inhabited by tribes of cut-throat Arabs who, though nominally Persian subjects, own allegiance to no one, and had only to knock a few holes in the pipe to interfere with the oil supply.

Persia at this time was full of German and Turkish agents with plenty of money to spend, the country was in a state of chronic unrest, the Swedish *Gendarmerie* was in parts strongly anti-British, so conditions were favourable; it is surprising that the pipe-line was not interfered with more than actually was the case, and it speaks volumes for the energy of the troops later employed round Ahwaz and for the diplomacy of the Oil Company's officials, that the supply was only once seriously interfered with.

Our voyage was soon to end, for at 1 p.m., while still ten miles below Muhammera, we came to a stop and heard we were to await further orders before proceeding; in the meanwhile, we were confined to the ship and there was nothing to do but look at the palm trees and count the other ships ahead of us and wonder when our turn would come to get on—as we could see fourteen transports upstream of us, our chance did not look hopeful. But even in our most pessimistic moments we had not contemplated a long imprisonment and, thank goodness, we did not know that we had a week of intense boredom and impatience before us, as in the end turned out to be the case.

Every day, it seemed, something happened to prevent us from going on: first it was that the embarkation staff had lost, or temporarily mislaid, the ship containing our brigadier and his staff; then half a regiment went astray; then a ship-load of camels and horses was rammed by another ship and had to be beached, thus blocking the fairway: then finally, when we were all assembled and thought we were all nicely straightened out and would be allowed to go on, came the retort, "Await further orders."

Just about this time the weather turned very cold, and every day broke with an icy wind blowing down river, and as we shivered about the decks we wondered for the first time who was the particular ass who told us that Mesopotamia was a scorching furnace and had sent us into this climate of icy wind and rain with nothing but cotton kit to wear.

Physical drill in the early morning was the only incident of the day to relieve the monotony of sitting still and looking at palm trees; even the messages which now arrived, by wireless and lamp, from the world outside, soon failed to move us—Italy came into the war at least three times in two days, there were insurrections in Constantinople, Persia had declared war on Turkey, Kaiser Bill had been assassinated. We had all these at frequent and uncertain intervals, repeated with variations, so that we finally believed nothing at all; when a long-promised mail was dumped on to the ship it was a pleasant surprise, and had a most beneficial effect on the somewhat jaundiced outlook of our ship's company It was reassuring to feel that we were not destined to play

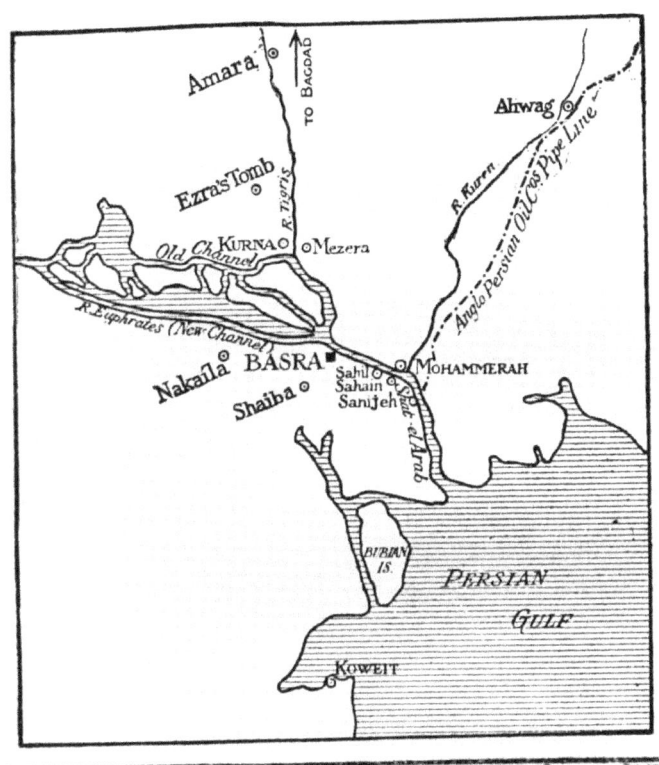
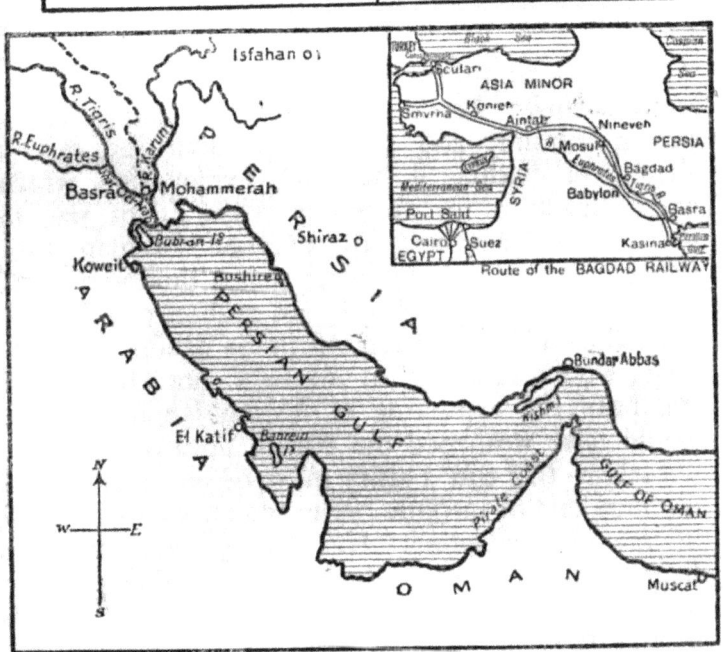

the part of Ancient Mariners for ever. For some anxiety had been felt on this score, as a fishing enthusiast, after spending many weary hours dangling a line over the stern of the boat with commendable patience but no success, had finally hooked and landed a fine seagull: it was felt that this might be an omen.

Almost opposite to where we were anchored the engagement had been fought on 17th November which decided the fate of Basra, when the 16th and 18th Brigades had attacked the Turkish forces in a strongly entrenched position and, though much hampered by the weather and absolute lack of cover, had turned them out and inflicted heavy losses—so heavy that the enemy were unable to offer further organised resistance, and Basra was evacuated four days later.

The name of the spot where the fight took place we heard was "Sahil"—somewhat vague, as "*sahil*" is merely the local word for "shore," and it seems likely that the same mistake has occurred here as happened once before. A surveying party on the Euphrates came to a village, not marked on the map; so, they hailed a local Arab and asked him politely, "What is the name of this village?"

"*M'adri*," replied the Arab.

So, the party marked the village on their map "Madri," and departed, quite content. But *M'adri*, being interpreted, means "I don't know"—which was what the obliging Arab meant to say. However, Madri it remains on the map for all time, and probably Sahil is also there by now.

At last our turn to move arrived, and on 3rd December we weighed anchor in the afternoon and set off up the river, bound, we believed, for Basra, though as it turned out we couldn't make it that night owing to the tide, and in the end had to lie to for the night just below the town. On the way we passed Muhammera, on the mouth of the Karun River, which here joins the Shatt-el-Arab, mixing its clear waters with the yellow flow of the Tigris. The Karun, though now metaphorically rather a backwater, is closely connected with the greatest periods of Persian history and was once the highway to cities the ruins of which, in the shape of great mounds, can be seen in the desert all round Ahwaz, and on the banks of the Kherkha. Ahwaz itself was long ago a city of importance but, until the last few years, had steadily declined in population and prosperity till it was nothing but a half-ruined village; lately, however, the activities of the Anglo-Persian Oil Company, and some increase of trade up the Karun to the Baktiari tribes, have re-established its importance to some degree, and, if all goes well, trade should increase and the country be opened up, as planned by Sir Henry Layard eighty years ago.

It is said, (among others, by Herodotus, Book 1), that the ancient kings of Persia had a particular liking for water from the Kherkha, and wherever they went silver flasks of the water were carried for the royal table: Cyrus, Darius, Xerxes, on all their campaigns drank nothing else, and wherever they were a mounted post was maintained between the Persian camp and the river to bring a constant supply of the precious water; but if you ask any of those whose unhappy lot it was to traverse the Ahwaz district through the summer of 1915 they will probably tell you that they are quite unable to understand such tastes, and that Kherkha water is over-rated stuff.

Muhammera as seen from the river looked rather a pleasant spot, with plenty of trees, and, rumour had it, a very nice Club and a cheery European colony; but what caught the eye most was a wonderful and gaudy building said to be the Sheikh's palace—or rather one of them—with a battery of ancient muzzle-loaders arranged in front, about a mile upstream of the town.

As they pass, the B.I. mailboats always fire a salute, and our transport followed the usual custom: it appears that many years ago the grandfather of the present Sheikh of Muhammera saved a B.I. ship from an attack by pirates, and, in memory of this, all ships of this line pay their respects to his successor. The present Sheikh, Sheikh Gazal, is to all intents and purposes an independent ruler though his territory is technically in Persia; he is hereditary chief of the numerous K'ab tribe of Arabs, and, thoroughly British in his sympathies, has done all he can to prevent German and Turkish propaganda.

It was Sheikh Gazal's father, Mizal, who, some years before the war, put a sudden and unceremonious stop to certain shady German plans to secure "concessions" from the Persian Government to irrigate the Karun valley. Sheikh Mizal intimated that if he wanted his territory irrigated he would manage the affair himself—and employ British engineers.

Muhammera, or its immediate vicinity, is the site of ancient cities, which succeeded each other on the banks of the Karun. Here Alexander the Great founded an Alexandria: it was destroyed by floods and rebuilt by Antiochus (the Seleucid) under the name of Antiochia: it was again destroyed and rebuilt by the Parthians and called Charax—then captured by an Arab who changed its name to Spasini Charax. Finally, in *A.D.* 235, Ardeshir (Sasanian) rebuilt it with again a change

British Royal Engineers at Work

of name—Astrabad or Bahmashir.

But 1914 was not the first occasion that Muhammera had seen a British Army; for in 1857 a British and Indian force fought an action here in which it completely routed the Persian Army. This six months' campaign, which arose indirectly from the capture of Kars and the persistence of the *Shah* in sending an army against Herat, has been almost forgotten.

On 1st November 1856 war was declared, and soon afterwards a division (under General Stalker) sailed from India and occupied Kerak Island and Bushire. A second division (and Sir James Outram, Commander-in-Chief) arrived on 31st January 1857, and an advance was immediately made on the Persians at Brasjaon, 50 miles from Bushire. However, as soon as our force came in sight of the camp on 5th February the Persians retreated hurriedly leaving everything behind them. Not a shot was fired. On the evening of the 7th the force started to march back to Bushire, and on the way the Persians made a half-hearted attack on the columns at Khoshab; this was defeated mainly by our artillery and a charge of the 3rd Bombay Cavalry, which did great execution.

It was then decided to attack the Persians at Muhammera, though it was strongly defended by nine batteries and an entrenched camp held by 13,000 enemy.

On 26th March, at dawn, a bombardment was opened by our ships (Indian Navy), which in a few hours silenced the batteries, so that the transports could move up the river to the point of disembarkation. (The ships were: H.C.S.S, *Clive*, *Assaye*, *Semiramis*, *Falkland*, *Feroze*, *Ajdaha*, and *Comet*.) The troops, about 5000 strong, under the command of Sir Henry Havelock, were formed up, but before the attack could be delivered the enemy broke and fled, leaving the camp and stores in our hands. A few days later 300 British produced the same effect on 7000 Persians at Ahwaz, and on 5th April news was received that peace had been signed.

It is rather a strange coincidence that two regiments (British regiments were: H.M. 78th Highlanders, H.M. 64th Regiment, and H.M. 14th Dragoons), that saw service in this campaign were again in the same part of the world in 1915—the 3rd Cavalry, who won fame at Khoshab, and carry it as a battle honour, are now the 33rd Q.V.O. Cavalry, attached to the VIth Division, and the 14th Dragoons are now the 14th Hussars, who marched up the Tigris later in the year. The *Comet*, which led Havelock's transports past the forts at Muhammera, has its counterpart in the armed launch of the same name in action at Ahwaz in March 1915, almost exactly fifty-eight years later. But to return to modern history.

Soon after passing Muhammera we reached the spot where the Turks, on their retreat upstream, had attempted to block the fairway by sinking three ships; of these the *Ekbatana*, an 8000-ton German boat, still remained with all her upper deck and bridge still above water-level, though of the others, a tug and a lightship, only the top of the tug's funnel was showing. Unfortunately for the Turks they had made some miscalculation: the big ship had failed to settle down, and the action of the tide and the strong current had shifted its position so that, instead of being broadside on to the channel, its bows were pointing half upstream, and, with care, there was plenty of room for our gunboats and transports to get through; as it was, the Turks wasted three good boats, and did themselves no good.

As we approached Basra signs of civilization began to appear—substantial houses, gaudily painted, with balconies and latticed windows, in place of tumble-down mud huts, walled gardens and here and there patches of lucerne (alfalfa) and other vegetables instead of the eternal date palms, though these were still very much in evidence. However, the short twilight was ending, and it was plain that we should not make camp that night, especially as we had just heard we were to disembark three miles upstream of the town. So once more, and for the last time, we dropped anchor in the river.

Next morning, 4th December, we got under way early, passed Basra as it was just getting light, and were soon lying at anchor about three miles above the town, opposite a date plantation, a wharf, and two tin huts, European pattern. This we heard was Magil, where we were to disembark and go into camp.

"Disembark" sounded delightful, and easy enough—camp quite tempting; but the stern realities of unloading ourselves, kits, and stores, not to mention mules, from a 3000-ton transport until the same was empty of all it contained, and clearing an exceedingly jungly date garden so that we could be neatly disposed in a strictly limited space—well, by the end of the first day we wondered if it was as good as it sounded. To add to our difficulties, we were lying a good 150 yards out in the stream, and every man had to be ferried across to the shore in launches, as there was not enough water for the ship to come alongside the wharf. All the horses and mules and stores had to be transhipped into barges and native boats, towed to shore, and there unloaded.

But Magil in truth had many advantages, which it would be ungrateful to a kind fate to disregard: a wharf, a steam crane, a complete system of trolley-lines, a huge iron-roofed shed, two very spick-and-span tin and brick houses, and, last but not least, an almost unlimited supply of steel rails and iron sleepers, all ready to the hand of the invader. If the question should arise, "Why all this kind preparation?" the answer is—the Boche, who, poor soul, had all unwittingly made things so nice and easy for us.

Before the war Magil was a sort of depot of the Baghdad Railway Company; here rails and sleepers and materials sent from Germany were transhipped into iron barges and tugs to be towed upstream to Baghdad, and hence the wharf and shed and crane and the two neat shanties where the German foremen lived; as far as we were concerned nothing could have been better.

Soon the work of disembarkation and unloading was going on well, and as soon as the steam crane and trolleys had been got going, things worked smoothly and rapidly; the crane was simply invaluable in hoisting the horses and mules and heavy stores out of the barges, and the trolleys conveyed the stores from the wharf to the big shed, which had been handed over to the Supply and Transport. When it is remembered that besides all ordinary stores, ammunition, material, food for British and Indian troops, we had also to bring every stick of wood-fuel we needed with us from India,—the country being quite treeless with the exception of date palms,—it can be understood that the stores of even one brigade needed some handling. For the next three or four days this work went on, and by the light of powerful acetylene lamps, well into the night. In the meanwhile, the site for our camp was cleared and tents pitched.

We found ourselves in a thickly planted date plantation— part of the belt which extends all up both banks of the river, from the mouth to Magil—with the river behind us, a creek on our left flank, and another creek, beyond which lay a small village and some walled gardens, on our right; in front the date palms extended for about a mile until the open desert was reached beyond. In every direction the view was much restricted, as there is always a good deal of undergrowth, young trees, bushes, and weeds in these palm belts; communications were difficult and hazardous, as deep water-cuts, irrigation ditches for the palm trees, divided the whole place into squares of 50 yards or so, and most of them were a good deal too broad to jump.

The first thing to be done was to clear the undergrowth, open up the view, make roads in all directions, and bridge the larger of the water-cuts: for this last purpose the iron sleepers, so kindly left by the Germans, answered admirably, and we very soon had all the broadest ditches safely bridged. Without them we should really have been in difficulties, as palm-logs, the only form of wood available, weigh about a ton each and are an awful job to handle. The local Arab, of course, never thinks of any other form of bridge but a single wobbly palm log thrown from bank to bank, and over this he passes with a hop, skip, and jump of his bare feet. But, having watched three members of the mess light-heartedly attempt the Arab stunt, and having assisted in wiping the mud off them afterwards, we came to the conclusion that this was hardly good enough.

The weather now was delightful. Though the nights were certainly chilly and an overcoat was quite welcome until well on in the morning, the days were warm and still with a wonderful freshness in the air; at midday the sun was hot but not powerful enough to make the wearing of a helmet necessary; as soon as the sun dropped below the horizon it was cold, but a dry and windless cold which was not at all unpleasant. Early morning and sunset produced the most wonderful colours in sky and river—a first sample of the gorgeous yet delicate colouring of this world of immense featureless distances, the real beauty of which we were to see more of as we moved upriver. The climate now was very much the climate of the Riviera in February or March—bright sunshine, intensely blue skies, wonderful colouring in the mornings and evenings, and always bright starlit nights; but even the horror of the hot weather, scorching sun, storms of dust-laden wind, fever, mosquitos, thirst—even the sum of all these could not blot out the first impression of that strange and haunting beauty which possesses this desolate Land of the Two Rivers.

Chapter 3

December 1914

By the arrival of the 17th Brigade at Magil on 4th December the VIth (Poona) Division was completed; the 16th and 18th Brigades and most of the divisional troops being already in the country—the whole force known as I.E.F. "D," and under the command of Sir Arthur Barrett. Before going any further, it will be as well to give the composition of the three brigades and a short account of the doings of the 16th and 18th Brigades previous to the 17th Brigade's arrival.

To take the brigades in order of their numbers, the 16th Brigade, under the command of Brigadier-General Delamain, consisted of the following regiments:—

> 16th (Poona) Brigade:
> 2nd Dorset Regiment.
> 104th (Wellesley's) Rifles.
> 20th Punjabis.
> 117th Mahrattas.

The 17th Brigade, commanded by Brigadier General Dobbie, was composed of:—

> 17th (Ahmednagar) Brigade:
> 1st Oxfordshire and Buckinghamshire Light Infantry.
> 103rd Mahratta Light Infantry.
> 119th Infantry.
> 22nd Punjabis (in place of 130th Baluchis).

And the 18th Brigade—Major-General Fry—of the following:—

> 18th (Belgaum) Brigade:
> 2nd Norfolk Regiment.
> 7th Rajputs.

Lieut.-General Sir W. S. Delamain K.C.B., K.C.M.G.

> 120th Infantry.
> 110th Mahrattas.

The Divisional troops were:—

> 10th Brigade, R.F.A.
> 23rd and 30th Mountain Batteries.
> 33rd Light Cavalry.
> 34th Divisional Signalling Company.
> 17th and 22nd Companies Sappers and Miners.
> 48th Pioneers.
> 6th Divisional Ammunition Column.
> 3rd Field Ambulance.
> 30th Mule Corps and Jaipur (Imperial Service) Transport.

Owing to the very suspicious activities of Turkey in September and October, and in view of the important interests which had to be protected in the Persian Gulf and beyond, the 16th (Poona Brigade) with the 23rd and 30th Mountain Batteries left India during the latter month for Bahrein Island—a wise Government deciding to have forces available near at hand in case something should happen.

Turkey declared war on 30th October, and on 7th November General Delamain arrived with his force from Bahrein at the mouth of the river. The Turkish fort here was rapidly silenced by H.M.S. *Odin* and the armed launch *Sirdar*, a landing party put ashore to occupy the telegraph station; the brigade proceeded at once upriver just past Abadan, where it disembarked on the right bank at Sanyeh without opposition. The enemy had evidently not expected such a rapid advance, although he had full information of the strength and composition of General Delamain's force through an agent of the Wonckhaus firm at Bushire, for it was not until 11th November that the Turks showed up. In the early hours of the morning the camp was attacked by a small force which was soon beaten off by a counter-attack of the 20th Punjabis, in which that regiment lost a most gallant officer, Major Ducat, who died of wounds received while leading a bayonet charge; otherwise our casualties were slight.

On 15th November General Delamain's Brigade was reinforced by the arrival of Sir Arthur Barrett with the 18th (Belgaum) Brigade, under Major-General Fry, 10th Brigade R.F.A., 17th Company Sappers and Miners, and one squadron of the 33rd Cavalry: these troops were at once disembarked, and Sir Arthur Barrett took over command.

The next day a "reconnaissance in force" by the 16th Brigade es-

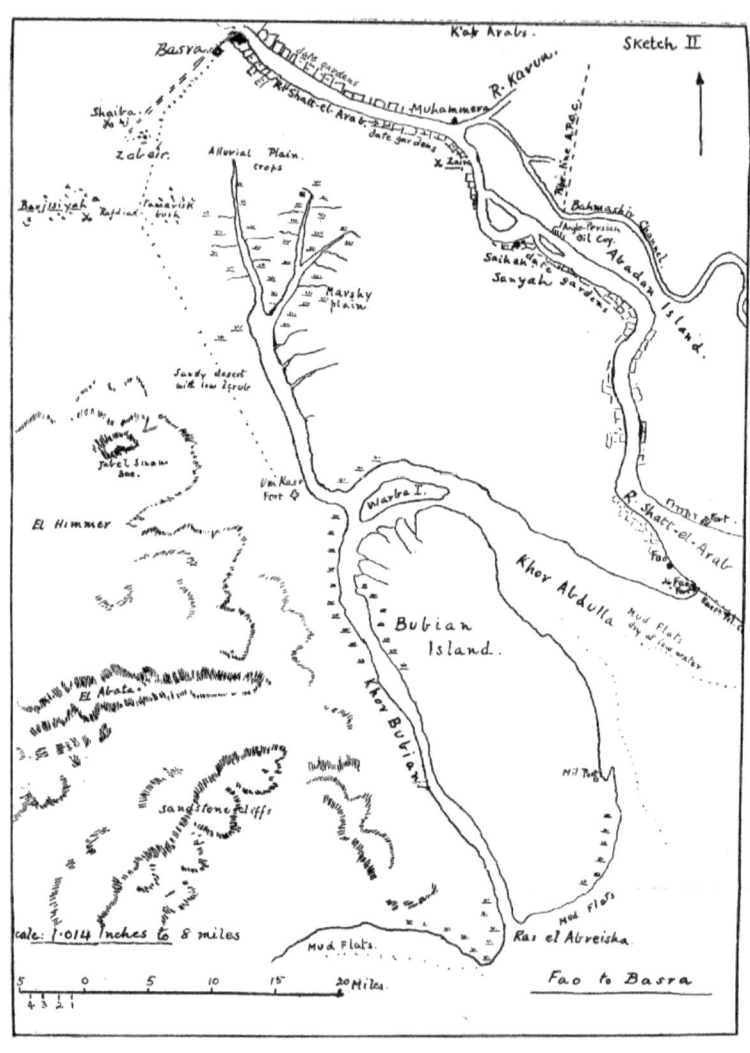

HRB SKETCH FAO TO BASRA

tablished that the enemy in some force were upstream near Zain, and accordingly on the morning of the 17th the whole force marched out of camp to deal with them. The start was made at 5.30 and the six miles across the desert to Zain covered without any opposition or sign of the enemy. Zain village was found to be evacuated, but soon after passing it the force came under fire from the Turkish artillery at Sahil, estimated at twelve guns, and the columns deployed to attack the enemy's position, which could now be seen in the form of a wide semicircle of trenches, the left flank turned back to the river.

Just as the deployment began, a heavy rainstorm broke in a perfect deluge over the desert, and what a moment before had been good going was turned in an instant into a slithering mass of mud, over, which the infantry could only move very slowly and with the greatest difficulty, while the gun-teams could not get on at all and the guns had to be manhandled.

Owing to this, the advance was painfully slow over the 2000 yards of absolutely flat, bare desert without a suspicion of cover; luckily the Turkish shrapnel was bursting too high to do much harm, and their rifle fire was, in the earlier stages of the attack, exceedingly wild. To add to our difficulties there was a bad mirage, and it was often impossible to see the Turkish trenches—at one moment the desert appeared to be a sea of shimmering water, then gradually it resolved itself into a forest of low bushes, then again, a row of smoke-puffs would show from a trench apparently suspended in the sky. In spite of all, the firing-line pressed on, though as they neared the enemy trenches the fire of snipers became very accurate and casualties increased; the Dorsets particularly distinguished themselves by their admirable steadiness, though badly enfiladed and suffering heavily.

However, the Turks were not having it all their own way, as a battery, moved well out to the left, was able to enfilade their right (desert) flank. The firing-line worked up to within 400 yards and, just as it was about to assault, the Turks jumped up and quitted. It was no orderly retirement. They scrambled from the trenches and streamed away across the desert under a tremendous fusillade of rifle-fire and a hurricane of shrapnel which did much damage. But here again the mirage came to their help and saved them; for suddenly—and miraculously it seemed—they disappeared from view and our guns ceased fire; owing to the state of the ground pursuit was out of the question—the infantry was tired out and the cavalry could not move.

The Turks were defeated and suffered heavy losses, over 200 be-

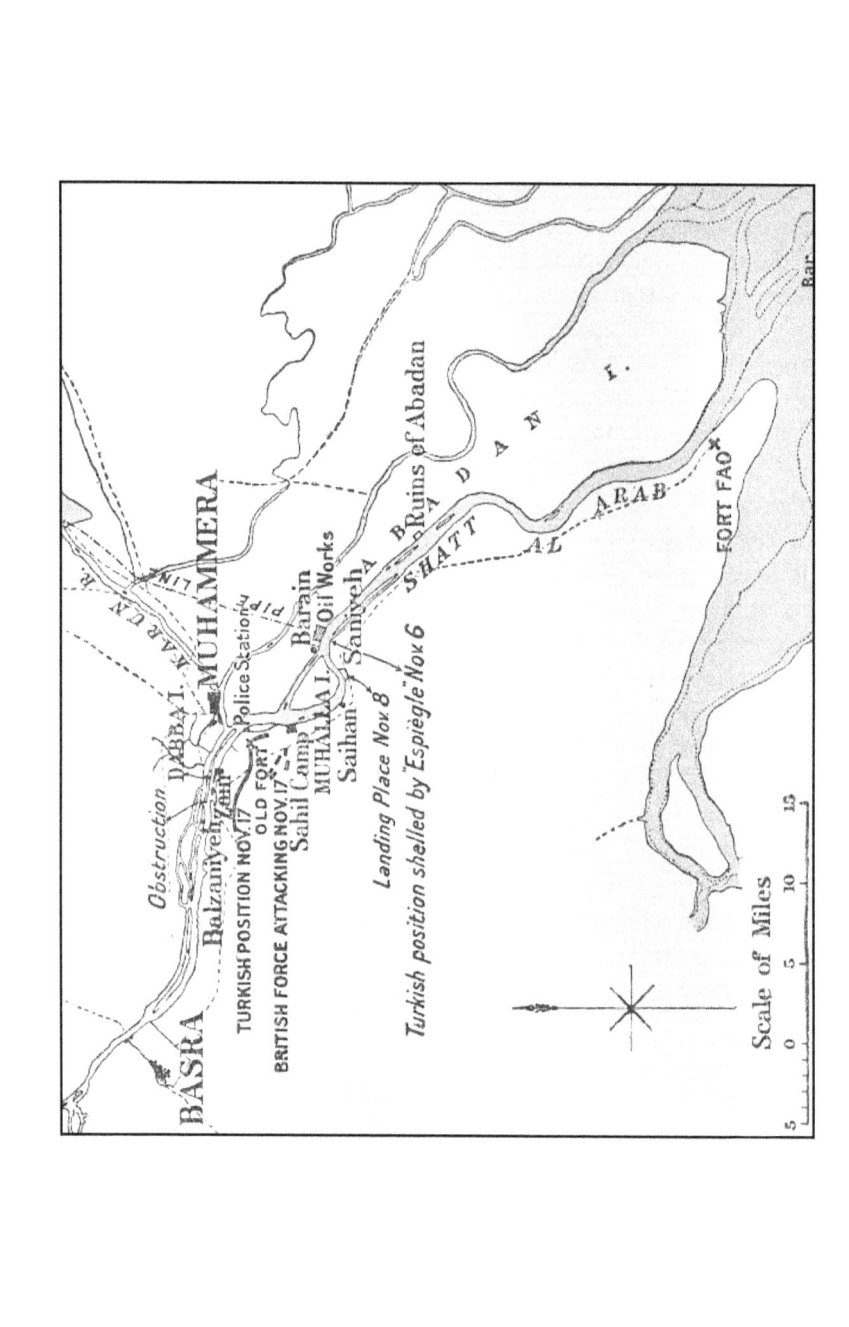

ing buried and the wounded estimated at 1000, besides 150 prisoners and the loss of two guns; but there can be little doubt that without the help of mirage and weather their whole force would have been destroyed. However, though it was not then realised, the engagement of Zain or Sahil decided the fate of Basra and gave us a secure footing in Mesopotamia.

Our own losses were—officers, killed 3, wounded 15; other ranks, killed 40, wounded 300. The wounded suffered severely, as the storm of wind and rain increased and the cold was intense; many lay out on the desert all night, others were carried as far as the river bank, but could not be embarked owing to the high sea running in the river, and the evacuation of the serious cases was thus held up. The expedition was in its infancy and organisation as yet incomplete.

It was on 21st November that the first news was received that Basra was being evacuated by the Turks, and Sir Arthur Barrett immediately decided to press on. General Fry and his staff with the Norfolks and a section of guns were embarked on the *Mejedieh* and the 110th Mahrattas on the *Blosse Lynch*, and the same evening at 9.30 they set off upriver escorted by H.M.S. *Odin* and *Espiègle* and the *Laurence* to take possession of Basra: the remainder of the force was to move across the desert, a 30-mile march. Mention of the *Blosse Lynch* and the *Mejedieh* suggests some reference to the splendid work done by these two river steamers and others of the same line, and an acknowledgment of how much Force "D" owes to Messrs. Lynch.

At this period, they and one other of the same line, the *Malamir*, were the only steamers of any capacity available, and had they not been there we should indeed have been up a tree. In addition to the value of the ships, their officers and others of Messrs. Lynch's personnel possessed a thorough knowledge of the river, the country, and the local Arabs, which was simply invaluable: whether or not this knowledge and their means of securing information was used to the most advantage is a matter of opinion—but it was certainly available and freely offered. It is almost impossible to think of the Mesopotamian campaign in its initial stages without these three Lynch boats, for they were practically the one and only means for the rapid movement of troops and stores.

Comparisons are frequently inconvenient—but why was it that Messrs. Wonckhaus, the leading German firm of the country, were backed through thick and thin by their Government, financed and supported and advised, while Messrs. Lynch, the British firm, was

The "Mejedieh"

gradually being shouldered out of the river-trade by Turco-German restrictions and not a vestige of remonstrance or a shadow of help was forthcoming from England? Wonckhaus, we know now, was a clearing-house for "information," and not only mother-of-pearl and cheap glass ware: Lynch, unsupported and nearly driven off the river, gave the most invaluable help at a critical time. Perhaps it is not too rash to hope that in better days to come the British Government may put two and two together.

The voyage of the two ships with the Norfolks and the 110th was not all plain sailing. At 1 a.m., eight miles upstream of Sahil, they reached the obstruction in the river, where the Turks had sunk the three ships, hoping to bar further progress. But the Turk is seldom very thorough, and he had failed to make a job of it here, although it was considered inadvisable to try to pass the obstruction in the dark, and the flotilla lay to for the night.

H.M.S. *Odin* negotiated it successfully next morning as soon as it was light, and by 7 a.m. on the 22nd all the ships were through. Two hours' steaming brought them in sight of Basra, and clouds of smoke were seen rising from the town; already a message had been received from the American Consul that the Arabs had started looting, so H.M.S. *Odin* and *Espiègle* and *Laurence* pressed on and arrived off Basra soon after nine. There a few rounds of blank from the 4-inch guns frightened the looters into good behaviour, though it was only just in time, as they had already broken into and set on fire the Custom House, and the Consulates were expecting their turn next.

General Fry's force was immediately landed from the ships, and piquets and patrols at once occupied the town, soon restoring order amongst a population which, with the exception of a few rowdy elements bent on looting, were evidently much relieved that British troops had put in an appearance. By noon the remainder of the force arrived, after a forced march of 30 miles—an exhausting journey by a route for which no maps were available and native guides not forthcoming, though the column was led throughout the night without serious loss of direction by an officer of the 33rd.

As men and horses were pretty well finished, and no billets had as yet been allotted in the town, the column camped for the day outside the walls and the official entry was postponed. On the morning of 23rd November, the troops marched in and were drawn up near the Turkish barracks; then in the presence of the various big-wigs of the town a proclamation was read, in Arabic and English, setting forth our aims and objects, and the reason for our presence. The Union Jack was run up, and the ships fired a salute of guns. Basra and its people had changed empires.

The next week was occupied in reorganisation, landing stores, clearing the Turkish barracks and other billets for the troops, and generally setting the place in order. Nothing more was heard of the rabble which had fled over the desert from Sahil until the beginning of December.

Some 40 miles upstream of Basra the "old" Euphrates joins the Tigris. The point between the two rivers is occupied by the village of Kurna (pronounced "Gurna"), the surrounding country being low-lying desert and marsh, bare and open, except immediately round Kurna and Mazéra (Muzeera), a village opposite it on the left bank of the Tigris, where there are considerable plantations of date palms.

The terms "old" and "new" Euphrates are at first rather confusing. The "old" Euphrates, which joins the Tigris at Kurna, is now scarcely navigable, and has become almost a backwater owing to the river having in fairly recent times changed its course farther to the south-west, and cut a new channel for itself through which it discharges most of its stream into the Tigris at Gurmat Ali, five miles or so above Basra; this channel is known as the "new" Euphrates.

At present it is ill defined and constantly shifting, so that it is almost impossible for navigation, and a great deal of the water escapes over the surrounding desert, which for half the year is one immense lake. The Euphrates, then, in its lower reaches, being useless for practical purposes of supply and communication, the Turks were forced to fall back along the Tigris, and if possible get themselves dug in in a defensive position where they could bar our advance up-river and at the same time get reinforcements and stores down quickly, and also— a most important consideration to the Oriental soldier—a position where there was not much chance of us getting behind them and coming in through the back door when they might want to get out!

Subhi Bey, the Vali of Basra, after his defeat on 17th November, had collected the disorganised remnants of his force, and leaving Basra to its fate, had cleared off upstream as fast as his boats could take him, as far as Kurna. In this he was no doubt wise, for the Kurna-Mazera line certainly had possibilities, and his troops had had a shaking and could do with a breather; but he miscalculated the possible speed of our pursuit.

News of the enemy's concentration at Kurna was no sooner received than a force was immediately sent to deal with it. Again,

Turkish prisoners

the *Blosse Lynch* and *Medjedieh* were to the fore; each mounted an 18-pounder, well protected with sandbags, and with the 104th and 110th, a detachment of Norfolks, and half a company of Sappers and Miners on board, they left for Kurna at 8 p.m. on 3rd December. The force was under the command of Lieutenant-Colonel Frazer, of the 110th, and was supported by a strong flotilla—H.M.S. *Espiègle* and *Odin*, and the armed tugs *Miner*, *Shaitan*, and *Lewis Petty*.

On the morning of December 4th, the force landed on the north bank of the Swaib, (actually the overflow of the Kherkha), a river that runs into the Tigris on the left bank, and a move was at once made against Mazera. By river, the armed launches pushed forward most gallantly and were soon in the thick of it, as indeed the navy always had been, and always was. Throughout the campaign, on so many occasions—here and elsewhere—the ships did half the work from the river, while the army did the other half on land—it was a most effective and loyal partnership. The Turkish guns had opened fire as soon as the ships had come in sight of Kurna, and, carefully concealed in the date palms and difficult to locate, succeeded in securing a good many hits. The *Miner* was holed below the water-line, and had to retire, temporarily, from the fight.

But in the meantime the *Espiègle*, firing 4-inch lyddite, had set fire to Mazera village, which went up in a cloud of smoke, and soon the surrounding date gardens were cleared of the enemy; apparently their preparations were but half completed, for the trenches were too shallow to give any protection against our shrapnel. Soon the attacking troops had worked across the intervening ground, and reached the left bank of the Tigris again, on the farther side of the elbow bend and opposite Kurna. But it was a case of thus far and no farther. As soon as they showed up on the bank they were met by very heavy rifle-fire from Kurna, where every house and wall was loopholed and evidently strongly held. If the opposition had been slight before, they were obviously "up against it" now. No boats, no bridge, three hundred yards of yellow racing Tigris, and a storm of rifle-fire were too great obstacles for the small force, and there was nothing for it but to turn back. So, the order was given to retire, and night found them back once more in their camp on the banks of the Swaib, where they had disembarked that morning.

If the Turks had underestimated the speed with which we should move, we had also underestimated the strength of the opposition to be met: Colonel Frazer's small force was obviously not man enough

Turkish prisoners with British Guards

in point of numbers for the job, and reinforcements were wired for.

That night and the following day passed without incident except for desultory shelling, and on the 6th General Fry arrived from Basra with the remainder of the Norfolks, the 7th Rajputs, one battery of field artillery, and another of mountain guns. But in the meanwhile, the Turks had also been reinforced from upstream and had again crossed the river and occupied the charred remains of Mazera. On the morning of the 7th General Fry attacked, and the engagement of the 4th was fought over again with very much the same result. The launches pushed up towards Kurna again with great dash and were allowed by the Turks to get quite near before they opened a tremendous fire from guns and rifles which forced them to retire; but the *Shaitan*, leading, was badly caught in the storm, and her commander, Lieutenant-Commander Elkes, R.N.R., was killed on the bridge by a direct hit from a shell, which wrecked the steering gear.

The launch narrowly escaped running aground within close range of the enemy's guns, but she was successfully brought down stream by her second in command and later patched up; but Commander Elkes' death was a loss very hard to replace. By land the trenches round Mazera were cleared again, the enemy driven across the river, but again our advance was held up by heavy fire from Kurna and a retirement was ordered. But this time a strong detachment was left on the bank opposite Kurna to prevent the enemy re-crossing, and a movement was made towards "the back door."

In the early hours of the morning of the 8th, the 110th and 104th, accompanied by a section of mountain guns and some sappers and miners, marched up the left bank, well away from the river, then, turning left-handed, reached the stream. There a flying bridge was quickly constructed by Lieutenant Campbell and the sappers, and the troops were ferried across to the opposite bank. Before the Turks realised what had happened they found that this force had marched down the right bank on their rear and were astride the northern approaches to Kurna: their communications were cut and the back door held fast against them.

The end was not long in coming. At midnight a brightly illuminated launch was seen heading downstream; on board were Turkish officers, sent by their commander, Subhi Bey, with a request for a parley. The Turks realised the hopelessness of their position; Subhi Bey was willing to surrender if his troops might march out under arms; Kurna should be evacuated. But General Fry very rightly would not listen to this suggestion but demanded unconditional surrender. After some discussion this was agreed to, and at 1 p.m. on the 19th the Turkish troops marched out of Kurna and laid down their arms. Many escaped during the night and in the early morning, and were seen marching off upstream by our patrols, but no cavalry being available pursuit was unfortunately out of the question, and they made good their escape.

Forty-two officers, including Subhi Bey, and 1100 men, surrendered, and their losses in Kurna and in the two engagements at Mazera had been heavy; 12 guns, all obsolete Krupps, were captured. Our own losses in the engagements of the 4th and 7th were three officers killed, including Lieutenant-Commander Elkes, R.N.R., and six wounded; other ranks, fifty killed and about two hundred and twenty wounded.

Kurna was occupied immediately, cleared of undesirable characters, and steps taken to clean up the appalling mess left by the Turkish troops and introduce some kind of sanitation. At its best Kurna is only a collection of filthy lanes and hovels, but, as left by its late occupiers, it was far from at its best. Many thought that the campaign was over or that at least no further advance was to be made, so it seemed wise to make the place as fit as possible for a prolonged stay.

Chapter 4

Basra

In the meantime, the 17th Brigade remained downstream at Magil leading a life of peace, with a certain amount of hard work thrown in. At first, we fully expected to be sent up to reinforce the troops fighting at Kurna, and although reinforcements were sent we were not the lucky ones, and after a few days more suspense we heard, on 10th December, of Subhi Bey's defeat and surrender.

The news was received with very mixed feelings. In those early days we imagined that our *raison d'être* was to protect the oil works at Abadan and the pipe-line from any interference, and the Turkish forces having now been driven well out of the district it seemed probable that we should sit down and hold on to what we'd got. Kurna was taken, the Shatt-el-Arab was controlled, and I believe it is a fact that at the time no further advance was contemplated; at any rate, we looked forward in those days to a dreary prospect of garrison work in Mesopotamia.

The time was spent now in improving the camp, roadmaking, and furnishing fatigue parties for unloading ships, and in battalion and company drill in the desert. Marching out of camp in the morning the road led first through a mile or two of date palms, with here and there a few plots of lucerne surrounded by fences of palm branches—enclosed country, with nothing to see but tree trunks in every direction. Then suddenly the trees came to an end, and one found oneself marching into illimitable space, over the open brown earth of the desert, which stretched away, it seemed, for ever into the distance. To the left one could see the outskirts of Basra and its minarets, and to the right some tall brick-kilns marked the course of the river, but directly ahead there was nothing but sky and earth, a vast expanse of blue and brown.

This sudden change, as one emerged from the narrow winding paths through the date grove, with its subdued light and close atmosphere, into the vast open expanse of desert, with the shimmering glare of the sun and the fresh breeze, was very striking—almost unconsciously one found oneself thinking of the sea, of standing on some shore, looking over miles of open water, listening to the rush of the wind. But this was winter; in the summer we were to find the desert a very different place.

Basra, to anyone who does not know, or hate, the East, is well worth seeing; but in truth it is rather an Ichabod of a town. Its glory is departed, and its state fallen since the days when Sinbad sailed from its port and the learned doctors argued in its schools.

Properly speaking, Basra is divided into two parts: the town itself, standing about two miles from the river on the Ashar Creek, and the port, Ashar, on the river bank—though, as a rule, "Basra" (pronounced "Bussra") includes the two. Ashar itself is a small town, the back streets of the usual grubby picturesque Oriental type, though the river frontage boasts a few fine buildings—the Turkish Naval Commandant's house, the German Embassy, the offices of two or three big English merchants; the small European colony live here, and there is also an English Club—with a tennis court and excellent drinks.

The ancient Basra, originally founded by the Caliph Omar in 636 A.D., was situated eight miles of its present site, where now the ruins of "Old Basra" and Zobeir stand. In those days the river ran farther to the west, but gradually changing its course to its present bed the city was left high and dry—the fate of so many of the cities in this country which trusted their lives to these erratic streams.

It was in the earlier years of its existence that Basra rose to fame as the city of wealth and magnificence and learning, a product of the period when the glory of the great *Caliphs* was spread through the world, and fables of "the gorgeous East" were never too strange, too wonderful to be believed. Much that can be read in the *Thousand-and-One Nights*, though half fiction, is a true picture of those earlier days in Basra, portraits of the life and times in its bazaars and schools and palaces and ships, in the years before the Caliph Mansur built his greater city in the north. Sinbad was a real man who sailed away on his voyages in just such a high-prowed "*mahéla*" as you may see to this day, moored in the river opposite, jostling a 4000-ton B.I. mail-boat; and in his wanderings and adventures and discoveries you may read the great overseas trade, the fleet of ships, the sailors and the merchandise that thronged the port and the bazaars.

It was at the zenith of the Omayyad Caliphate, after the massacre of Husain and his followers at Kerbela, that Basra was famous for its theologians and philosophers such as Hasan and Jahiz—learned men who wandered from the narrow path of the True Faith. Then came unsettled times after Yazid's death, when all Arabia and Syria were plunged in civil war; to the general *mêlée* Basra contributed the Kharijite schismatics, whose rebellions and disturbances kept the surrounding country in a state of seething unrest till they were finally put down, after an eighteen-months' campaign, by Mohallab in 697.

It was soon after this that Basra, reduced by years of disorder, received a heavy blow by the transference of the government of Irak to the newly-founded Wasit, a city built by Hajjaj, Abd-el-Malik's great viceroy, to facilitate the government of the country, Basra having become too turbulent a place for comfort.

Later, Basra again occupies an important page in Mesopotamian history. It was in 758, when the Omayyads were no more and the second Abbásid Caliph, Mansur, was hunting the last of the family of Ali, that Ibrahim (son of Abdallah, grandson of the Prophet) raised the standard of revolution in Basra, only to be defeated and slain a few months later by Isa; Ibrahim's brother Mohammed, together with their father Abdallah, had suffered the same fate, and the cause of the house of Ali was lost. Thus, his last enemies accounted for, Mansur at once turned his attention to the building of his new capital, Baghdad, which was completed in 766 A.D. and henceforward became the first city of Mesopotamia; Basra, both politically and economically, becoming of very secondary importance.

We hear little of the city during the Middle Ages, and the next episode of importance in its history is its capture by the Turks in 1668; in 1777, after a siege of eight months, it was taken by the Persians but retaken by the Turks in 1778.

But under Turkish government the city's importance has gradually dwindled, until now the population has shrunk to a bare 30,000: you may walk through the streets and look in vain for the two hundred mosques, the colleges, the libraries and palaces which once stood within the walls, and in the maze of the narrow, filthy bazaars it is hard to recognise the once wealthy markets of a great city.

And yet Basra even as it now stands, or as it was in 1914, for it has been "improved" since then, holds still some mysterious charm, some links with its past which recall the scenes of the stories. In the twilight of the mat-roofed bazaars the water-carrier, his little donkey laden with two dripping skins, will jostle you against the narrow cupboard-like shops where grave men sit before their wares piled in baskets at their feet—just like Alnaschar with his glassware, who "chose a very little shop and sat with his basket before him and his back against the wall till someone should come and buy his wares." So, you may see them sitting now, silent and contemplative and apparently not at all anxious to sell, before their heaps of melons and cucumbers, or their cases of cheap European goods, or piles of carpets—the dim, hazy light softening the glaring colour of the German aniline dyes.

Then you can walk through the silk bazaar, where fat merchants in large turbans blink shifty eyes—and just such a one must have been that greedy merchant who met the *dervish* with the magic ointment on his way from "Balsorah." The crowd has probably changed little enough—through the streets pass Jew and Indian, Syrian and African and Persian, porters with their heavy loads, with their continual cry of "*Bárluk, Bárluk!*" to clear the way, donkeymen, grave Arabs in their flowing *abbas*, and the shuffling forms of the veiled women.

Up many a dark alley you will catch a glimpse of massive doors, heavily barred and studded with iron, dark archways, and high, windowless walls which might hide many a court of fountains and cool marbles—might, though you know that such things are past and gone. But still one may be pretty sure that though Nur-ed-din and The Fair Persian are dead, such stories as theirs are still enacted behind those broad-latticed windows which lean mysteriously over the palm-fringed creeks, and that still the counterparts of the garrulous barber and his six brothers live somewhere in these twilit streets.

But, turning from fancies to facts, the well-stocked bazaars show that the trade of Basra, though it may have dwindled since those far-off days, is not by any means dead; indeed, it has increased considerably in the last few years, and is recovering gradually from the depression caused long ago by the discovery of the Cape route to India.

Dates, of course, are the chief article of export: every year from the palms of Basra and the surrounding country a huge harvest is gathered, packed (in boxes brought ready-made from Norway) and exported, mainly to America, England, and Somaliland. There is no doubt that the date-business of Mesopotamia has a great future before it and ought to go ahead after the war, when, under British rule (we will hope), the country will be more settled and shipping facilities enormously increased. Dates are inexpensive to raise and apparently need skilled labour only during a short period each season, (for the process of fertilisation, which has to be done by hand), provided that, as the Arabs say, "their heads are in the fire and their feet in the water"—two conditions easily fulfilled with the sun and the river as allies; and the palms, once grown, are very prolific.

Besides dates, Basra exports wheat and barley and large quantities of liquorice; in 1912 £1,118,000 was the figure for barley— and here again there is no doubt that the security afforded by British rule, better communications, and modern methods will increase the growing and export of grain a hundredfold. Hundreds of thousands of acres of corn-growing land, some of it the best in the world, lie ready to be ploughed, and a tremendous area of land can be reclaimed by draining and irrigation.

Irrigation, though it is far from being so easy a matter as it sounds, is, of course, the key to this country of so-called desert. Desert the Mongols made it and desert the Turks have allowed it to remain, but there is no doubt that it is some of the most fertile land in the world— the same land that supported the teeming populations of Babylon and Assyria, and of Sumer and Akkad before them; but these people knew the secret of irrigation and covered the country with a network of canals, of which now only the ruins and dry skeletons remain.

Given irrigation and population the soil and climate can produce a wonderful variety. Round Basra in irrigated gardens, mostly belonging to Jews, you may see apples, peaches, nectarines, grapes, figs, pomegranates, dates, plums, and melons of several kinds; tomatoes, peas, beans, broccoli, lettuce, cucumbers, onions, garlic, artichokes, lucerne; while on the banks of the irrigation ditches clover grows in the grass under the willows, and roses and hollyhocks make one think of home. In fact, one is rather puzzled to know what will not grow in this Garden of Eden.

Among exports must not be forgotten the valuable trade in Arab ponies; though most of the trade at present is centred in Koweit, the two big Basra firms have a large business with the horse dealers. These ponies are not a local product, coming mainly from the interior of Arabia and the Western Desert, but there would seem to be possibilities in the future for other stock along the banks of the rivers, and especially for sheep, judging by the quality of the mutton which we sampled on many occasions. As for minerals, their development, too, is greatly a matter for the future, though we know that oil exists in huge quantities and that there are large deposits of bitumen at other places besides Hit, which might be profitably worked. I met one enthusiast, a skipper of a river tug, who persuaded me (over two bottles of beer) that it was certainly from the Pusht-i-Kuh that Solomon got his gold—he was most convincing at the time, but I have since heard that there are reasonable grounds for doubt.

In 1912 the exports of Basra totalled 3¼ millions, the imports considerably over 2½ millions, making a total annual trade of nearly six millions: then the country was extremely unsettled, the resources undeveloped, communications bad and slow, shipping facilities at Basra very limited; and last, but assuredly not least, the country was under the blighting influence of Turkish rule, that poisonous regime of neglect, corruption, bigotry, and bullying which has strangled a great civilization and made a desert of a world's granary.

After the war we must look forward to a British Mesopotamia—must, because for three years we have shown the people what it is to live under honest administration, and taught them to rely on justice, and have begun to make the desert blossom as the rose; and to surrender the people and the country again into the frauds from which we rescued them would be not merely a shirking of responsibility but an act of national cowardice, a deliberate and cynical refusal to fulfil our obligations.

No doubt there is a large reward waiting for the rescuers of Mesopotamia: so large a reward that many will find there, motives of "land-grabbing" and Imperialism in its worst aspects and see good reason to decry British rapacity. Others will own that European intervention is necessary, but shrinking from a great responsibility, or fearful lest their own country should reap any advantage, will suggest international action.

To both the answer might be in the form of advice to read and learn how for nearly 300 years Great Britain has policed the seas that lead to Mesopotamia, protected the trade of all nations alike, and unwisely indeed but in good faith, produced that order by which the Turks, and not the British, were enabled to carry on a policy of land-grabbing. For 150 years Great Britain has been mistress of the Gulf and its coasts, its harbours and its trade waters, but a mistress who has ruled for others, opened and kept open the way for others and never appropriated territory for herself: it was only when Germany, profiting by British policy and the Pax Britannica, began to "jump" claims on the Gulf coast or to secure concessions of land from Turkey to which Turkey itself had no vestige of claim that Great Britain very

A "Goofah" at Amara—The Circular Boat mentioned by Herodotus.

mildly asserted herself. Only by the outbreak of the *Kaiser's* War was the medium of this assertion changed from notes and diplomatic interviews to guns and battlefields.

As for a future international administration of Mesopotamia it is, of course, a possible alternative, but it suggests a few questions. Firstly, have those who support it any personal knowledge of the country and its needs, and have they heard the wishes of the Arabs themselves expressed? Do they know that for many years before the war it was to Great Britain that the tribes of Mesopotamia looked for relief, and that it was to the British residency at Baghdad, not to the Turkish, German, Russian, French, or Italian authorities, that they came for help? Does not history suggest that Great Britain is the most successful of Western peoples in dealing with Orientals? Does not our long and extensive contact with the Mahommedan religion, ideas, and civilization particularly qualify us to administer Mahommedan affairs? That the great mass of Arabian opinion is in favour of British administration, that it would prefer it to any other nation's, is a fact: that Great Britain has succeeded better than other European Powers in its dealings with Oriental and Mahommedan populations seems hard to deny; and the evidence of history is not favourable to condominiums.

There seems one great obstacle to Mesopotamia becoming a British Protectorate, and that is political cowardice—fear that we may be accused of land-grabbing, fear that we may do the unpopular thing, fear that others may be jealous, perhaps fear of responsibility.

This cowardice, these combinations of fears, all had their place in the luggage of our politicians before the war; let us hope that in the turmoil of war some of their baggage has been lost, and that never again shall we find a British Minister so pitifully ready with surrender—a secret and craven surrender, who would readily give everything to the Big Bully, "if only you'll promise not to hit me."

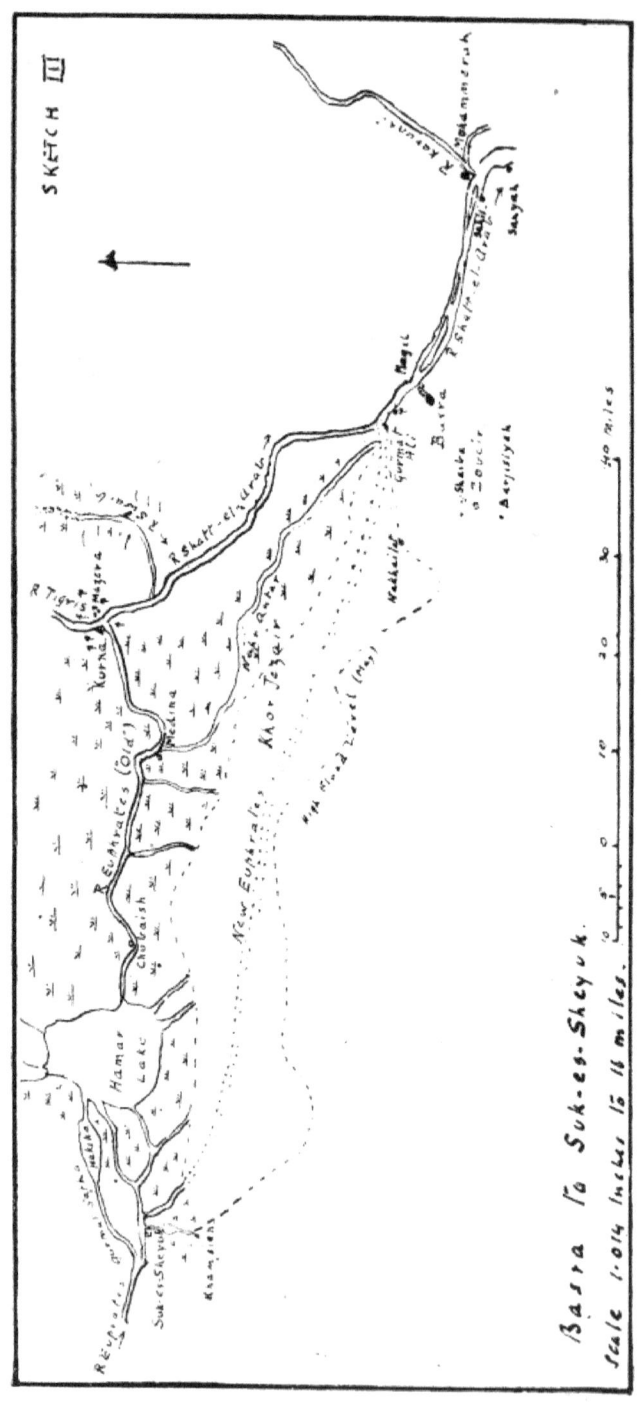

HRB sketch Basra to Suk-es-Sheyuk

CHAPTER 5

17th Brigade Move to Mazera

Having as it were found our legs and explored our immediate surroundings, those provident ones who had included guns in their kit began to question the sporting possibilities of the country. On the way upriver we had seen any amount of strange water-fowl of sorts—the scoffers called them "paddy-birds"—but there had certainly been some duck amongst them; and lately the sound of flighting wings had been heard in the early mornings. Besides, much of the country bordering the river looked decidedly "snipe-y."

So at length it was decided to try a muddy, marshy-looking island about a mile up from Magil, and, one afternoon, having collected our scatter-guns, cartridges, a *bellum*, and three villainous-looking Arabs, we set forth to see what we could find. It was a cloudy, blustering afternoon, so we made slow headway upstream, poling along the bank, and our journey was not hastened by the crew striking half-way with a demand for twice as much as they had bargained for; however, they were very soon persuaded that they had made a mistake, and, continuing our voyage, we at last arrived.

We had hardly set foot on the island before it was quite evident that we had come to the right place; snipe flicked up in every direction, hundreds of them, and we were soon busy. It's as well to get excuses over at once, and I will begin with the bad light; then there was a nasty gusty wind, and it was very cold; also we were using No. 5 shot; both of us were nearly drowned on several occasions by falling into water-cuts; the Arab appears to be a congenital idiot when it comes to marking and picking up birds—he doesn't understand English (even if one shouts very loud); our ammunition was limited; and, lastly, perhaps we didn't hold quite as straight as we might have—anyhow, we splashed and waded about the island for two hours, and returned to our boat with 14½ couple of snipe, one snippet, and one various: the price being 100 cartridges, rather more than less.

However, it was quite a successful afternoon, for we had established beyond any doubt that there were snipe to be had in plenty and close at hand, so that while our enforced peace conditions continued we proposed to have other and more successful outings after them; also, we had reliable information of duck up the "New" Euphrates.

In case the casual reader should think that we did nothing but lay plans for "*shikar*" and carry out the same, I must hastily add that there was plenty of work, clearing ground, road-making, unshipping wood and stores, doing outpost duty and numerous fatigues. But as we were a long way from the fighting there is nothing exciting to chronicle, the routine of fatigues and parades is of no interest, and only the intervals when we were able to emerge from the seclusion of our date grove afforded incidents to be noted in restricted diary-space.

On 20th December a preliminary reconnaissance after duck up the New Euphrates gave us a chance of seeing more of the country, and, I think, some idea of the vast flatness of it all. Having borrowed a staff steam-launch, the *Asp*, we started in the morning and headed upstream, past the island where we had shot the snipe, and, arriving at Gurmat Ali, left the Tigris on our right and rounding a wooded island were soon steaming up the Euphrates. The view was extraordinarily beautiful: to the left stretched miles of unbroken desert, chequered by the flitting shadows of the clouds, ahead of us the Euphrates lay very still and blue in the morning sunlight, and on the right were low scrub-jungles of thorn bushes, with here and there a group of palms.

It was one of the typical landscapes of this country which we were later to know so well—a strangely featureless picture in values of brown and blue, but now in the early morning a haze of such beautiful shades and gradations which, without having seen, is hard to imagine, impossible to describe. Later in the year, when the fiery sun is in full power, these delicate tones would be changed to fierce splashes of brazen yellow, hard stony blue, glaring purples.

Our smoke left a black trail over the blue waters behind us as we chugged upstream, with not a sound to be heard but the beat of our engine. Close to the banks on either side we could see the big black-and-white kingfishers busy at work, hovering high over the water, then dropping like stones to their dive. In the distance a group of dark specks in the water created some excitement at first, but on getting nearer they turned out to be coot, with which, farther on, the river was crowded.

As we went on, the palms and most of the scrub disappeared, and their place was taken by beds of tremendous reeds, especially on the left bank, where rushes and marsh stretched away to the horizon. On the right bank the belt of marsh was narrow, and beyond we could see rice-fields and a few villages, the houses built of reeds.

After about three hours' steaming we saw through the haze ahead of us that the channel appeared to divide, and, on getting a better view, we made out five distinct streams branching off from the main channel, like the five fingers of a hand. This meant that we had got as far as we could safely go, for it is here that the New Euphrates is still in process of deciding which road it really prefers, and the river flows through many constantly shifting unnavigable channels—unnavigable, that is to say, unless you "know all about it."

Accordingly, we called a halt, and embarking in the *bellum* which had been towed astern, paddled across to the right bank. We very soon saw some duck feeding upstream, and we also very soon discovered that duck-shooting in these parts was not quite so easy as it seemed; the birds were not at all tame, and always insisted on flying too high or too soon, which proved disastrous to our day's sport. Though we saw plenty of teal, gadwell, mallard, and brahmini, and other species we could not recognise, we found it impossible to get near them, and by 3.30 had only managed to "down" one teal, which, with 5½ couple of snipe, one black partridge, and four various, made the sum of our bag. No doubt there are ways and means of getting at the duck here, but the tremendous area of the marshes and pools on the left bank, the size of the river and the many channels, make it extraordinarily difficult in the middle of the day. Probably great fun could have been had at flighting-time, but naturally no leave was obtainable at such hours.

Christmas Day was now approaching, and the problem of Christmas dinners loomed large. Company officers were to be seen stealing off to Basra to try persuasion on the stony-hearted Supply and Transport with a view to hams and anything else that could be bought for their men—generally, I am afraid, with little success, as extras were scarce. However, at the eleventh hour the situation was saved by the arrival of Lady Willingdon's excellent plum puddings, a most welcome surprise, which was much appreciated by everyone, and helped us to realise it really was Christmas.

There was a certain amount of feeling owing to the non-appearance of a promised turkey. This turkey had been bought a fortnight before in Basra at a huge price and dedicated by the generous purchaser to the mess. But in the meantime, he and the mess sergeant had made a pet of the bird and discovered her to be the possessor of so many endearing qualities that, when it came to the point, they felt themselves unable to kill one who had become their constant and affectionate companion! "Elizabeth" was spared to accompany us for many months, to take part in all our journeys and to share the vicissitudes of war. She favoured each officer in turn by sleeping on or under his camp bed and could always be found at mealtimes in the mess-tent, where she stalked up and down pecking flies off our backs or dozing among the papers in the corner.

At last one day she fell ill; her legs swelled, and we thought it was gout; but when she died, mourned by all ranks, the doctor who conducted a post-mortem examination gave it as his opinion that death was due to three dozen gramophone needles, four regimental buttons and two trouser *ditto*, all found in the deceased's possession at the end.

On Christmas Day the *Asp* carried another cargo of cheerful sportsmen up the Euphrates. This time we were bolder, and, trusting to the assurances of the Chaldaean skipper-engineer-fireman that he knew all about the river, we essayed one of the branching channels. All went well till suddenly the launch gave a heave and a lurch, slowed down, and finally stopped with a hiss and splutter, hard aground on a mud-bank. For two hours we tried to get her off, until someone noticed that the tide was ebbing, the boat heeling over more and more, and it became plain that a little more at the same pace and the launch would be high and dry on her side and her cargo in the mud.

Leaving our Chaldean to his fate, we hastily evacuated and paddled ashore in the *bellum*. There our luck with the ducks was not conspicuous, but that element of danger, which is said to be so attractive to sport, was present. With us was a representative of the British Navy, a cheerful soul and an addition to any party. He had a gun which he had picked up cheap, in Bushire, I think he said. Anyhow, he told us it was a very good gun, the only thing against it being that *sometimes* it went off when he closed the breech. We stood behind him while he had three tries to load the weapon and wasted six cartridges. After that we left him, and for a long time heard heavy explosions at frequent and uncertain intervals. Later he said he had been shooting coot, which weren't worth picking up, of course!

Late in the afternoon, with 3½ brace of duck and some snipe to our bag, we waded back across the mud to where the *Asp* was lying on her side. Our skipper told us cheerfully that the tide would float her off about 3 a.m. next morning, and that he would be quite comfortable for the night. There was nothing for it but to row and pole the twelve miles back in our *bellum*, with the hope that it would dry our soaking clothes, for consolation. The pink and gold of sunset were staining the clear blue sky as we started off on the long homeward voyage, and when we made Gurmat Ali and the helpful stream of the Shatt-el-Arab the moon was up, changing the river to a sheet of bluish silver, down which we drifted close under the dark shadow of the palms till Magil was reached. And so ended Christmas Day.

However, we had almost come to the end of our sylvan life in Magil, which, though pleasant in some respects, was hardly what we imagined we had been sent from India for. It was in the early hours of the morning, 28th December, that we were roused by the dulcet tones of our respective orderly corporals announcing that the regiment would parade in full marching order at 8 a.m.; further, that kits would be stacked for loading at 7 a.m., and that by 8.30 we should be embarked on the *Blosse Lynch* bound upstream. As there had been no whisper or rumour of a move the night before, this was rather a surprise.

The morning air struck horribly chilly as I emerged from the comfortable fug of a 40-lb. tent into the starlit darkness and toyed with a bucket of water on which there was a quarter-inch of ice. Why had we been sent to this tropical climate with nothing but cotton drill? But it was no time to go into such matters now, as there was plenty to be done in getting kits together, "packing up" the camp, getting the mules and horses and ammunition on board, cooking and eating breakfasts, and a thousand and one other things necessary before we left our happy home. It was difficult work in the dark at first, but as soon as the sun rose everything went well, and smoothly and in a surprisingly short space of time all was complete, and, leaving a depot of sick and sundries to follow later with tents and heavy baggage, we embarked on the boat and started off upstream, bound for Kurna. The remaining regiments of the brigade were to follow as quickly as the limited transport would permit.

The journey from Magil to Kurna is, from the point of scenery, very uninteresting. The usual belts of palms continue for some way on either bank, gradually giving way to scrub and marsh, which on the right bank stretches to the New Euphrates and covers a tract of country which later in the year is under water. In fact, the whole desert between the "Old" Euphrates and the "New" Euphrates is one great triangle of marsh and reeds, with Suk-es-Sheyuk, Kurna, and Basra at the three angles. Though the left bank is not so marshy at this time of the year, and the cultivable land stretches farther into the desert on that side, still there is a tremendous area there too which is, as the map has it, "liable to floods"—that is to say, that between February and May it is half water. Marsh and palms, a grey sky and a cold wind, is about all that can be said of the voyage up, which was uninteresting in the extreme, until towards evening we rounded a bend and saw Kurna ahead of us, jutting out on its peninsula between the two rivers, the blue, leisurely Old Euphrates and the racing, tawny Tigris.

We steamed about a mile upstream past Kurna, till beyond the palm trees we could see the straggling form of a camp dimly showing in the dusk. This was Camp Tigris, and here we were to disembark. The prospect was dismal to a degree; it had been raining heavily and the ground was a mass of slush and slithering mud, while overhead the palms hung their lank dripping heads against a grey sky, an icy wind blowing in puffs downstream. The camp we found an irregular, straggling affair, pitched in the desert just beyond the palm-belt, while beyond it in the distance to west and north a bank of blue haze showed where the marshes lay. Directly behind the camp lay a native village, and to the east ran the river.

We were immediately told off to some trenches on the western face, where, owing to the irregular formation of the camp, there was an awkward gap in the defences, and no perimeter built; we were warned to expect a night attack. Having reached our ground, we found that the trenches were a myth, and under the occasional light of the watery moon had to do our best with the entrenching tools. We seemed to have struck the only solid piece of desert—two inches under the surface it was as hard as rock—and, scratch as we might, we could not make much impression. We lay there all night and waited for the promised attack, which never came off.

Next morning, we began to glean some of the rumours, and to hear the reasons, real or supposed, which had brought us to Camp Tigris. The rumours were to the effect that the Aleppo Army Corps was concentrating somewhere up-river—the actual place of concentration and the number of troops varied with the teller of the tale—but all agreed that a descent upon Kurna was imminent, and that was why we had been invited. The actual facts, as opposed to rumours, seemed to be that a force of enemy estimated at 2000 infantry with guns were holding a position about six miles upstream on the right bank, with

A British Infantry Trench

alternative positions on the left bank. These trenches were sited at a bend of the river and protected on each bank by broad creeks, while the river was blocked downstream by sunken boats.

So far so good. At eleven that morning, 29th December, we heard we were to move out at one and march four miles upstream, where we were to protect a bridge-building party and remain out after the bridge's completion to hold the bridgehead. Kits, cooks, reserve ammunition, and stores were accordingly re-embarked on the *Malamir*. However, just as that had been completed, at 12.15 a message came from the Brigade to say that the move was postponed, and most of the stuff had to be unloaded again and carried back to camp.

That day it poured in torrents and blew a hurricane, a particularly cold one, from morning till night, and we discovered that palm trees are but a poor shelter from rain. However, it was some consolation to hear that there was to be no sitting still, for the whole force was to move at 5 a.m. next morning, and, after bridging the creeks, a "reconnaissance in force" of the Turkish position was to be carried out. Kits were to be roped overnight and put on board at 4 a.m.

But the uncertainty of war was to be again demonstrated, for at 4 a.m., just as the kits were going down to the ship, came a cryptic order to "lie down," followed by a more intelligible one to "stand fast," and finally word was passed that the move was again off. The order, indeed, had been given the previous night, but someone had forgotten to hand it on. The rain cleared off about midday, and, though everything was in a pretty bad state, the camp began to assume a more regular shape as we got to work on our perimeter, a most necessary precaution in view of the habits of the local Arabs.

A few nights before our arrival some of these scallywags had crept through the village in rear of camp, and finding a convenient gap, were all over the place in no time, and succeeded in killing two or three men, wounding more, and getting off with several rifles. There was an article in an English newspaper about this time describing "the warm welcome accorded by the Arabs to British troops"; it was due only to the fact that the Arab's ammunition is mostly home-made and strictly limited that their welcome was not considerably warmer—as it was, they sniped us whenever convenient.

At last, on 1st January, the promised reconnaissance took place, a small force of all arms leaving camp at 6 a.m. and marching northwards up the right bank towards the Turkish position. Two creeks had been successfully bridged and were passed, but further investigation showed another creek some 1000 yards in front of the enemy's position, besides the one directly in front of their trenches. The former was a particularly broad one, too deep to ford, and was pronounced impossible to bridge without pontoons. As there was no such thing in the country, operations came to a sudden stop, and after the exchange of a few shots by the opposing guns, the reconnoitring force marched back to Camp Tigris, not very much the wiser for their day's outing. Why no information had been forthcoming as to the existence and nature of this very obvious obstacle was not clear.

We were still hard at work with the spade improving the perimeter of the camp, and, if any were at first inclined to take matters fairly easily, a few nights' experience was guaranteed to change their frame of mind. The sniping had grown to be rather more than a nuisance. What at first had been the casual "popping off" of half-a-dozen rifles in the direction of camp had gradually increased in volume and accuracy until there was an almost nightly demonstration. The Arabs engaged in these enterprises had a curious mode of procedure, which was decidedly entertaining to their spectators but must have been costly to themselves. Regularly every evening at about 4.30—half an hour or so before sunset—straggling bands could be seen collecting on the edge of the marshes north-west of camp. When a crowd was assembled it would start drifting towards us, halting every now and then and working itself up into a state of apparent frenzy, shouting, stamping, and dancing, retreating a few hundred yards and then advancing again.

At this stage there was never any shooting; generally, after the hoisting of many banners, green and white and black, the assembled crowd would gradually disperse and disappear into the rising mists towards the marshes; but almost invariably after these "Salvation Army meetings," as they were christened, there would follow a night of furious sniping. Consequently, it was considered advisable to break up these meetings, and one evening these religious enthusiasts received an unpleasant surprise from the attentions of a section of field guns. The shrapnel cannot have failed to do great execution among them, but on no occasion was there ever a "pick-up" the next morning—their dead and wounded were all removed without exception.

After a few fine days the weather had broken again, and then followed a period of pelting rain and icy cold winds. Fortunately, on 3rd January, a boat arrived with our tents, and getting them pitched made a considerable difference to our comfort, though the first appearance of the tents proved a great attraction to the snipers.

British troops marching in Mesopotamia

That evening a particularly buzzing swarm had been dissipated by the guns, and we counted on our first comfortable night under canvas. We were sitting in the newly pitched mess-tent, feeling rather pleased with life, when there suddenly came a shout from outside, "Lights out everywhere!" We tumbled out through the darkness as best we could, and floundering through ditches and pools and trenches sought our allotted places: once there, what was the scare about? A pitch-dark night, blusters of wind and rain, but not a shot broke the stillness; then on the wind came a sound weird and uncanny—the rising and falling chant of hundreds of voices. Gradually the sound came nearer, and we heard it swelling into a roar, "*Allah Illahi! Allah Illahi!*" beginning suddenly out of the black silence, ending as suddenly in silence.

Boom! from the other side of camp; and high over the desert burst a star-shell, drooping gracefully and dazzlingly to earth. Then with a roar and rattle the silence was snapped—for there in the glaring light, banners and all, stood and crouched and slunk the ranks of our visitors. It was sharp and very short: their heavy Martini bullets droned through the air, varied by the occasional fizz of a Mauser; thudding on to a tent here, and there smacking into a parapet. But the Arab at his best moments is the worst shot on earth and prefers to point his gun to heaven; now, on a dark night, facing magazine fire, his efforts were ineffectual. The moon bursting through a rift in the racing clouds finished the business, and after a few more departing shots, silence reigned once more. We retired to bed, cursing the "warm welcome" of the local inhabitant, but thankful that "three rounds rapid" could so signally defeat him.

The Aleppo Army Corps apparently got lost or was taking a long rest on the way, for there was no sign of its approach; The small force upstream slumbered securely behind its unbridgeable moats, and only the Arab's nightly serenade stayed our hands from beating our swords into ploughshares. Indeed, preparations were going forward a mile downstream that suggested much use for the latter instrument. Now that Camp Tigris was sufficiently provided for, fatigue-parties might daily be seen wending their way towards Kurna, where a system of field fortification was being pushed on as quickly as possible: in time we all visited the scene of labour.

Kurna is a filthy village on a peninsula formed by the Tigris and Old Euphrates. A few brick houses—the barracks, the custom-house and telegraph office, the governor's residence—front the Tigris bank, but these needed a good deal of repair after having recently afforded

INSIDE No. 6 REDOUBT, MAZERA.

targets to H.M. gun-boats; the rest is a tangle of horrible lanes and still more horrible mud and reed houses, which straggle in an irregular triangular shape among the palm trees down to the meeting-place of the two rivers—the apex of the triangle.

The eastern and southern sides of the peninsula are protected by the Tigris and Euphrates, the western by a creek running into the Euphrates, and on the north stretched, then, the desert, looking towards Camp Tigris and the marshes beyond.

As we found it at this time of year Kurna could be said to have definite features as boundaries; but later in the season, as the marshes encroached and the rivers and creeks rose, we were to learn that Kurna and all that therein was, including ourselves, were but an accident on the face of the waters, flotsam of the flood which might, or might not, close over our heads.

But in those days, we all of us had much to learn, and despite the fact that water was met with at two feet or less beneath the surface, we suspected nothing, and everyone went to work with a will. As digging down was very obviously out of the question, building up, equally obviously, was indicated. However, the problem was solved by the fact that the northern and western faces were surrounded by a broad bank of earth standing well above water-level, probably the remains of some very ancient wall, though it is hard to imagine Kurna at any time as a prosperous city.

In these broad ramparts a good deal of digging could be done, and trenches of a quite serviceable pattern cut in the hard earth which needed little or no revetting. Furthermore, there were several big brick-kilns built at intervals on the bank which were easily converted into observation and machine-gun posts. These kilns are very solidly built of brick—squat, square towers smaller at the top than at the base, and a peculiar feature of the country. from a distance they look exactly like the keep of some Norman castle.

As work progressed, the scheme of fortification was developed to include the left bank of the Tigris also, and a system of trenches and redoubts was designed with its left flank on the river opposite Kurna, and its right flank bending back to meet the Shatt-el-Arab again below the junction of the Old Euphrates—describing an arc of which Mazera was, roughly, the centre.

Very soon after this scheme was decided on, the 17th Brigade was sent across the river to do the necessary digging, and for the next two months Kurna knew us no more. When next we took up our resi-

A Marsh Arab Village—A "Mashoof" in the Foreground.

dence there we found it a very different place.

Our move across the river was at short notice and at an early hour. As moves go it was a small affair, and yet it had its memorable moments, spasms of several varieties. In those early days there was still no bridge across the river; everything had to be passed over by boat. As no barges were available, it followed that everything, men, horses, mules, ammunition, stores, and tents, had to be embarked in an orderly manner on the *Blosse Lynch*, steam raised, the anchor weighed, and a course pointed for the opposite bank. Someone remarked that to look at us anyone would think we were going to Baghdad!

The voyage was successful—except that the two last cases of soda-water were dropped overboard and drowned —but the work really began when the farther shore was reached. The mules, of course, made a vulgar demonstration on the gangways, which demoralised the otherwise well-behaved ponies, and it was some time before, that uproar settled, the ship was emptied of men and mountains of kits and stores; and then we had scarcely begun, for we found that orders directed us to camp in the palm trees a mile and a half from where we had been landed! There were no carts, and consequently everything had to be manhandled across the shadeless stretch of intervening desert; there we made the discovery that we were travelling with quite a surprising amount of luggage.

All day backwards and forwards to the ship trudged fatigue-parties, their bowed forms disguised under loads of kits, tents, ammunition boxes, water-tanks, till at last as the sun set everything had been transported. I saw "Elizabeth," the turkey, perched in her travelling cage, being borne along on a man's head, to her evident satisfaction. Her slave was also carrying his equipment and rifle, 120 rounds of ammunition, his kit, and a "*dicksee*," and he sang "We are but little children weak" all the way from the ship to camp.

The road led us past some of the Turkish trenches used in the two engagements at Mazera. The Turks had buried their dead very inadequately, and as pi-dogs and jackals had since been at work, there were many grisly sights and scents. It was not a pleasant scene, but apparently it was taken as part of the day's work, nothing out of the common; and Private Dash as he tripped over a skull remarked chattily, "'Strewth! there's a bloke's napper—with 'is 'air on, too! what 'ud mother say if she saw me now?" What, indeed!

That night the snipers left us alone—luckily, as there had hardly been time to dig much of a perimeter,—and next morning we started in to get a camp pitched two or three hundred yards back, on the border of the Mazera date groves.

This necessitated a good deal of clearing, as the ground had previously been used for the same purpose by the Turks, and the filth left by them is quite indescribable. Many strange relics were brought to light, and, among others, in a ditch was found the limber of a Krupp field-gun. This was at once pounced upon by a lynx-eyed Mess President of an inventive turn of mind, and, with the aid of the Pioneer-Sergeant, it was presently converted into a most excellent cooking-range, on which the cook performed miracles: such a come-down in the world for an apostle of blood and iron will doubtless grieve Fräulein Bertha—if we ever tell her.

It was in Mazera we first came up against two new plagues of the country, in flies and pi-dogs. The flies were, we thought, bad enough, little knowing what Mesopotamia could really do in this direction, but they were particularly loathsome here, as we knew only too well the reason of their fat and sleek appearance; accordingly, exhumation and re-burial parties were sent out to tidy the place up. They did their unpleasant work well and truly—we will leave it at that.

But the pi-dogs remained as bad as ever, slinking about by day and rushing in yelping, howling packs through camp by night, ever loathsome and unsightly companions. The poor beasts had originally belonged to Mazera, and since its destruction were homeless and starving. Packs of fifty or sixty could often be seen round camp, mostly big, shaggy dogs, red-eyed and mangy, snuffling about in the desert on the track of shallow graves. After a bit we could stand it no longer, and a parade of all "marksmen" was ordered, with all officers who had sporting guns, and a *battue* was held in which nearly thirty dogs were killed: it was an unpleasant business, but necessary.

Soon the whole brigade was tucked away among the palm trees and the surrounding gardens, and work was immediately started on the new defences, which at first comprised four redoubts (later extended) and a system of wing trenches, communication trenches, gun emplacements, and much wiring—in fact, the whole line was covered by a wire fence later, as it was found that snipers crawled in between the self-contained redoubts. The camp was situated about 600 yards behind the line, and the garden walls, with some knocking down here and building up there, formed an inner perimeter for the northern and eastern sides, while on the west was the Tigris, and on the south the Shatt-el-Arab (Tigris + Euphrates).

Once the gardens and date grove had been cleared they afforded an excellent camping-ground, and every one soon settled down to a steady routine of digging, building, and wiring, with intervals for sport. About five miles east of Mazera the Swaib River joins the main stream, and here we found any number of snipe and duck, particularly in the marshes which the river forms a mile or two from its mouth. Here reeds and pools and backwaters stretched for miles north and east, the dwelling-place of innumerable duck and snipe and other water-fowl, and also of huge pig, jackal, and wild cats. Later, when the flood season arrived, these marshes grew visibly while we watched, and all the desert, over which we walked and rode now, became one immense lake.

The duck we never quite managed to circumvent, but good bags of snipe were made until they left in the first week of February, and excellent sport was had with the pig. The tactics were to ride out early in the morning, when the pig came out on to the desert, and to get between them and the marshes: then the fun began. They had a firm objection to being driven far from home and would always try to turn back. Anything in the way they charged most gallantly, and there were many upsets and several cut legs in the stable.

They were certainly fine pig, nearly all stuck being about 36 inches and carrying tremendous coats, rather like ragged door-mats. In spite of some prejudice at first, it was very soon discovered that they made excellent eating—indeed there was no reason they shouldn't, as they fed exclusively in the marshes—and each day after the "cavalry" had been at work, an artillery waggon would go out and gather up the slain, which were distributed later among those of us whose religion and appetites permitted pork. I think ten was the record bag for one day.

At this time the weather was perfect: cold, starlit nights, an unclouded sky by day with a warm sun, though not powerful enough to make a helmet necessary, and a splendid freshness in the air. So far, mosquitoes had hardly made themselves felt. We wondered could this Riviera like climate really be capable of the horrors of which we had heard, and this pleasant land of hazy distances, blue waters, and green palms be that wilderness—Mesopotamia?

CHAPTER 6

January 1915

At Kurna and Mazera we were now in the middle of the marsh country, which, though now in the early days of January still comparatively firm underfoot, was soon to become one immense inland sea. Even now one could not go far afield without meeting permanent swamp, depressions from which the annual inundation is never drained off, dreary stretches of reeds intersected by sluggish streams which appear to have no beginning and no end. These constitute as it were the focal points of the immense marsh country, and outside them now on this so-called desert could be seen the roots of dry rushes springing from the fissured soil, with here and there jungles of dead reeds: beyond this belt of dry marsh vegetation was only a very small area of desert proper, where the date palms grew round the villages, protected by banks.

The villages themselves are above the high-water mark, but everything else, including the date groves, is in time covered by the rising floods which make their appearance in February, are at their height in May, after which they recede, until in October the country again begins to assume the aspect of *terra firma* (more or less) in which we now found it.

The area of land involved by these floods is tremendous and can be roughly divided into three districts, though at the height of the flood season the waters merge, and one immense reedy sea results in the country below Amara.

The three districts are roughly—from Museyib (40 miles south of Baghdad) to the southern end of the Bahr Shinafia, an area of about 90 miles from north to south, by 50 miles east to west; from Suk-es-Sheyuk south-east to Gurmat Ali and east to Kurna, 100 miles by 40, and the Swaib River marshes, which stretch from Kurna north-east to the Persian border 50 miles distant, and are of varying breadth; the third district is that north and north-west of Kut-el-Amara, 40 by 50 miles.

These areas are, of course, very greatly increased when the floods are at their height in May, and, with the exception of the Kut area, as they increase they become connected, until there is very little dry land between the Euphrates and the Tigris. By the middle of May every year quite 10,000 square miles of land must be under water, and of this about three thousand square miles is permanent marsh and unproductive, except for a certain amount of rice grown on the Euphrates.

The cause of these tremendous inundations is not uncontrollable. We can be pretty certain that in Babylonian and pre-Babylonian times the country did not suffer in this way as a general rule, though no doubt there were exceptional seasons, when the arrangements made for carrying off the water broke down. The country being exceptionally flat and without natural barriers, when once the water got "out of bounds" and started to spread, no doubt it spread with alarming rapidity and with an effect devastating to a crowded and unprepared population. It is considered by some that the story of the Flood as we have it in Genesis is the true account of some such occurrence in the valley of the Tigris: a great, but local, disaster.

The rise in the rivers is caused by the melting of the snows in the mountains on their upper waters, and not by abnormal rainfall occasioned by any comparatively recent climatic change of the country. That being so, it is plain that the floods are no new and abnormal problem, and that the ancient civilizations had to deal with a like volume of waters; not less, certainly, and very probably more. That they succeeded is evident from the almost uninterrupted prosperity of the country from the earliest days, and the questions naturally arise as to how it was done, and why it is no longer possible.

The answer to both questions seems to lie in the keyword to Mesopotamia—irrigation.

We know that before the dawn of its ancient history the country was intersected in all directions by a huge system of canals. Who first built them we do not know, but they were so old that in the first millennium B.C. their origin was considered to be mysterious and divine. For thousands of years this network of irrigation channels and canals had been repaired and developed, and the two rivers were harnessed to do the work of civilization: to irrigate the vast crops, to serve as highways about the land, to carry merchandise, to afford communications. The great waters were not the masters then.

It is remarkable that throughout the changing fortunes of the country, under the succeeding rules of new masters, its conquerors were wise enough to leave its lifeblood alone: the system of canals was not interfered with. Persians, Seleucids, Parthians, Sasanians, Omayyad Caliphs—all were conquerors of the land within a period of little more than a thousand years, but, with comparatively minor exceptions, all these newcomers were content to leave the irrigation as they found it; perhaps they were wise enough to realise that the waters might become their master.

But there came one who did not understand, or perhaps did not care. In the year 1257 A D., Huláku Khan, at the head of Mongol hordes, turned his eyes westward. Persia, disintegrated and effete, fell at the first blow of these armies, organised, brave, and well-armed. Nothing could withstand the fierce rush of the conquerors, who conquered only to spoil and grew more impetuous as each success brought wealth and loot. It was an orgy of destruction and wanton cruelty before which the old civilizations fell, but an orgy directed by unwavering determination, and carried out with savage and unscrupulous thoroughness. The rush turned south-west, ever gathering to its numbers the outcasts of conquered peoples and broke into Mesopotamia. That the country had enjoyed civilization and prosperity and wealth for the last five thousand years meant to Huláku's armies that it was the greatest prize that had yet fallen to them. That it was a great prize pointed only to the greater necessity of unpitying savagery and unrestrained pillage. And so, the work was done thoroughly. Baghdad was taken, the inhabitants massacred, the town sacked and burnt.

In a year Huláku had done his work. When he marched back to Persia he left behind him only the ruins of that wonderful system which had raised and supported the greatest civilization of the world. The canals were cut, their high banks levelled, the irrigation channels blocked, and the waters diverted. What the Mongols had not done personally, Nature effected in a few years; for now, the great waters were again unharnessed—they were masters.

So, it is that Mesopotamia, the birthplace and home of a great civilization, a granary of the world, has been reduced to a howling wilderness of dust and scrub and marsh—"Thorns shall come up in her palaces, nettles and brambles in the fortresses thereof: and it shall be an habitation of dragons and a court for owls"—because seven centuries ago a savage from Central Asia let loose the rivers.

That it has remained a comparatively unproductive waste is hardly to the credit of the Turks, though they cannot be held responsible until the early eighteenth century, when first they secured a considerable foothold in the country. But from that time until a few years before the war, they had done nothing to reclaim this valuable possession, and the irrigation work which was then initiated (with Sir W. Willcox as chief adviser) very soon had to be abandoned—a good deal owing to the unbusinesslike methods of the Ottoman Government, and to the corruptness of its officials. But if Turkey did not realise the potential richness of this outlying corner of her empire, and had no use for its strategical importance, somebody thought otherwise, and that somebody was Germany, who, by a most consistent policy for ten years before the war, showed that the Imperial Government was alive to the value of these thousands of miles of desert and marsh.

As it is now, it is certainly a desolate country as soon as one gets away from the river; and that part of it in which we now found ourselves, with its wide expanses of silent and apparently lifeless marsh, its stagnant, endless creeks, is peculiarly depressing. But if the country is strange its inhabitants are scarcely less so, and, assuredly, not less unpleasant. It is peopled by a strange race generally known as Marsh Arabs, who live an amphibious life among the reeds and swamps which border the rivers, calling themselves often by the names of well-known tribes and subdivisions from which, maybe, they originally sprung, but to whom now they have little relationship. Indeed, they are a different people from the Bedou, by whom they are regarded as scum of the earth, reviled as of no religion, and commonly held to be born with webbed feet!

On the whole, the Bedouin's estimate seems a fairly just one. The Marsh Arabs are by occupation herdsmen of water-buffaloes, shepherds, fishermen, and odd-jobbers, by predilection thieves and robbers, and, by nature, lowdown scoundrels, though perhaps environment and treatment have something to do with this. As a race they are finely made, tall men, with tremendously big bones, (the Tigris valley is very rich in lime), and evidently of great strength, very different from the light and rather dried-up-looking Bedouin of the desert beyond. They live in small island-villages in the marshes for the most part, and on the banks of the river. These villages are not permanent, but are constantly shifted, and, as the houses are built exclusively of reeds, it is very little trouble for their inhabitants to remove, which they do by pulling down their houses, packing them into boats for the journey, and then re-erecting them elsewhere.

Some of them are permanent residents in small riverside towns such as Kurna, and these, engaging in river trade, are comparatively sophisticated (though none the less blackguards for that), but, for the most part, they are a slinking, disreputable crew, living an obscure life away in their swamps and marshes, continually bickering among themselves, and robbing any stranger who is so unwise as to venture among them. Living as they do a practically amphibious existence, they are naturally boatmen before all else, and their narrow black *mashoofs*, in which they journey, work, fight, and often live, are everywhere to be seen. Every small village of reed huts seemed to possess a fleet of these of various sizes, from small skiffs only big enough for one man, to large, heavy craft big enough for a family of half a dozen and two or three cows as well!

As for the fighting, a good deal of inter-tribal and inter-village scrapping seemed to go on, each small village apparently having its *Sheikh* and being at loggerheads with the next village. There being plenty of Martinis about, this results in a good deal of shooting, and very often at night we could hear a battle going on somewhere away in the marshes, or a blaze on the horizon would mark the burning of a village. Later, we were ourselves to become involved in the troubled politics of the neighbourhood, and to learn how battles are fought and honour satisfied. But, at this time, domestic disputes quite lost their attraction for the Marsh Arabs, who found the rival forces of Briton and Turk far more worthy of attention.

There is good reason to believe that we were not the only sufferers, but certainly the sniping now became a regular nightly performance, and an exceedingly annoying one, for the snipers showed extraordinary cunning in avoiding the outer line of redoubts and creeping up close to camp. This necessitated a strong defence of the perimeter in addition to the outpost companies occupying the redoubts, whose primary business was to "watch out" for Turks. Consequently "nights in bed" were few and far between, and we began to hate the local scallywag with a very bitter hatred; the only exception perhaps being a character who became known as "Blunderbuss Bill" and was a great source of entertainment to the men.

He was never seen alive, but every night without fail the thunderous boom of his weapon would be heard and the swish of an immense lump of scrap-iron high over the palms. Interested time-keepers recorded that it took him 57½ minutes to reload his piece! He was one of the few of these nocturnal visitors to pay the penalty, for one night he came too near, and a lucky shot from a sentry in the 119th lines laid him low: at least next morning an old Arab was found outside the wire; beside him lay an ancient rifle of about .600 bore; and after that the boom of "Blunderbuss Bill" was never heard again.

But if the natives were out for blood by night they changed their demeanour by day: those in the neighbourhood of camp and the loungers about Kurna made a great show of civility, almost of affection towards us, while others farther afield would often bring strange tidings of our enemies, whom they swore were indeed children of Iblis. Of course, they were playing a double game, and were quick to learn that "Intelligence" was valuable—to both parties; and for both parties, British and Turk, they acted with conspicuous impartiality.

They were in a difficult position. Their hatred of the Turk was genuine, and, on the whole, their sympathies were with us: but against that must be set the facts that the Turks were Moslems, that evil in the form of Turkish misrule was perhaps preferable to the unknown possibilities of British rule, and last, and most telling of all, they did not know what we meant to do. Naturally these people wished to back the right horse: but if they threw in their lot with the British and helped them unreservedly against the Turk and then the British were to back out (or be driven out) of Mesopotamia, they knew only too well the fate that was in store for them from their revengeful masters. We had given them no definite promise as to the permanency of our occupation; and they had their suspicions. It is notorious that news travels apace in the East, and the British desertion of the friendly tribes in Somaliland, the breaking of a solemnly pledged promise, was still recent history: between Somaliland and Mesopotamia news, as well as dates, is exchanged—further comment is unnecessary.

In addition to this, our first intervention in local politics was decidedly unfortunate. About this time, the middle of January, it became evident that the *Sheikh* of a village some way up the Old Euphrates, Chubaish, was sheltering Turkish agents and was undoubtedly their fervent ally. Accordingly, measures were taken to stop his game. An expedition consisting of two gunboats and a landing party was sent up river, and, arriving off Chubaish early one morning, summoned the *Sheikh* to surrender immediately. He had been taken completely by surprise and there was nothing for it but to obey, which he accordingly did; and in due course he was sent to India as a political prisoner. In his place was put the rival claimant to the "throne," a cousin of the late *Sheikh's*, though a proved and loyal adherent of the British; but within a week he had his throat cut by assassins sent by the Turks for that purpose. This was a bad beginning and not calculated to inspire confidence in others or to encourage them to follow the murdered man's example.

As for the origin of the Marsh Arabs they are difficult people to trace exactly, their degraded life not tending much towards the careful preservation of tribal and sub-tribal tradition, but they are all probably offshoots of the Muntafik, Albu Mahommed, and Beni Làm tribes.

The Muntafik is a large tribe still mainly nomadic, which inhabits vast stretches of country to the south of the Euphrates from the Khor Shinafia, where its neighbours are the warlike Anaize, to the desert just west of Basra; also across the Euphrates up both banks of the Shatt-el-Hai. Though, for the most part, this tribe are still nomads, a great number in the last fifty years have settled down to become tillers of the soil, despised of the Bedou, and from these, spring many of the small divisions of the Marsh Arabs. Their name is legion, but among them may be mentioned, on the Euphrates, from Suk-es-Sheyuk eastward—the Beni Said, El Duayish, El Basal, Beni Mansur; and, on the Tigris, from Kut-el-Amara southward—the Rubea, Beni Famin, Makusis, Abu Diraye; and the Beni Taruf, on the Persian border about Hawiza, who perhaps are hardly Marsh Arabs, but have most of their unpleasant characteristics.

The Albu Mohammed tribe inhabits both banks of the Tigris from some way above Kurna up to Amara. The same remarks apply to them as to the Muntafik, though they were never as numerous or warlike a tribe as the latter and are now mainly engaged in agriculture: they are not quite such villains as the Muntafik offshoots. The Beni Làm, living on the left bank of the Tigris, from north-east of Kut to Amara and eastward to the Persian border, are the villains of the country, and among the Arabs themselves they are considered low-down thieves and murderers, without any vestige of honour—and that sort of reputation means something in a land where robbery with murder is a gentlemanly pastime.

CHAPTER 7

February 1915

It was very soon evident that Turkey had no intention of respecting Persian neutrality, and by December news had arrived of Turkish troops having moved across the frontier and occupied various towns in western Persia, where they were engaged in collecting and organising local irregulars to help them.

The scene of these activities pointed to their objective—namely, the pipe-line of the Anglo-Persian Oil Company, which runs through Ahwaz, on the Karun River, to Abadan, the refining station beforementioned, on the Shatt-el-Arab. Already attempts had been made to bribe the K'ab Arabs into revolt and outrage, and evidently a more serious attempt was to follow.

Accordingly, it was considered necessary that some force should be detached in order to guard against any surprise in this direction, which, besides being serious for the pipeline, would also have endangered our lines of communication. At the end of January, a small force, consisting of the 7th Rajputs, less two companies, one platoon of the Dorsets, one troop 33rd Cavalry, 23rd Mountain Battery, and one section 82nd Battery R.F.A., was sent up to Ahwaz to keep an eye on the surrounding country. The remainder of the 18th Brigade remained as garrison at Basra, and, with 16th and 17th Brigades at Kurna and Mazera respectively, our small force, still one division, and without its proper complement of guns, was fairly widely distributed.

Ahwaz, now little more than a tumble-down village, has played a great part in ancient Persian history. It was near here that Nearchus, marching up the Karun (then known as the Pasitigris) joined forces with Alexander, who had bridged the river, and from here the army marched to Babylon, where Alexander died.

Under the Abbasid Caliphs, $A.D.$ 750, when it was known as Agi-

THE FIRING-LINE—RECONNAISSANCE OF RATTA.

nis, Ahwaz reached the height of its prosperity. Abulfeda, the Arab historian, describes it as "adorned with gardens and enriched by plantations of sugar-cane," besides mentioning the magnificence of its buildings and society. It is interesting to note that African negroes were employed on these sugar plantations, and it was due to their rebellion against the Caliphate that Ahwaz was destroyed. The rebellion was crushed, but the city never recovered its ancient state.

In modern times Ahwaz has no history of importance, unless the "battle" there in the Anglo-Persian War of 1857 he considered such, when 300 of our troops sailed up the river against 7000 Persians entrenched on the right bank. No sooner did the Persians see them disembark than they fled incontinently, and the battle ended.

But to return to Kurna and Mazera. In the meanwhile, work was going steadily forward. On the right bank opposite we watched the gradual growth of a scaffolding which already showed above the palm-tops and was destined in course of time to become an observation tower, nearly 100 feet high, from which a tremendous view could be commanded over the dead flat country. There were also preparations under way to bridge the river between the two villages, a bridging-train having arrived from India. But a hitch had occurred owing to there not being enough pontoons, so that big "*mahelas*" had to be brought up and moored by each bank to carry the shore ends of the bridge.

Day in and day out, Sunday included, we worked at the Mazera defences, the nine redoubts and trenches being allotted to the same regiments both for work and for defence, so that in the event of attack (unlikely as it seemed to us) we should be told off to the works we had ourselves constructed.

At this time there was a good deal of movement among the Arabs, besides the sniping, and, almost nightly, reports were brought in warning the brigade to be prepared for an attack. The attacks did not materialize, but, in consequence of these warnings, everyone was kept rather too consistently on the *qui vive*, the garrisons of the redoubts and the picquets on the perimeter were increased at sundown, while any heavy outburst of sniping was the signal for everyone to stand-to, so that very often not more than two nights out of seven were spent in sleeping.

The chief scene of activity seemed to be the Swaib River, away on our right, and from that quarter the cavalry patrols were always bringing in reports of numbers of Arabs crossing the stream; as they seemed as a rule to be crossing away from us towards the other bank, it seemed

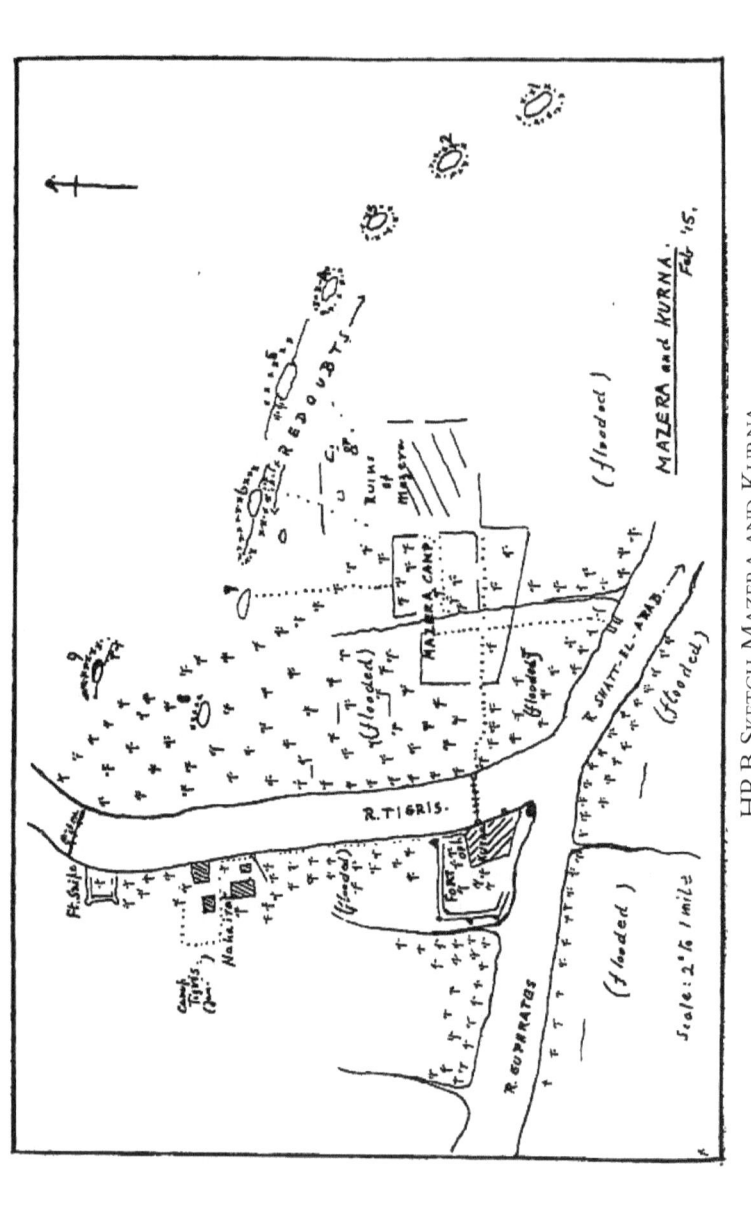

unnecessary to interfere, but later on it became pretty evident what had been going on.

The centre redoubt of the line, No. 6, was the strongest, and its importance was soon further enhanced by the arrival of a searchlight, which was duly installed and fired off by night in obedience to frenzied telephone calls from commanders of other redoubts up and down the line who, from time to time, were convinced that they heard Arabs cutting their wire. The Arabs were always pi-dogs or jackals, but, all the same, it was well worthwhile. The searchlight was manned by Calcutta volunteer Engineers, who were good men, and took their responsibilities most seriously. The man who ran the dynamo engine was known as "Young Percy"—no other name was he ever addressed by.

Whenever a call came through on the telephone the same thing happened; shadowy forms leapt at the searchlight and appeared to be wrestling with it, while the engine started puffing in its dug-out below. Presently a fizzling spark would appear, flicker for a minute, and then go out. Thereupon a wail would be heard through the darkness, "For Gawd's sake, young Percy, can't you give us some more (qualified) voltage?" By the time this had arrived and the light was working, a message would come through saying that "Captain —— was so sorry but it was only a dog after all. The dog had now run away." Poor young Percy! His life was made hideous brooding over his (qualified) voltage: but his troubles much enlivened our weary vigils in No. 6 Redoubt.

19th January brought us at last the welcome news that we were to be employed on something else besides digging and making mud bricks. A "reconnaissance in force" was billed for the next day, and all ranks were relieved at the prospect, for this favourite form of operation in Mesopotamia had not yet lost its novelty; and, apparently, for some it never did.

The previous reconnaissance on 1st January up the right bank had proved a failure, owing to lack of bridging material, and now it was proposed to repeat the operation, it was hoped this time with success, up the left bank. The Turkish position on this bank had been strengthened since the 17th Brigade had come over to Mazera, but they were occupying the same line as formerly, namely, a line of trenches taking off from the bank just beyond a bend in the river, and protected in front by the Ratta Canal, a broad and deep creek: behind the trenches there were reed villages on both sides of the river where the Turkish camp could be seen. Below the Ratta Canal (on our side, that is) and separated from it by 1000 yards of semi-dry marsh, a low ridge of sand-hills 1000 yards long stretched from west to east across the front: lately the Turks had been occupying these in some force and firing on our patrols. Our objective, we were told, was to drive the enemy from this ridge and on no account was any further advance to be made: the navy, represented by H.M.S. *Espiègle*, and the gunboats *Miner* and *Lewis Pelly*, and assisted by the *Medjedieh* mounting a section of field guns, would co-operate from the river and protect our left flank.

The "Order of battle" was as follows: Advance guard, 33rd Cavalry, less two squadrons, and two companies 1st Oxford and Bucks Light Infantry. Firing line and supports, 103rd Mahratta Light Infantry, 1st Oxford and Bucks Light Infantry, less two companies; reserve, 2nd Norfolks and 7th Rajputs, less two companies rear guard. Artillery: two batteries less one section R.F.A., and one battery mountain guns.

Next morning it was pitch dark and decidedly chilly when we paraded outside the perimeter at 4.30 a.m. and waited about while the advance guard got off. Staff officers dodged about with feverish whispers and jealously guarded lights, darting from group to group with all the rapid stealth proper to the villains of melodrama-—indeed, before we had started, we all felt we were midnight marauders engaged in some dark plot. At last we got a move on and started out slowly across the desert. Once clear of the redoubts we split up into artillery formation, and, when the small columns had shaken into place, the pace improved, though, as it was pitch dark, we naturally moved slowly.

We had been marching for about an hour when the sound of brisk rifle fire ahead showed that the advance guard had come up against something. This continued for a couple of minutes or so, and then died down to desultory popping. The columns immediately deployed, and, as the long lines went forward, the sun burst up above the eastern horizon with its usual wonderful suddenness, turning the dark desert to a sheet of gold and transforming the figures of men into brazen marching statues. The suddenness and brilliance of the change was wonderful.

There was some light upon the scene now, and we could see what was happening. A few hundred yards away the sand-hills stretched across our front, lined, not with Turks, but with our own men, the former having put up no kind of show, as we heard later, but only waiting hurriedly to loose off their rifles before retiring at the double. The only casualty caused by their hasty fusillade was an "over" which hit a man 1000 yards back in the main body!

We were soon up to the sand-hills and extended on our fronts behind them, the 103rd on the extreme left, the Oxfordshire Light Infantry on the right, and the 22nd Punjabis brought up to fill a gap in the centre, while the guns took up their position covered by the highest point of the ridge and opened fire on the camp behind the Ratta Canal at 7.30. We had not long to wait before the enemy woke up and began shelling us. Of course, they had the exact range of the ridge, and only the fact that they burst their shrapnel much too high saved the gunners from a good many casualties, while the common shell with which they bombarded our prostrate forms were nearly all duds; but, all the same, one realised what a horribly flat place a desert is!

Mutual bombardment continued for an hour and a half, but, in the meanwhile, the *Espiègle* had done great execution with 4-inch lyddite, and the village on the opposite bank was going up in smoke, while the Turkish artillery had become very spasmodic. Then, contrary to expectation, the order was given to advance and the ridge was crossed, and we began to move across the intervening marsh towards the Ratta Canal. It was good going at first but gradually it grew wetter and wetter under foot, until we were squelching through mud and reeds nearly up to our knees—but no one minded that if, as it seemed, we were really going to make a job of it.

Down on the left, near the river, matters were not quite so easy, as there were a lot of snipers behind some brick walls on the opposite bank who were enfilading the line and picking off a good many of the 103rd, though there was very little rifle fire from beyond the canal. There it was obvious all was not well, for we could see figures running to and fro in disorder, and mounted Arabs riding away to the northeast, while only one gun was replying to the fire of our field batteries. At a point about 1000 yards from the canal a firing line was formed and rifle fire opened on the evidently confused mob on the other side, though observation was so difficult that it was hard to say if it caused them much inconvenience; but the shell fire certainly did, as we saw several direct hits on laden "*mahelas*" in the canal, and the village in the palms behind was on fire.

But, much to our surprise and disappointment, no further advance was made, and at 11.30 came the order to retire. So, we ploughed our way back through the marsh—a slow business but encouraged by the enfilading snipers afore-mentioned—and over the sand-hills. One gun still barked spasmodically at our retreating forms, but that was soon left behind and we reformed on the desert beyond. And so home, after a thirsty march, to camp and tiffin, rather surprised at this first mild sample of battle-fighting and full of curiosity as to what exactly had been accomplished.

Our casualties were eight killed and fifty-five wounded; and we heard later, through prisoners' reports, that the Turks had lost four hundred men out of a force of between 3000 and 4000, including Arabs; also that their commander had been wounded by shrapnel; that the whole place was in a state of confusion, and that the Arabs had run off and that the guns had no ammunition left; finally, that the Turks could not understand why we had not come on and finished the job, and could only attribute it to the fact that we had lost very heavily—a conclusion which was, of course, circulated among the Arabs.

Figures in such reports are naturally never reliable and, as we found later, must be generally at least halved: but it was afterwards established that their commander, Suliman Askeri, had been wounded there, and as we had certainly seen much confusion and the guns had ceased fire, perhaps there was a good deal in the rest of the story. But what exactly this "reconnaissance in force" had effected, or what information had been gleaned, we never heard.

Perhaps it served some valuable purpose; but, to the Arabs, who take little account of "retirements according to plan" or of the intricacies of strategy, we appeared to have set out to attack the Turks, to have made a lot of noise, and then—to have returned without accomplishing our purpose. The conclusion was obvious: the Turks were too strong for us, and we had been beaten—suffering, so the report said, heavy casualties: the Turks were still in their position astride the river.

There is little doubt that in some such way our prestige suffered among the Arabs. The rumours spread quickly and in the next few weeks we were shown, quite unmistakably, which way the wind was blowing.

Sunday, 24th January, was the first Sunday we had kept as a holiday since we had landed—but, of course, as we had no work to do the weather kindly obliged with a real soaker of a day, and it rained from dawn till night without ceasing. Besides being peculiarly unpleasant, for the desert was turned into a sheet of slippery mud, rain was becoming rather a serious matter, as we began to realise that there was quite enough water about without the addition of any more from above, and at about this time "Floods" first began to be spoken of with some apprehension. Earlier, indeed, when first the fortifications round Mazera were begun, some of the better disposed of the local Arabs had hinted that we were likely to have a dampish time of it; in fact had predicted most solemnly that as the site of our trenches had annually, within the memory of themselves and their fathers, been under water, it was improbable that there would be any exception this year; particularly as, they pointed out, the bunds "or dams of sun-baked earth, which were usually built in autumn, had not been built or repaired the previous year. But, either from a suspicion that they were leg-pulling, or owing to the supreme importance of occupying this position for rather less than two months, such warnings were disregarded and work continued; and the workers were quite convinced, poor dears, that the result of their labours would remain as their monument for ever and ever, amen.

Towards the end of January an important addition to the defences arrived in the shape of a battery of 4-inch guns, Kurna and Mazera each getting one section.

They were of the type familiarly known as "cow-guns," from their teams of sixteen oxen—tremendous great grey beasts whose triumphant and stately entrance to camp made a great impression. Officially the guns are described as "4-inch B.L."—B.L. signifying breech-loading as distinguished from Q.F., quick-firing; though a carping critic said that of course the guns were so obsolete that unless due stress was laid on the breech-loading someone might have rammed a cannon ball down their spouts and tried to touch them off with a squib!

However, it was just as well not to look our gift horse in the mouth, for it was 1916 before the army in Mesopotamia got anything more modern in the shape of heavy guns.

Hardly had we recovered from the excitement and admiration occasioned by the "cow-guns," when we had another surprise. On the night of 29th January, a message was received to say that an attack might be expected at 10 a.m., and all precautions were immediately to be taken. We gathered from the context, as it were, that 10 a.m. was a misprint for 10 p.m., but as it was now 9 p.m. there was not much time to be lost.

So far, little reason for surprise, as such warnings were common; but the surprise came, when, after two or three hours' vigil, a sudden and furious rifle and machine-gun fire broke out from the eastern perimeter, which was quite adequately replied to by a force apparently right up against camp. We outside in the northern redoubts stared hard at our wire, but saw, unfortunately, nothing of interest, while there was quite a lot of firing going on behind us; though whether the bullets that came over from camp were foes or friends it didn't much matter—bullets from behind are much the same when there is no *parados!*

After a few minutes the firing, except for an occasional burst from a machine-gun, ceased, and we waited till the morning and our return to camp to hear what it had all been about. There we found that there had been quite a good "pick-up" of Turks, five killed and eight wounded, including an officer, and from him an account of sorts of the affair was gleaned. He said that he was leading a patrol—which was sent out every night—of about 200 men (rather a large number), that they had lost their way, and, quite by mistake, slipped in between the redoubts on the east side.

They had almost bumped into the perimeter, and then his men had lost their heads and started shooting. He, personally, had been much frightened, and strongly objected to the 103rd machine-guns' traversing fire! That was, roughly, his story, and not a particularly likely one, as we had pretty full information of this "accident" some six hours before it happened, and we knew very well that the Turks were not in the habit of sending nightly patrols to look us up.

However, whatever the game was, they had left eight prisoners and five dead with us, and one more was bayoneted in the wire of a redoubt, though the rest got away as mysteriously as they had arrived. Probably they had a very good idea of our positions from the Arabs. Later in the morning, but perhaps rather too late, a squadron of the 33rd was sent in pursuit, and came up with some stragglers who put up a fight. Six of them were killed and several wounded, while the 33rd lost one native officer killed and three *sawars* wounded.

Out casualties in camp the night before were eight wounded, including Major Farmar of the 84th Battery, who had only arrived the previous day, while three horses and one camel were killed. One or two men in the redoubts were wounded—rumour says that when the bullets were extracted they were found to be .303. Certainly, some of the shooting had seemed a trifle wild!

Within the next three nights there were two more alarms, based on the observance of large movements of Arabs across the Swaib, and our garrison at Mazera was strengthened by additions from Kurna; but nothing came of either, and we were left in peace, though it was obvious that there was a good deal more "movement" round about us than there had been previously, and decided unrest among the Arabs.

This was rather disconcerting, because we had just heard that H.E. the Viceroy, after a visit to Basra, was coming up to inspect Kurna and Mazera, and any vulgar interruption on the part of the locals was, we felt, untimely. But, in spite of a monster "Salvation Army meeting" on 5th February opposite Kurna, attended by thousands of Arabs and flags, and suitably dealt with by the *Miner's* 6-pounder and machine-gun at close range, all was quiet when the Viceroy with his Staff arrived on the 6th and walked round the defences of Kurna and Mazera. H.E. remained till the next day, and attended church parade, after which he left again for Basra in R.I.M.S. *Laurence*, now a gunboat armed with 4-inch guns. It was on the viceroy's departure that the pontoon bridge, lately completed, was "cut" for the first time to allow the passage of a big ship, and I believe grave doubts were entertained as to whether a ship of the *Laurence's* beam could get through the narrow opening with the stream behind her. It must have been a ticklish job but was accomplished successfully.

At Basra the viceroy had inspected troops and received various loyal Arab Sheikhs, to whom "robes of honour" were presented as rewards for services rendered. But the main reason for his visit was, we were told, that he might personally examine the situation in Mesopotamia and its requirements.

There is little doubt that already at this stage an advance on Baghdad was decided on, unless anything very unforeseen occurred. His visit, we hoped, heralded some return to activity on our part, for business had certainly been slack ever since the taking of Kurna two months before, and we had still no clear idea as to whether a further advance was contemplated. So far we knew we were of no account to the world without, and it was distinctly galling when fond relations wrote and said, "We are so glad that you are not going to the 'front'!" So, we hoped for an offensive policy. But whatever plans man, in the shape of the Staff, might make, it became increasingly plain that Nature was not here to assist. For the last fortnight the water from the Swaib marshes had been spreading, and slowly the desert to the east became covered. First depressions here and there, dry one night, would appear as ponds next morning, then gradually we watched an uninterrupted lake that day by day edged farther westward and northward towards the line of the redoubts. The same thing was happening over the way at Kurna. The river had begun to rise rapidly.

Dawn in those days was a memorable sight. "Stand to" in the redoubts found one waiting stiff and cold under a pitch-black sky, in which the stars shone with a marvellous brilliance from horizon to horizon.

Gradually over the east would steal a rosy glow, quickly changing to a gold, pale at first, but deepening with every minute to a gorgeous orange, which spread and seemed to roll towards one, covering earth and sky. And then one realised that beneath the golden sky, as far as the eye could reach, stretched a vast expanse of flashing golden water. The sun rose with a rush above the eastern horizon, and day began— a miracle of blue sky, mass upon mass of towering sunlit clouds, and leagues of water, each little ripple a flaming point of gold and blue. A great artist might paint the picture, but no one would believe him.

CHAPTER 8

Transport Difficulties

The first signs of the activity long hoped for were manifested in a re-shuffling of the troops, which were now distributed in the Kurna-Mazera, Basra, and Ahwaz districts. On 31st January the 12th Brigade of the XIIth Division had disembarked at Basra—a valuable reinforcement to our small force; but, better still, came the rumour that this Brigade would soon be joined by the other two brigades of the division, so that we could look forward to having two divisions in the country, and I.E.F. "D" would become an army corps.

The 12th Brigade, under the command of Brigadier-General Davison, consisted of the 2nd Royal West Kents, the 90th Punjabis, the 4th Rajputs, and the 44th Mewaras.

On 9th February the West Kents and 90th Punjabis arrived, and came into camp with us at Mazera, where they had to put up with rather close quarters; at the same time the two companies of the 7th Rajputs at Kurna were sent downstream to join the remainder of their regiment at Ahwaz, where the pipe-line had again been attacked. The Norfolks also left ten days later for the Basra district, where most of the 16th and 18th Brigades were soon concentrated.

But it was evident that the "activity" which called for these changes was not entirely due to our own intentions. Ahwaz had had to be reinforced owing to the appearance in its vicinity of large forces of Arabs, which were soon strengthened by Turks—there was a general drift of many forces towards the Karun from the Amara district, which was considered now to account in some measure for the movements which had been noticed parallel with our front across the Swaib River in the previous month. News also came that there was a big concentration in progress at Baghdad—the Aleppo Army Corps again—and some signs of movement on the Euphrates above Suk-es-Sheyuk;

though, naturally enough, none but the Staff knew any details.

At first sight it does not appear very clear why the VIth Aleppo Army Corps should have been causing us anxiety, as, on the map, Aleppo is a long way from Basra. Baghdad is also the headquarters of an Army Corps, and this should have been our natural enemy.

But the Baghdad (13th) Corps of the Turkish Army is largely locally recruited, and numbers many Arabs, together with Arab officers, in its ranks. Enver Pasha considered these troops would fight better if removed from "home influence," and they were accordingly sent north to the Caucasus. Here they suffered terribly in the ice and snow of the mountain passes during the winter campaign of 1914-15. They were ill-treated in every possible way by their Turkish commanders, insulted, and frequently murdered, and finally they shared in the disastrous defeats at Sarikamuish in December 1914 and January 1915, where their losses were appalling; the XXXVIIth Division attached to the 11th (Van) Corps being literally annihilated.

In their place it was decided, originally, to send the Aleppo Corps to defend Mesopotamia; but it was long before any move in that direction was made, and, finally, during 1915, various reinforcements were sent down piecemeal, some from Constantinople, some from Aleppo, some from Mosul, so that the organisation of the Turkish forces (until the beginning of 1916) was mixed, and it was extremely difficult to identify units and formations.

Indeed, the whole organisation of the Turkish Army at the beginning of war was difficult to fathom. It was fairly simple on paper, but extensive reforms were still being carried out, many of them as secretly as possible, and information was scarce as to how far the paper army corps and divisions corresponded to the actual formations.

Probably till after its defeat at Kut in September, the Turkish Army in Mesopotamia was represented by three "Muretteb" Divisions, with some locally recruited Arabs. "Muretteb" Divisions were formed of reservists strengthened by Nizam (Regulars) or by recruits with a considerable stiffening of older Nizam, though the proportion probably varied considerably. The artillery of this army was throughout bad: until July 1915 there were no quick-firing guns in the country.

After their defeat at Kut in September the Turkish forces were reorganised and considerably strengthened, and an army of very different quality opposed the advance on Baghdad in November 1915.

Whatever happened, though, it was becoming increasingly plain that any movement from, or for that matter against, the Kurna front,

Flooded Date Gardens at Mazera.

was going to be a matter of difficulty. The river was still rising rapidly and, from Baghdad, came ominous reports of a tremendous flood, the worst for thirty years, which had swamped the outskirts of the city and washed away houses. From Mazera we watched the water spread across the desert in shining curves, ever edging towards our positions. We were fully alive now to the flood danger, and realised that, to hold Mazera, we should have to fight the river—a far more formidable adversary than the Turk.

Mazera Camp was connected with the pontoon bridge and Kurna by a road which ran through the palm trees, and by another similar road to a pier on the Shatt-el-Arab. These roads were our only communications with the outside world, and they were rapidly becoming too water-logged to carry wheeled transport. Gradually, the palm groves on either side were becoming flooded, and the roads had to be raised and the edges carefully revetted— hard work and needing a lot of labour. But the need increased as time went on, and it was found necessary to employ outside labour in the form of Arabs, who were kept constantly at work on the roads, raising them by inches every day till they were causeways running through the floods which extended among the palms on each side. It was a tremendous work, not only in regard to the actual labour of building, but because every bit of dry earth used had to be brought either from across the river or over a mile from the desert, where we still kept some *terra firma.*

The Sappers were the hardest-worked men in the Force, and laboured day and night at a heart-breaking job. The work was urgent and absolutely essential, so there could be no picking and choosing as regards labourers. A huge gang of Marsh Arabs was employed under British and Indian N.CO.'s, at the princely wages of *As*. 12 a day (the current rate in these parts previously having been four *annas* a day!); though they were qualified mud-larkers they were the slowest workers on earth. They strolled about and jabbered, staggered under loads which a child could have handled, and showed a wonderful keenness at helping each other do one man's job: their taskmasters the N.C.O.'s, were wonderfully patient—too patient, perhaps, for the Marsh Arab somehow seems to understand orders much more rapidly when a thick stick is handy.

Among this very mixed gathering there is little doubt that we got hold of some bad 'uns,—they were too big a crowd to be carefully examined,—and that information of sorts got through to the enemy by this channel; but apparently not much harm was done in this way,

Hut Building at Kurna.

as the workers hadn't much opportunity of learning anything important, though, of course, there was the possibility of a spy being taken on as a *coolie*.

Very soon, with the exception of these two roads, any movement by land became a matter of ankle-deep wading and was obviously soon to become a matter of swimming. Under such conditions we couldn't get at the Turk and the Turk couldn't get at us, so we were quits. But the webbed-footed Arabs had the laugh of us; with their fleets of light "*mashoofs*" this was the sort of going which just suited them, and they knew every channel and every hiding-place in the marshes—they could come to us, but we could not go to them.

This was, of course, a state of affairs which could not be allowed to continue, and the only remedy appeared to be for us also to become proficient in aquatic sports. Accordingly, we set about it.

In the second week in February arrived an order that each regiment would train and organise crews for four "*bellums*"—one crew per company—each regimental detachment of four boats being under the command of a subaltern, the whole fleet of sixteen boats to be commanded by a captain, the Brigade Bellum Officer.

I well remember our first practice. It was on a gusty day with squalls of rain at intervals, and a high "sea" was running in the river, where the strong stream met the wind and was converted into steep, choppy waves. Though the boats had been provided, as yet no paddles were forthcoming, and we were bidden to do our best, or worst, with whatever we could find. So, we pushed out from shore and faced the dangers of the deep armed with shovels, G.S., for paddles. It was an unhappy voyage, and an inauspicious beginning to our enterprise. It would take somebody of the nature of an "expert" to use a clumsy-headed, short-handled shovel as a paddle; but, out of the eight that comprised our crew, four had never been in a boat before, and no one had ever used a paddle.

Then the handles were too short, and, only by leaning well over the side, could the water be reached—a difficult manoeuvre when the boat was bobbing and rocking like a cork. It ended by everyone taking a jab at the water whenever it appeared to him he could do so with reasonable chances of hitting it without falling in. Our progress was somewhat irregular, but a source of amusement to spectators.

However, in time, and in better weather, we learned the rudiments of the game, and, when the paddles had been fashioned by the pioneers, things went better, so that it became no unusual sight to see

British troops crossing a flooded area

a *bellum* accomplish quite 200 yards in one, and presumably the intended, direction, without any of the crew falling off their seats, dropping their paddles, or knocking out their front teeth. The Tigris was rather out of favour as a practice course, owing to the strong stream, but, morning and afternoon, crews could be seen ploughing furrows in the glassy waters of the Euphrates, while the *staccato* counting of the coxswains, their commands to "Keep it long" and not to "wash out," gave quite a Henley tone to the proceedings. We started none too soon. For some time, the river had been perilously near the level of the low-lying desert. About the 10th of February it reached that level, and we knew that now our last dry land, a strip between the river and the ever-encroaching Swaib marshes, was only secured by a *bund*—a low bank of dry earth on the river's edge: if that broke, the fate of Mazera was sealed.

Lately, as the floods had encroached, all the game had been driven to the little dry land that yet remained. The snipe had left, but their place had been taken by sandgrouse, which were now beginning to arrive, and any spare time we had was employed in chasing these; also, the pig, which could no longer be ridden, but still supplied useful fresh meat.

We had been out early one morning to see what could be picked up for the pot, when, on our return, we found the camp in a state of apparent confusion—at least things looked unusual. There was little need to ask what was up, for it was easy to see: towards the redoubts, from the direction of the river, trickled a broad stream of water—all hands were engaged in fighting this new enemy. But, strive as we might all day long with dams of sandbags and mud, nothing could be done. In the early hours of the morning the *bund* had been cut, and now the river was enlarging the gap every minute. We could say with truth "an enemy hath done this," and, while heaping vain curses upon his head, scarcely wonder at his simple and effective tactics.

Nos. 5 and 4 Redoubts were out of action, and we knew it was only a matter of time— and not much time at that—before the whole position would have to be evacuated. In a few days this became the official view, and orders were issued for as much material as possible to be saved and taken over to Kurna. The guns, together with "Percy" and his searchlight (and, we will hope, his voltage too), were the first to be got out, and much heaving and hauling it took; then came the salvage of lighter stuff, and we set to to save as much of the wire and wood as we could, and generally to pull down the edifice we had so carefully built up in the last two months. No doubt the situation had its humorous side, but, at the time, I don't think we saw it.

To add to the cheerfulness of life we got a bout of rain. Every night it poured and pelted, so that we waded more than knee-deep in the trenches that were still occupied until we should have finally cleared out; and mud was everywhere—the rich, adhesive article that must be slept in to be really appreciated. The cavalry and R.F.A. had been sent downstream as unsuited to such an amphibious life, and were transferred to Ahwaz and the Basra district, and the West Kents and 90th Punjabis (12th Brigade) left us soon after for the same destination, where events suggested the need of more troops at no very distant date.

Finally, on the 27th February, the 17th Brigade, having saved as much as possible from the wreck of their home, received orders to cross the river to Kurna, leaving one regiment perched upon Mazera's small plot of solid ground, to protect the bridgehead. The unfortunate regiment chosen was the 22nd Punjabis, and the rest of us crossed the bridge and took over as garrison to Kurna, relieving other troops to be sent downstream to a new centre of attraction, which now began to assume importance.

If transport had, up to this date, been hardly adequate, it now became obvious that we were distinctly short of it—and short of it in its most important form, namely, river steamers and barges. When troops and stores had to be conveyed up and down river and between places so widely separated as Ahwaz and Kurna, difficulties immediately appeared.

It is true that the country itself had been "drawn" very carefully for anything in the shape of a steamer, but they were not particularly common articles in Mesopotamia. At the start of the campaign our resources in this direction, exclusive of small launches, had been represented by the three Lynch boats, *Blosse Lynch*, *Medjedieh*, and *Malamir*. By March this fleet had been augmented by the addition of the following, a mixed lot, of odd appearance and queer antecedents and no uncertain age. The *Julnar*, a twin-screw Lynch ship, the biggest and fastest craft on the river, was now out of dock and again in commission. This ship was of invaluable service, in spite of being rather unhandy at the sharp turns. The *Salimi* was a fair-sized paddleboat, owned before the war by a Persian who ran her on the Karun. She was about the best of the lot, though her skipper, Mr. Hasan-bin-Ghulami, preferred to keep her in a state of indescribable filth. Then there was the *Massoudieh*, a very, very ancient and small stern-wheeler, once known as the "Basra 'Bus," for she used to do ferry work between Muhammera and Basra.

The *Shushan*, another very old stern-wheeler, full of years and history, was originally built for the Gordon Relief Expedition, and had been spending her life, since 1898, in navigating the Upper Karun, where the rude inhabitants of Shustar christened her "The Red Pig." These, with some iron barges, lent by the Anglo-Persian Oil Company, constituted our transport, while the armed launches had been reinforced by the *Sumana* and the *Comet*,—originally the launch of the British Resident at Baghdad,—though, on various occasions, the old *Shushan* and the *Massoudieh* became ships of war.

But, in spite of these additions, our state was really worse than before. Distances had increased, and more troops were arriving. Already, at the end of January, the 12th Brigade of the XIIth Division had arrived, soon followed by a Cavalry Brigade, and during March the two other brigades of the division were to land, besides divisional and army troops, so that we soon had more than twice the number of men in the country. These had to be fed, and moved, almost entirely by river, so the problem was a knotty one. What about hospital ships? If a lot of wounded had to be moved by river, what would happen? Perhaps the question was asked then; anyhow, it was to be answered one day. But "that is another story."

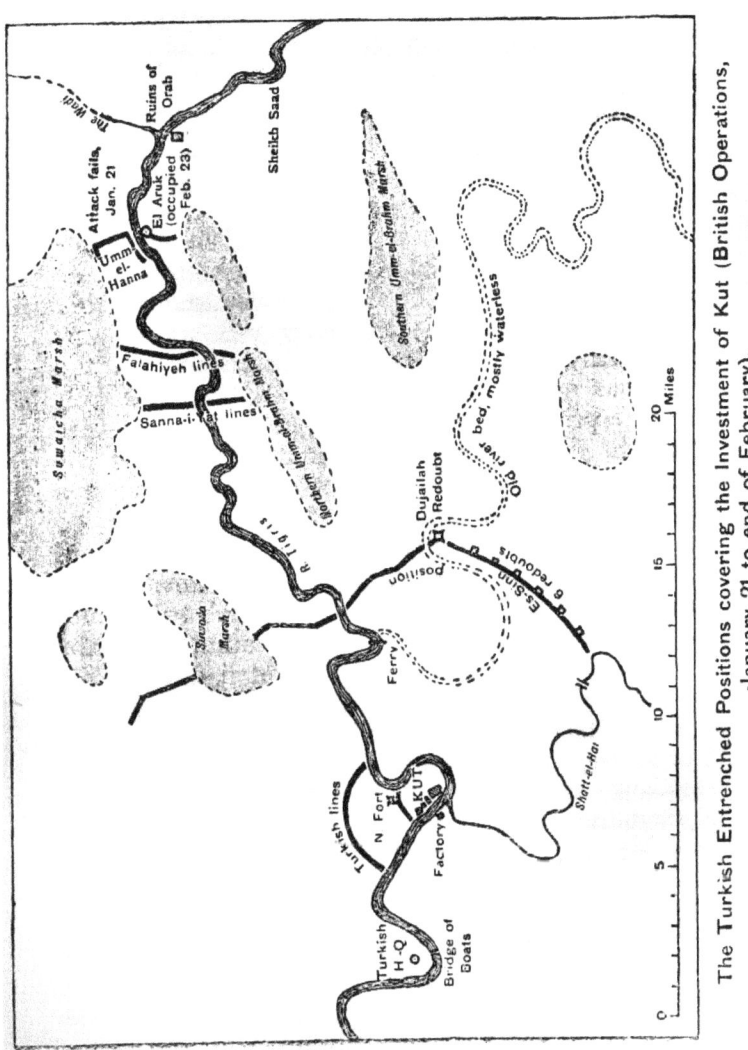

The Turkish Entrenched Positions covering the Investment of Kut (British Operations, January 21 to end of February).

CHAPTER 9

March 1915

March 1 was, I remember, the first day on which the hot weather made itself felt. We had plenty of cool days and cold nights later before the heat really began, and this day was only an unseasonable freak; but an oppressive stillness in the air and a steaming heat, coincided, rather unfortunately, with the taking up of our new quarters at Kurna.

These we found at the northern end of the village among the date palms, on a bit of ground intersected in all directions by irrigation ditches, brimful and odoriferous, the breeding-ground of clouds of mosquitoes. As we could walk hardly five yards in any direction without meeting one of these ditches, the pitching of tents was a matter of difficulty, and, in addition, the palms, too precious to be felled, had also to be avoided. On the whole the prospect was not very tempting.

Kurna and its surroundings had altered considerably since we left in the early days of January. Camp Tigris was no more, for, with all the desert to the north, it was under water, and, as far as the eye could reach, stretched the glittering floods with green tips of reeds just beginning to show above the surface. A little dry land remained along the edge of the Tigris, and, on the extremity of this, Fort Snipe, a small redoubt, was still held. It was our "farthest north,"—about 1000 yards from the Kurna perimeter—and its garrison led a damp and harassed existence with water on three sides and only a very boggy and uncertain tow-path to connect them with their friends.

Farther north, across the swamp, was Norfolk Hill, a low mound standing up above flood-level, once occupied by the Norfolks but now evacuated, and beyond this again two sandy ridges showed on the horizon—Tower Hill and Gun Hill, respectively 3500 and 5000 yards from Kurna, which at present were "no man's land." Behind Gun Hill and out of sight we knew lay Bahràn, a considerable area of high ground which was never likely to be flooded out, and was now held by the Turks. These mounds were our only landmarks, all else was water and reeds, with only a few palm trees upon the bank to mark the course of the Tigris.

Westward, we were bounded by a broad creek, and, beyond it again, lay miles of reedy marsh, soon to become one vast lake. On the south ran the Old Euphrates, its far bank green with palm groves and cultivated fields for a mile or so inland, but they soon ceased where the shimmering waters of the Khor Jezair spread far southward to meet the "New" River. North and west and south was water, and east ran the Tigris, with its one bridge leading only to the post at Mazera, round which lapped the floods from which we had just fled. We had escaped them, but it looked as if we should have to stand a siege.

Within Kurna itself, though the defences were now complete and adequate, the prospect was not inviting. On the northern and western faces in the high banks beforementioned, trenches and posts had been cut, and the brick kilns turned into observation towers and machine-gun positions, while directly within the perimeter a road had been constructed—an encircling causeway giving direct access to the northern and western trenches and bordering the Tigris on the east and the Euphrates on the south, with transverse roads running north and south, east and west.

Within this encircling causeway on the northern and western sides lay an expanse of horrid bog, which gradually became a stagnant lake, forming a lagoon within the perimeter and the causeway; and on the scarcely solid core of this lagoon, surrounded by stagnant water and moated with many ditches, we sat for three months, while waters rose about us and heat increased and mosquitoes multiplied.

"If," as a soldier remarked, "Kurna was the Garden of Eden, it wouldn't take no blinkin' fiery sword to keep me out of it!"

As for the defences, they were mainly constituted by the trenches in the perimeter facing the marshes, and by the converted brick-kilns, which were, we found, all named after various distinguished officers. There were four of these kilns: One on the Tigris bank at the north-east angle, one at north-west angle, one half-way down the western face, and one at the south-west angle at the junction of the creek and the Euphrates, named, respectively, Fort Winsloe, Fort Frazer, Observation Post, and Fort Peebles.

At the junction of the Tigris and Euphrates was a strong redoubt, Fort Fry, but otherwise the Euphrates and Tigris banks were not held, except by picquets at night, as there was no danger with their broad streams between us and possible marauders. Artillery we were not rich in, but indeed this was not exactly the terrain for field batteries, which were urgently needed elsewhere. A section of 4-inch guns on the northern face, later reinforced by a section of 5-inch, together with the ships' guns, provided all the artillery necessary. A boom across the river above Nahairat protected the ships from mines.

Here, then, we had arrived, but how long we were to stay and what we were to do were alike wrapt in mystery, for it seemed that no enemy without a fleet could possibly contemplate an attack on us, while we were only too plainly imprisoned by the surrounding waters. Within the walls of our prison we had an area of some 100 acres, some of it dry land, where we could play about. We could lean over the walls and make faces in the direction in which we believed the enemy to be; but, beyond that, we fancied, there was not much to be done.

Soon we learnt we were wrong. The first thing we found out was that it would only be by hard and constant work, by much making of bricks without straw, by weary hours of tamping and puddling and mud-slinging, that we should remain in the Garden of Eden at all; for the rising water was ever craftily sapping our foundations, insinuating itself into our defences, and could only be kept at bay by careful and constant plumbing. So, we plumbed: for three months, in an atmosphere of mixed steam and mosquitoes, we were slingers of mud and stoppers of water, and so we saved Kurna from inundation—though it must be understood that it was for our own sakes and not for Kurna's that we did this. As far as we were concerned, Kurna and its natives were welcome to a millstone and the deepest ocean!

However, those who had been chosen as temporary "*matlots*" led a more interesting existence and escaped in some measure the confined bounds and irksome labours of Kurna. Morning and afternoon and evening we took to our boats and the open sea until a warning from Headquarters forbade us to go farther upstream than the creek. Information was to hand that certain Marsh Arabs were lying up for us— no doubt from jealousy at our superb skill; but Brigade Headquarters seemed to take a less favourable view of our proficiency, and we were not yet considered fit to take the web-footed ones on at their own game: that, we hoped, would come later.

In the meantime, while we have been settling in comfortably at Kurna, things had been happening elsewhere. It was on 5th March that we first heard rumours that there had been fighting downstream; no one seemed to have definite information except that some sort of action had been fought both at Ahwaz and Shaiba, the eastern and western extremities of our line, and that things had not gone too well.

Official reticence gave rise to forebodings, which were increased during the next few days by fresh crops of rumours which reported "regrettable incidents" on both flanks, and numerous casualties, among which were the names of many friends. It was soon impossible to believe that something unfortunate had not happened, but equally impossible to find out the facts. In consequence, Kurna was soon persuaded that the worst was being withheld, and that it must be pretty bad. This unhealthy gossip of mystery and disaster was the talk of all ranks and by no means unknown to the local inhabitant.

Secrecy is at times advisable or necessary; but it became absurd and unnecessary when one morning the *Comet* came alongside the landing-stage. She came direct from the scene of action at Ahwaz, where her crew had taken part in, or witnessed, the whole of the recent operations there. There followed a strange situation: while the natives of her crew—engineers and such-like—were giving a full description of their adventures to the local crowd, Brigade Headquarters were unable to give any information at all—not because they would not, but because they had not yet received any official news whatever that any fighting had taken place downstream. If the staff wanted to know, no doubt they could go and hear what the Arabs on the quay were saying!

But at last our discreet authorities unbent, and we were given an official account of both engagements. It arrived on 9th March. Both affairs had taken place on 3rd March, one on our extreme right flank at Ahwaz, the other, 100 miles away, on our extreme left near Shaiba: evidently neither had been a success for us.

At Ahwaz, news had been received that large concentrations of Arabs, stiffened by Turks, were taking place in the hills to the northwest. A "reconnaissance in force" was decided on. Leaving a company to protect camp, a force consisting of 4th Rajputs, 7th Rajputs, one platoon of the Dorsets, one troop 33rd Cavalry, one section of field guns, and the 23rd Mountain Battery, under Brigadier-General Robinson, started out on the morning of 3rd March. After marching about eight miles, and just after entering a narrow valley in the hills, the column was surprised. Without any warning— though presumably all proper precautions had been taken—an avalanche of Arabs, estimated at about 12,000, descended with a rush upon the small force. To cut a long story short and to speak bluntly, there was a panic: a howling mob of Arabs was round the column and across the road back to Ahwaz, and unexpected Turkish guns began to open fire. Eyewitnesses who were there say that a few rounds of well-controlled "rapid fire" were all that was necessary to stop the rush, for half the Arabs were only armed with knives and stones; but that was not forthcoming, and the column was almost smothered.

Few would ever have got back if it had not been for the splendid behaviour of the platoon of the Dorsets, who, under Lieutenant Thomson, fought a rear-guard action for six miles against thousands, and steadfastly refused to be rushed, and the fine work of Lieutenant Sheepshanks (12th Cavalry) who, with a troop of the 33rd, charged again and again. These, together with stalwarts of the 7th Rajputs, and a mixed force of medical officers and stretcher-bearers, saw the thing through and accounted for a good many of the enemy—one medical officer killed twenty-four Arabs with his revolver, and, then fired over 200 rounds from a rifle at point-blank range.

The column got back to Ahwaz with about 200 wounded—but it left behind it five British Officers and eighty men killed, one field gun with limber and a wagon, with ammunition intact, and the breech end of a mountain gun; the other half, Captain Hunt, though severely wounded, managed at great personal risk to get away.

That was Ahwaz. At Shaiba things had not gone so badly, though they might have gone better. Here, again, signs of a strong enemy concentration at Nakhailat suggested another "reconnaissance in force," and, on 3rd March, the Cavalry Brigade set out to clear up the situation. They had ridden some twelve miles out from Shaiba without meeting with any opposition, though constantly catching sight of mounted Arabs who immediately made themselves scarce, in which they were aided by a particularly bad mirage.

Perhaps it was owing to this mirage that the main force of the enemy were not seen sooner; but, at all events, before anyone realised what was up, an immense cloud of Arab horsemen appeared, spreading far round the flanks as they came. The order was given to retire—the walk changed to a trot, the trot to a canter, the canter to a gallop, and they were riding a finish with the enemy closing from the flanks and already among them, when suddenly guns and rifle fire opened on the pursuing Arabs. Under cover of this, the cavalry were able to break off while the enemy galloped away in confusion.

60 POUNDER GUN FIRING IN MESOPOTAMIA

Later, it transpired that it was all a carefully laid plan: the Arabs were to be enticed to follow our squadrons, who were to lead them into entrenched infantry, sent out for this purpose from Shaiba. But this stratagem was never confided to the Cavalry Brigade—at all events not to regimental officers, with the consequence that they had no idea that any infantry support was near at hand on which they could retire slowly with safety. It proved an expensive omission, for again the loss in British officers was severe—four killed and several wounded—with a pretty heavy casualty list among other ranks. A machine-gun also was lost.

The established presence of enemy in considerable numbers at these two points, together with information of a concentration at Suk-es-Sheyuk, on the Euphrates, pointed to their evident intention at some future date of attacking. The force opposite Ahwaz, though considerable in numbers, was of poor quality, being mostly Arabs, but there were signs that an army of better stuff was gradually being assembled on the Euphrates. That was the obvious "kick-off" for any force moving from the west against Basra, and so it seemed almost certain that the attack would come on our left flank, while "diversions" would be arranged, no doubt, to keep Kurna and Ahwaz busy.

By retaking Basra, the Turks would, at one blow, recover their lost prestige, capture a valuable base with its stores, and, most important of all, be able to interrupt all sea communications with India. Indeed, if ever Basra were to fall, the troops upriver would have a thin time of it, with no food and no way out—short of marching back to India by the Makran and Baluchistan!

So, it was that the enemy concentration on the Euphrates was watched with very particular care; and, by degrees, all available troops and guns which could possibly be spared from upstream were brought down to Basra and Shaiba, which now for the next six weeks became "the front." Ahwaz would have to take care of itself, and Kurna, girdled by its waters, was not likely to come to harm—so long as the garrison went on plumbing.

We had not long to wait before "diversions," no doubt intended to keep us busy, were started for our benefit: they were amusing, and helped us to take interest in life, but were otherwise, as far as I know, ineffective. The Arabs had been getting above themselves for some time and showed in various ways that they wished to annoy us. One night a party of them crossed the creek on the western face and got away with a motorboat and *mashoof* belonging to some officers of the Oxfordshire Light Infantry—rather a cunning performance, as the boats were securely moored in the creek scarcely ten yards from a sentry-post—and the next night the Turks from upstream floated two mines down the river, intended, no doubt, to destroy the bridge. However, they bumped the bank before their journey was accomplished, and, beyond blowing a hole in Mesopotamia and severely startling those of us who were asleep, no harm was done.

Sportsmen had for some time been obliged to abandon the chase as far as guns were concerned, but their attention was soon turned to the fish, and it was discovered that there were plenty about. The first adventurers were to be seen in these days armed with palm branches, string, and home-made hooks, but soon such primitive tackle was superseded by the real article, sent from India. Spinning was not a success at this time of year, the middle of March, but there was a fine hatch of fly every evening, especially of a big, fat-bodied, white-winged fly which covered the waters about sunset and produced a perfect maelstrom of big, hungry fish.

Night after night we tried for them off the point at the junction of the rivers, but the fish refused to look at our imitations. Gradually, by experiment, we discovered that a gaudy salmon fly—a "Silver Doctor" or "Jock Scott" and a *mahseer* fly "Smoky Dun" were the best, and I caught fish up to 5 lb. on these flies. What exactly the fish thus caught were I don't know: the Arabs called them "*shillig*." They are bright silver and in shape rather like a char but with very powerful jaws and teeth. There were many other kinds of fish in the rivers and the floods, including mud-fish, a sort of fresh-water pipe-fish, and carp of all kinds, among them a very flat, broad one, with big, bluish scales, which the Arabs seem to eat in quantities; and also some perfect monsters running up to 100 or 150 lb. which the natives catch with a paste of flour and dates, and sometimes with meat.

I saw one of these fish which was brought into the mess about six hours after it had been killed, and it then weighed 60 lb. It was a beautifully-shaped fish, with a dark back, brown flanks speckled with black, and a white belly. It was said to be a "*mahseer*," but judging from a plentiful supply of "whiskers" it was a bottom-feeder, and in shape so like the "*shillig*" that it seems probable that these so-called *mahseer* are *shillig* that have grown big and become bottom-feeders.

But to turn to more serious topics. It was on the 19th of March that the Turks first started shelling us. They opened fire from Gun Hill (which they had lately occupied) at 3 a.m. that morning and put a lot of shells over Fort Snipe, without doing much damage, and also favoured H.M.S. *Odin*, which was lying out in the stream above Kurna. The *Odin* retaliated, but the artillery duel produced little result on either side—except to warn us that we must now keep a weather eye on those little mounds among the floods which the enemy did not mean to leave unoccupied.

Towards the end of the month we heard that General Nixon was coming out to command force "D," while General Townshend would command the VIth Division and General Gorringe the XIIth Division, when it was complete; there were also cheering tales of well-armed river monitors and aeroplanes and a whole crop of rumours as to what the Turks were doing. An Arab was captured—intentionally, we suspected later—who gave quite bloodcurdling accounts of what was in store for us: guns as long as palm-trees, huge armies of Turks and a thousand German officers at Baghdad, together with many aeroplanes. Noticing, no doubt, the hit this scored, he rather unfortunately enlarged upon the aeroplanes, and described how he had seen them flying, and how "they flapped their wings like immense birds." However, even so, his news was believed in some quarters, and no working party was allowed on the perimeter without a percentage of rifles told off to look for the immense birds and instructed that it was necessary to aim ten lengths in front in order to bring them down; unfortunately, they never had a chance of proving the efficacy of this recipe.

A certain amount of sniping, casual and ineffective bombardments from Gun Hill, now and then the nightly mines which always exploded prematurely, and so life went on. We led our strange island existence very little troubled by the world without (for the wire to Basra was in a chronic state of being cut); within, we plastered and revetted and drained, and spent much time in building most beautiful reed huts, barrack-rooms for twenty men, orderly-rooms, officers' quarters, and mess. At first Arabs were secured to build some sealed-pattern huts, while an officer from each regiment and some N.C.O.'s looked on and learnt the method. Then huts were built by the men with an Arab present to give any necessary hints, and finally the Arabs could be dispensed with, and each regiment could boast of a company of expert hutters, who did all the necessary building.

Without, the boats' crews poled and punted and became expert watermen, much assisted by the safe practice to be had on the glassy surface of the flood, where the soldier or the *sepoy* could not possibly drown himself, punt he never so rashly.

Lieut.-General Sir G. F. Gorringe K.C.B., K.C.M.G., D.S.O.

The weather was heating up certainly; but the frequent thunderstorms, though they flooded camp and made living damper than ever, cooled the atmosphere. Nearly every evening huge banks of clouds would come drifting in from the north-west, slowly swelling up from the horizon and bursting with a rush of waters over the marshes. There were wonderful atmospheric effects—rainbows through the mists that hung over the waters, immense and towering banks of snow-white clouds, which blushed to the colour of a rose in the evening; and always at sunset a moment when the marshes became a deep, shadowy blue, with one vivid gold patch across them leading into the fiery disc of the setting sun.

There were other strange effects too. I remember fishing very peacefully in a channel in the marshes, while two hundred yards away crashed the 4-inch guns, and the enemy's shells burst with a whine over the palm trees by Fort Snipe. A little way off on the river front a band was playing "The Blue Danube," and, in an interval between gunfire and waltz music, I heard the *muezzin's* call to evening prayer from the mosque which is said to mark the site of the entry into the Garden of Eden. Which, if you come to think of it, is a strange mixture.

CHAPTER 10

April 1915

Downstream there was every sign that the Turks meant to have a big try to retake Basra. From their base at Nasryeh they were concentrating at Nakhailat on the Euphrates, while we were collecting every man and gun that could be spared at Shaiba, 11 miles north-west of Basra. From Kurna the 119th had been taken from the 17th Brigade and hurried off downriver to fill the place of a regiment in the 16th Brigade, while reserve ammunition and stores were reduced to the lowest possible proportions. So cut down, indeed, in ammunition was the force at Kurna that any determined push would have found it in a tight hole, but it was inconceivable that the enemy could do much against our island position. Ahwaz was in a different situation, as it was almost surrounded by enemy, and just had to grin and bear it until the more pressing business near Basra had been settled.

It was, indeed, pressing business. The Turkish forces, under Suleiman Askari Pasha, were estimated at 12,000 regulars, 24 field guns, together with some mountain guns and a battery of howitzers, besides a swarm of Arab cavalry supposed to number 10,000 men, Muntifik Bedouin under Ajaimi, a force to be reckoned with if the spirit should move them to fight.

To oppose these there were concentrated at Shaiba at the beginning of April the 16th Brigade (with the 119th Infantry in the place of the 20th Punjabis, at Basra), the 18th Brigade (less 7th Rajputs, at Ahwaz), with the 6th Cavalry Brigade and divisional troops of the VIth Division, the whole under the command of Major-General C. I. Fry.

This was not a large force with which to meet an attack by possibly 20,000 enemy. To make matters worse, communication with Basra, eleven miles distant, was exceedingly difficult, owing to the road being under water for nearly the whole distance. This meant that reinforcements from Basra had to wade the whole way, while nearly all stores and ammunition had to be punted across the floods in *bellums*.

By the beginning of April, it is true, there was about twice the number of troops in the country that there had been at the beginning of the year. By now I.E.F. "D" had become an army corps of two divisions (the VIth and the XIIth), and, with the exception of drafts, no further reinforcements were received until after the advance on Baghdad at the end of the year. So, there were actually plenty of men at this stage of the campaign; but the problem was to move and concentrate and feed, and with the hopeless lack of transport that was the difficulty.

This addition to our strength had been formed by the arrival, at the end of February and during March, of the Headquarters and two brigades of the XIIth Division, with some divisional troops. The third brigade, completing the division, arrived at the beginning of April.

XIIth DIVISION.
Major-General G. GORRINGE, C.B.

12th Brigade—
Major-General Davison.

(Arrived 31st January.)

- 2nd Royal West Kent Regiment.
- 90th Punjabis.
- 4th Rajputs.
- 44th Mewaras.

33rd Brigade—
Brigadier-General Lean, C.B.

(Arrived end of March.)

- 1/4th Hampshire Regiment (T.).
- [11th Rajputs.]
- 66th Punjabis.
- 67th Punjabis.

30th Brigade—
Major-General C. Mellis, V.C., C.B.

With 12th Company Sappers and Miners.
(Arrived beginning of April.)

- 24th Punjabis.
- 76th Punjabis.
- 2/7th Gurkhas.
- [126th Baluchis.]

6th Cavalry Brigade—
Brigadier-General H. Kennedy.

(Arrived end of February.)

- 7th Hariana Lancers.
- 16th Cavalry.
- 23rd Cavalry.
- "S" Battery R.H.A.

It will be noticed that the XIIth Division was very short of artillery: there were no Field Batteries at all, while one of its brigades, the 30th, was only three battalions strong and without a British battalion—the fourth battalion, the 126th Baluchis, having been stopped *en route* at Bushire to deal with local disturbances, engineered by the German Consul. Of the two British regiments in the division one was a Territorial unit, which had only arrived in India the previous autumn and, after four months to train and acclimatize, had been sent to serve in about the worst climate in the world just as the hot weather was coming on. The 33rd Brigade, too, was short, as the 11th Rajputs were also diverted to Bushire, and the 67th Punjabis developed cholera *en route* to Mesopotamia and were consequently for some time unavailable.

At the end of March and beginning of April, the 12th Brigade (less the 44th Mewaras at Basra) was concentrated at Ahwaz together with the 1/4th Hants and the 66th Punjabis of the 33rd Brigade, so that there were at Ahwaz at this time six battalions of infantry, one battery R.F.A., and one battery of mountain guns and a detachment of the 33rd Cavalry, the whole under the command of Brigadier-General Lean (until Major-General Gorringe arrived towards the middle of April). The 30th Brigade, not yet in the country, arrived soon afterwards, and one regiment was sent out to reinforce the two brigades of the VIth Division which were already concentrated to meet the enemy's attack, while the remaining brigade of the VIth Division was, as we have seen, upstream at Kurna.

But to turn again to the approaching crisis at Shaiba. Sir John Nixon had landed at Basra on 8th April and taken over command of the Army Corps on the 9th from Sir Arthur Barrett, who owing to ill-health was obliged to return to India immediately. As soon as he had taken over, it became plain that a big engagement was imminent.

Shaiba itself consists of half a dozen large houses and an old fort (the summer residences of Basra notables) some 11 miles north-west of the town. It is situated on the edge of the rolling sandy country which is the beginning of the desert proper and is surrounded by a certain amount of cultivation and trees.

After some preliminary reconnaissances in January the fort was put into a state of defence in February, and as signs of the Turkish concentration at Nakhailat became more clear the position was strengthened and trenches dug by the 16th Brigade, which was then in occupation. Gradually the garrison was increased and the positions extended, though in the meanwhile considerable difficulties had been caused by the gradual spreading of the inundation—the waters descending from the "New" Euphrates floods gradually intervened between the positions and Basra, until towards the end of March the road was under water for nine out of the eleven miles.

About this time a river-column was formed, consisting of two 4-inch guns and a section of 18-pounders mounted on barges and ships (under the command of Colonel Molesworth, R.G.A.), whose duty it was to patrol and blockade the "New" Euphrates and interfere as far as possible with the Turkish concentration at Nakhailat. A few camps were shelled and some grain boats sunk, though the most important work was done later, after the Turkish defeat.

By the beginning of April, the force at Shaiba had been increased to two infantry brigades, one Cavalry Brigade (two regiments strong), two batteries R.F.A., and one mountain battery—the whole, as before mentioned, under General Fry.

On 11th April the Turks were reported on the move from Nakhailat, and reconnaissance found them encamped in Birjisiyeh wood. The previous evening some of the cavalry were seen towards the west but retired on being shelled. In the meantime, picquets had been strengthened and the whole force stood to arms that night.

Next morning (12th) the attack began in earnest and was pressed nearly all day. At dawn the Turkish guns started a heavy bombardment of the camp and fort from the south-west, and it soon became evident that they had something heavier than field guns, though fortunately an extraordinary amount of "duds" came over. Soon after the infantry attack was developed. From the direction of picquets 2 and 3 long lines of skirmishers appeared on the desert with dense columns in rear—rather too far in rear, it appeared, to afford any timely support when the moment came. Luckily the moment did not come; the two picquets were safely withdrawn under cover of the perimeter, and our guns then proceeded to deal with the developing attack. They very soon had the range of the advancing lines and sprayed them with shrapnel so effectively that they were held up 1500 yards from their objective and forced to retire. The withdrawal was an orderly one, although their losses were pretty heavy.

In the meantime, the Arabs in large numbers, some mounted and others on foot, had worked round south of North Mound and were making a determined bid for House C, which they eventually occupied though they could make no further progress. With them they had Turkish machine-gun detachments and a stiffening of Turkish infantry. All the afternoon further attempts were made along the original line of attack, and a turning movement was also developed and strong attacks thrown against the south-east ("Dorset Position"). These, however, were all held up with wonderfully little loss to ourselves, and about 4.30 p.m. the fighting died down.

But the Turk hadn't given up yet. About 8 p.m. their guns opened again, supported by heavy rifle fire from the south and south-east: one of the first shots smashed the searchlight in the south salient of the fort. Nearly all night a heavy rifle fire was kept up, under cover of which detachments were sent forward to crawl up to our wire. Opposite Dorset Position (occupied by the Norfolks) they managed to cut the wire and effected an entrance, though once in the trenches they appeared to be at a loss what to do next! The Norfolks soon decided for them.

No other attacks were even partially successful. Before dawn the firing had died down, and by the morning of the 13th they had withdrawn to a safe distance. The previous evening (luckily in the short lull of the fighting) Major-General Mellis with the Headquarters of the 30th Brigade and the 24th Punjabis had arrived from Basra. Being senior to Major-General Fry, he now took over command.

As soon as it grew light enough to see on the 13th, the main body of the Turks were observed to be moving towards Old Basra (southeast of Shaiba), as though they contemplated an advance on Basra across the floods. Though a risky move on their part, if it had been successful it would have put us at Shaiba in an awkward hole. It seems possible that it was contemplated, as a large number of *bellums* was seen on the floods, manned by Arabs and Turks, while the main body of the Arabs kept up a hot fire from the north-west, round House C. Probably an attack from this quarter was intended to contain us, while the Turks were moving across our left rear.

If so the Arabs, as usual, let down their allies, for though a continuous fire was kept up no actual attack developed. However, this threatening attitude of the Arabs occasioned some anxiety, and as the guns could not get at them the Cavalry Brigade was ordered to clear them out. Forming up near Wood Picquet they trotted out north-west, and then turned due west to charge the enemy lying in the cultivated ground near House C. But almost immediately after reaching this point they came under very heavy rifle and machine-gun fire, losing many horses and men, so that it became necessary to order their withdrawal. The troops wheeled about and regained the shelter of a fold of ground near 1A Picquet.

It was on this occasion that Major Wheeler of the 7th Lancers gained a posthumous V.C. Riding far ahead of his squadron he knew nothing of the order to turn about, and accompanied by one native officer only, galloped straight at North Mound, which was occupied by a crowd of Arab riflemen supporting a large green standard. Though heavily fired on, the two reached the Mound and galloping into the Arabs sabred several. Major Wheeler shot the standard-bearer and grasped the standard but was himself immediately shot and killed.

The native officer was wounded and unhorsed, whereupon he was set upon by a crowd of those fanatical demons, soaked in oil, and set on fire. His still smouldering body was found later in the day, and a stern vengeance exacted from some of his torturers who were caught. This officer was later awarded the Indian Order of Merit.

After the failure of the cavalry an infantry counterattack was launched against House C and the vicinity, the 104th Rifles being detailed for the duty. Unfortunately, this proved far too weak, and the 104th, having suffered severely, was forced to retire. After these two costly attempts it was recognised that stronger measures must be taken, and after a thorough artillery preparation (the Arab hates the guns) the 2nd Dorsets and the 24th Punjabis made a sortie which was completely successful, clearing House C, the wood, and North Mound, and taking four hundred prisoners with two mountain guns, beside inflicting heavy casualties on the enemy. After this lesson the Arabs took no further part in the hostilities, until the Turkish Army was retreating, when they "changed sides" and did all they could to hinder it.

On the morning of the 14th there were no enemy in sight, and it was concluded that the Turks had probably had enough and chucked it. Askari Pasha had certainly had enough of attacking, but he now intended that the positions should be reversed and accordingly had laid something in the nature of a boobytrap—into which, presently, we were obliging enough to walk.

At 9 a.m. on the 14th the whole force, leaving the 104th and details to guard the camp, started out to reconnoitre the country to the south, towards Old Basra and South Mound. The force marched in artillery formation with the 16th Brigade (with 24th in place of 104th) on the right, the 18th Brigade on the left, each with two battalions in reserve; and the Cavalry Brigade covering the right flank.

About two miles out when nearing South Mound the 24th and the Dorsets (on the right of the right brigade) came under rifle fire from a ridge of low mounds; the leading platoons were extended, but the enemy was found to consist of only a few horsemen who rapidly made off, and the advance continued. The force marched on southwest, until at 11 a.m. the 16th Brigade came under a sudden and heavy fire from their right front, in the direction of Birjisiyeh Wood, which lies at the bottom of a long and slight slope. The 24th Punjabis suffered severely as they rapidly changed front towards the enemy, the remainder of the brigade conforming and continuing the advance by rushes, though nothing could be seen of the enemy.

The Turkish fire-discipline at this stage of the fight was exemplary: as each rush was made the fire was turned on as if from a tap and shut off again immediately there was no target. Their machine-guns were also much in evidence and well served, though the artillery, which had been heavily shelling the advance, was soon turned on to the reserves and Headquarters near South Mound, near which also our guns had come into action, though much hampered by mirage. The Cavalry Brigade who, supported by "S" Battery, were wide on the right flank, dismounting, opened fire at about 1400—too distant to be very effective.

By 1 p.m. the 16th Brigade had worked up to between 500 and 700 yards from the enemy's trenches, which could now be seen (when mirage allowed) almost at the bottom of the Birjisiyeh slope; a slight fold in the ground afforded some cover, but still casualties continued heavy.

The brigade was occupying a frontage of rather more than half a mile opposite the enemy's right flank, and the 18th Brigade, until they could be brought across to fill the gap between the 16th and the Cavalry, was comparatively ineffective. The 16th Brigade had orders to wait until this move had been effected.

But the Turkish fire showed no sign of weakening, and over the open glacis-like approach to their trenches the firing-line could make no progress. Ammunition was running very short, for although the *drabis* behaved most gallantly in bringing the mules forward, nearly every animal was killed on that open ground and the men killed or wounded. But a few got through or at least near enough to replenish from; and the *drabis*, hard-working but generally inglorious members of an army, earned undying fame that day as very gallant soldiers.

By 4 p.m., though within only 500 yards of the Turkish trenches, things looked bad. Casualties had been heavy, heat and thirst during the long four hours very severe, and practically every available man was already in the fight. There were no reserves and the attack was held up.

It is said that the order had already been given to retire—a retirement which would have entailed a six-mile fight back to Shaiba camp against a victorious enemy, our own men weak from thirst and sun and losses, with the doubtful sanctuary of Shaiba Fort at the end—and the Arabs take the hindermost.

Whether or not the order was given it never reached the Dorsets, for, just as things were looking at their worst, the regiment, led by Major Utterson, jumped up and assaulted the Turkish position. (Lieut.-

Colonel Kosher, commanding the Dorsets, had been killed earlier in the action.) The rest of the line took this fine lead and were soon into the trenches with the bayonet, most of the Turks quitting before they could be got at, though a considerable number were killed while others surrendered.

Preparations were at once made to repel the expected counter-attack; but it never came, and the Turkish reserves and those who had escaped the assault were seen moving off rapidly towards the northwest, evidently bound for Nakhailat. It was afterwards discovered from prisoners that this was owing to rather a curious and very lucky mistake: some Jaipur transport carts which had been brought up to pick up wounded were reported by the Turkish observers to be fresh batteries of artillery—this was too much for the reserves, who decided that flight was preferable to counter-attack.

The Turks' retirement was completely disorganised, a terrified rabble streaming over the desert; the Cavalry Brigade, however, did not pursue, and it was not until three days later that they reconnoitred as far as Nakhailat, where they found the Turkish camp burnt out and deserted.

As soon as the wounded could be collected the force marched back to Shaiba, which they reached in the evening, taking with them their 1300 prisoners, which, together with the wounded, were sent into Basra next day.

The Battle of Birjisiyeh completely disposed of any hopes the Turks may have had of retaking Basra, though their chances of success had looked not altogether unpromising. In Basra itself the betting was against us, and it was discovered that in some quarters elaborate preparations had been made to welcome the old regime once more. No doubt those quarters were disappointed when the doleful columns of prisoners were marched through the streets.

The Turkish losses in killed and wounded and prisoners were estimated at little less than six thousand—nearly half their force. Our own amounted to 194 killed and 1132 wounded, which was light considering the nature of the fighting.

Had the cavalry been enabled to pursue, probably very few of the enemy would have escaped; but what we omitted the Turk's allies accomplished. All the way to Nakhailat, where they burnt the camp, and on to Khamasieh, a distance of 90 miles, the Arab harassed the retreating columns, looting and murdering the stragglers.

★★★★★★

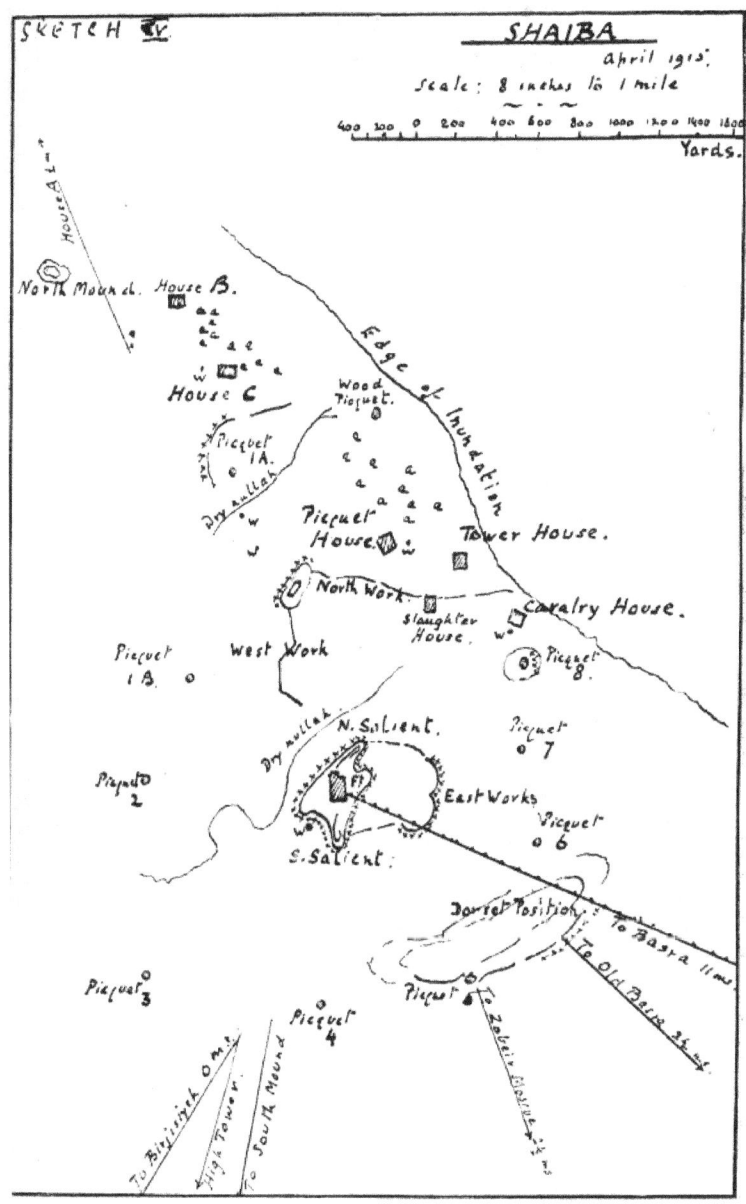

HRB sketch Shaiba

During the retreat from Nakhailat the River Column did excellent work in denying the river to the enemy's *mahelas*, several of which were sunk. The enemy were watched, and interfered with where possible, all the way back to Khamasieh, at the western end of the Hamar Lake, which henceforward was kept under observation.

★★★★★★

The Turkish commander, Suleiman Askari, after making an address to his officers in which he attributed his failure entirely to the Arabs holding back in the first place, coupled with their final treachery, professed himself unable to fight again under such conditions, and shot himself.

The Turks could never resist the fatal attraction of numbers. Though disillusioned time and again, they persisted in bringing into the field large bodies of Arabs who never did a hand's turn of fighting, and only waited in the offing to loot the vanquished.

Twelve thousand regulars was no doubt an exaggeration of the numbers of the enemy. Probably their force consisted of two "Muretteb" divisions, though the "stiffening" was of very good troops indeed. Among them was the Constantinople Fire Brigade—a corps of enlisted men (not conscripts) who have a reputation of being smart troops. Several of this regiment were taken prisoners.

The infantry fire-discipline was throughout the engagement noticeable for its excellence. The majority of the troops were armed with the 1908 Mauser, the machine-gun sections were provided with German guns of late pattern, far and away superior to anything we had.

Their equipment was rather mixed, but on the whole appeared serviceable, except for their boots, which were much worn, and their uniform, which was far too thick for campaigning in Mesopotamia. The entrenching tools also were bad and flimsy. Many of the regiments had been brought down from the north, and marched hard and fast. Several prisoners complained that they had scarcely any rest after a 500 miles' march before being hurried into action—probably the Arabs forced Askari Pasha to attack before he meant to by threats of leaving him. This at least was the report.

Except for their artillery, none of which was quick-firing, the enemy had been at no disadvantage as regards numbers, arms, ammunition, or equipment. They had occupied exceedingly well-sited trenches commanding a thousand yards of open desert and had been turned out and defeated simply because their attackers were better men.

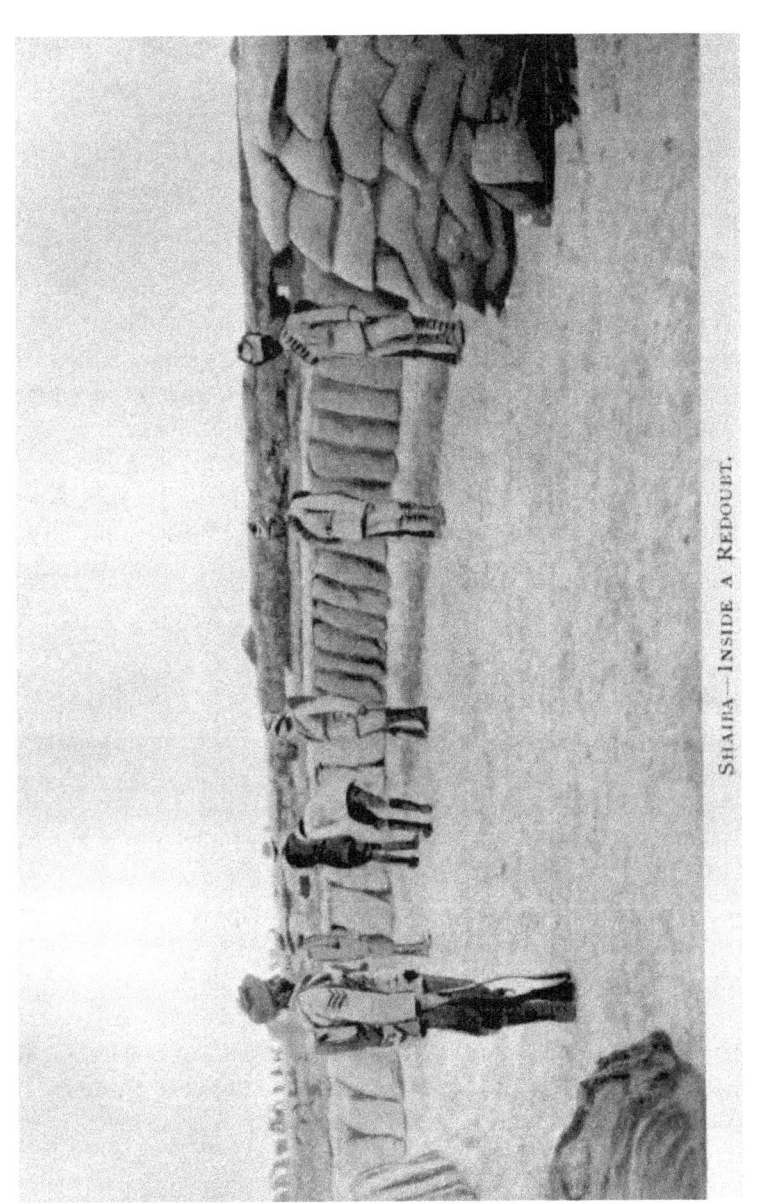

SHAIBA—INSIDE A REDOUBT.

Though the victory in itself was an important one, it becomes doubly so when the consequences of a defeat here are considered. Shaiba cut off by the floods from Basra would have been exceedingly difficult to hold against an enemy with their tails up. It would have been all but impossible to replenish stores from Basra or to retreat on the town. In Basra itself were only three battalions, who in the event of a reverse would no doubt have had their work cut out to deal with local trouble.

Had Basra fallen, communication with Kurna would have been cut, the troops at Ahwaz could easily have been isolated, and, most serious of all, the base with its stores and shipping would have been seized by the enemy.

Had such a disaster occurred it is difficult to see how the Expedition could have been provisioned, and the capture of at least a very large part of the army avoided. The effect of such a failure on our part in the East at that stage of the war would have been terrible.

Fortunately, the danger was past almost before it appeared, but those four hours before Birjisiyeh Wood were indeed critical. It looks as if the assault of the 2nd Dorsets decided great issues, and in fact averted a disaster, the possible consequences of which have never been realised.

While the fighting at Shaiba and Birjisiyeh had been in progress, the Turks had also made demonstrations against Ahwaz and Kurna. At Ahwaz a bombardment was opened on the 9th and continued spasmodically for the best part of a week; beyond sniping there was no infantry action.

At Kurna the Turks had worked down the river towards our positions on both banks and had occupied Tower Hill and Norfolk Hill on the right bank and One Tree Hill on the left. On Tower Hill they had mounted a gun. A bombardment opened on the morning of the 11th, which continued all day, the shells coming well into camp. The next morning the bridge was blown sky-high by a floating mine, and large bodies of Arabs were found to have occupied the woods on the north bank of the Euphrates and opposite the creek. These it appeared were Beni Lam, who had been brought down from the Amara district to do the amphibious fighting, the Turks preferring to sit on their mud islands.

However, H.M.S. *Odin* steamed up the Euphrates and subjected the Arabs' trenches to such a dose of shell fire that at about 2 p.m. they thought it time to go. As soon as the *mashoofs* appeared from the

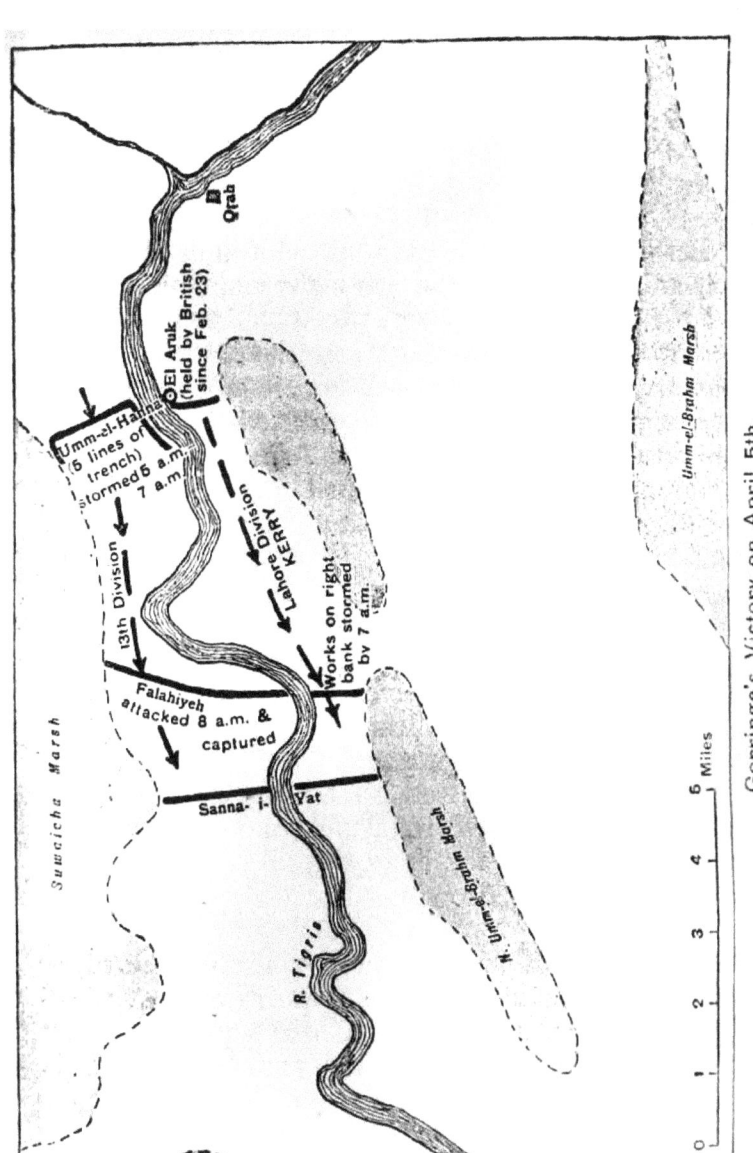

Gorringe's Victory on April 5th.

trees on to the open marsh they came under fire of 4-inch shrapnel and machine-guns from the fort, which did great execution. This was repeated by a second body about 4 p.m. with the same result, but on this occasion the Turks, seeing them retiring presumably not "according to plan," turned their guns on to them as well.

On the 13th, camp was again bombarded nearly all day with conspicuously little result, except for one direct hit on the observation tower: the shell passed between the observing officer's legs and through the platform without injuring him.

The programme was almost identical on the 14th. All day long at intervals the distant thud of guns was heard from the south, and we knew that something was doing in that direction, though it was three days before the result was known. The Turks, however, must have heard sooner, for on the 15th all was very quiet—no gun fire and no signs of Arabs. After this date there were no further "demonstrations"—the news of Birjisiyeh evidently had a discouraging effect, and Kurna was left in peace, to continue its mud-larking once more.

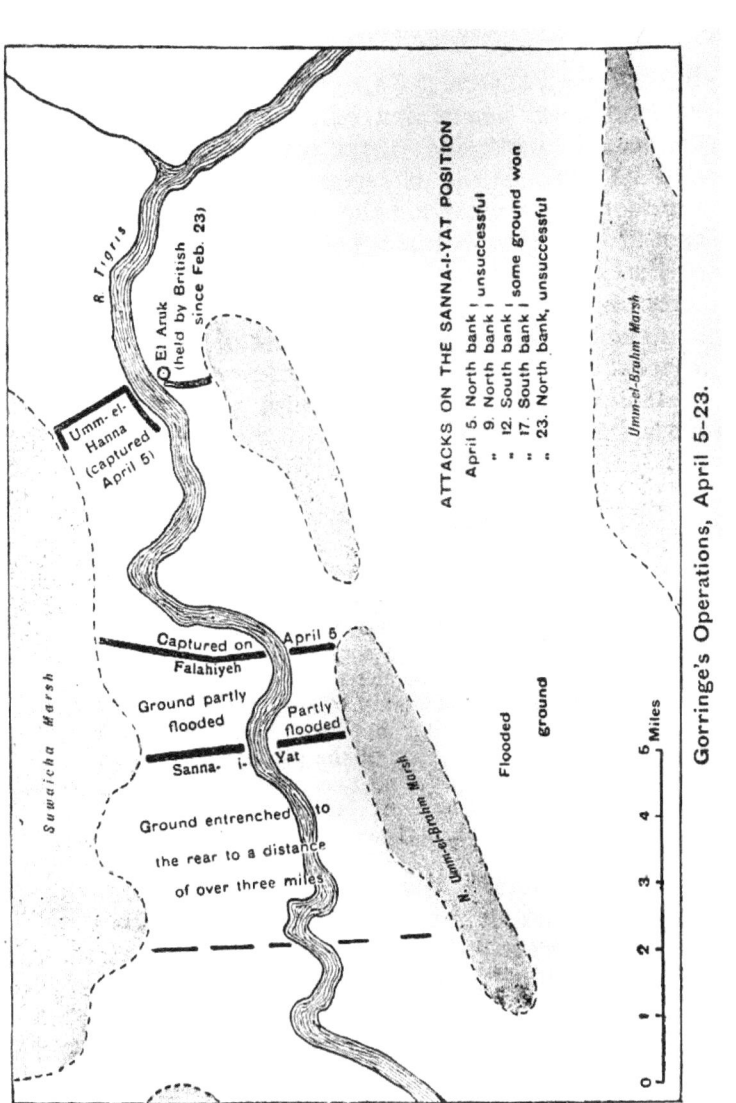

Gorringe's Operations, April 5-23.

CHAPTER 11

April and May 1915

The victory at Birjisiyeh completely altered the situation in Mesopotamia. Whereas for the last two months we had been forced to remain on the defensive and subordinate everything to meeting the Turkish attack on Basra, the danger was now disposed of, and freedom of manoeuvre, as far as transport difficulties and the state of the country would permit, was again ours.

To a great extent the rules of "savage warfare" applied to the operations in Mesopotamia at this stage of the campaign; and one generally recognised axiom of this kind of war is, that it is imperative to allow no gathering of hostile troops to go unattacked. Failure to attack the enemy wherever he can be got at is invariably taken as a sign of weakness and over-discretion—with the result that the enemy are encouraged and his ranks reinforced by every waverer.

Although the late Turkish defeat had proved a wholesome reminder to the local Arabs, there were still many who thought it worthwhile to sit on the fence a bit longer; some too, farther afield, who would no doubt be told plenty of good reasons to excuse the result of the battle; and others again, fewer but still a considerable number, who had not yet lost faith in the Turk and needed further proof of our intentions.

The main Turkish force was disposed of, but there were still considerable bodies round Ahwaz and Kurna who had suffered no loss and were detaining British forces at both these places. Accordingly, General Nixon determined to deal with them, and as soon as the Shaiba operations were at an end, plans were made for the VIth Division to circumvent the enemy on the Tigris and advance to Amara.

It was on 18th April that the 17th Brigade at Kurna first got an inkling that their turn was coming. On that day an order arrived that every regiment was to train 200 men to pole and paddle *bellums*—ostensibly to deal with the Arabs, but, rumour said, actually with a view to bigger game: it would all depend on what sort of a show the boatmen made. At first the matter of training 200 men per regiment was rather difficult, as we only had our original complement of four boats each. But *bellums* were being bought, hired, and stolen in Basra as quickly as possible, and when once they began to arrive, matters went extraordinarily well, and with the four crews per regiment already trained, it was not long before the fleet was in being.

There were at this time one or two little diversions which were rather valuable in taking one's mind off the continual round of routine—which consisted mainly of muddy fatigues—and in preventing one thinking too much of the weather, and wondering what would happen if the *bunds* were to break; for the water was two feet above the level of camp and still rising, while the weather was getting rather warm and steamy and very favourable to mosquitoes.

Indeed, it was a situation in which one could not sit about and ruminate, and any activity made life more bearable—so that the Euphrates blockade was quite a popular job. Those who took part in it would disappear from our midst for a week or ten days, during which they seemed to wander about on the Hamar Lake without the slightest idea as to where they were or what exactly they were expected to do, beyond getting out and pushing the steamer whenever it stuck in the mud. However, they always found their way back in the end, and appeared to have had a pleasant and mildly adventurous outing

There were other odd jobs to be done too among the Arabs, and during one of these we had a rather amusing insight into local politics, together with an exhibition of amphibious battle-fighting which was extraordinarily picturesque.

The situation was as follows. The *Sheikh* of a marsh tribe on the southern bank of the "Old" Euphrates had made himself a nuisance by looting the Basra-Shaiba convoys. At the same time, he had reopened an old feud with the Sheikh of Medina—anxious, so said the latter, to show what his looted rifles could do. Medina was very keen to humble this evil-doer, but too nervous to tackle him alone, so he approached the Political Officer and gave the show away. Accordingly, one morning early in May, an imposing fleet started up the Euphrates to "co-operate" with the Sheikh of Medina—H.M.S. *Odin* and *Espiègle*, followed by the *Salimi*, *Samana*, and *Massoudieh*, with one hundred men and a machine-gun section. Our orders were to stand by and assist if necessary—otherwise the *Sheikh's* army would do the fighting.

Two hours steaming up the still, glassy waters of the Euphrates brought us to a sharp bend of the river, and, rounding it, we were met by a surprising sight. The first impression was a motley of many shifting colours, and a far-off indistinct ripple of sound, scarcely breaking the intense stillness of the morning. As we drew nearer the sound increased to a deep buzz of talking, and the haze of colour divided itself into two distinct sections. First, in a long line beside the river bank were crowded two or three hundred *mashoofs*, in each a few men dressed in strange, sack-like patchwork garments, rusty red, brown, faded blue, or sporting voluminous striped "*abbas*," and blue "*chefiehs*" (head-cloths) held in place by coils of black wool. Behind the men in the boats rose a second tier of confused colours, formed by a crowd of men upon the banks; above all, their silver-topped poles flickering in the sunlight, flapped and sagged many silken banners, green and white and black, with here and there the white Star and Crescent on the red field—the White Ensign was flying in strange company!

As the *Odin* dropped anchor near the bank a hush fell upon the crowd, and almost immediately out shot a long *mashoof*, covered by a smart awning and poled by two huge negroes: it was the "state barge" of the *Sheikh*, who was going aboard the flagship to confer with his allies. The two commanders, British and Arab, met upon the deck and discussed the situation, while beneath them, on the still waters of the river, shone the reflections of the White Ensign and the Star and Crescent; and the two armies waited to learn what was to be done.

After some talk it was decided that, as the enemy village to be attacked lay in the marshes some way from the river, the *Sheikh's* fleet had better move up a creek and surround it so that no one should escape, and, when the investment was complete, the *Massoudieh* was to appear as a surprise and overawe the wicked enemy with the shadow of her two 3-pounders.

So that was settled. Now followed a period of confused uproar: words of command, bellowings of religious ecstasy, shouting, singing, and much brandishing of rifles, all entered into with such abandon that we wondered despairingly how long the performance would last. Quite suddenly, however, and apparently without any definite word of command, they got a move on. In a cloud the boats shot out into the stream, their crews paddling with short, quick strokes, which made an odd sobbing noise in the water. Overhead the red and green banners floated out like wings above the long black shapes, and the brightly coloured forms of the crews swayed rhythmically over their paddles.

As they drew away from us towards the creek, this strange fleet looked for all the world like a bunch of gorgeous butterflies hovering on the green water, and not at all like an army on the warpath.

When, after a suitable interval, the *Massoudieh* thrashed her way up the creek after them, we found there had been a mistake, for the village was not surrounded: there was our butterfly fleet peacefully resting in the sun, discussing a variety of subjects: but, fighting, not at all. Inquiries made it clear that they considered an investment of the village a rather too hazardous operation—after all, a cornered enemy must fight; so far better leave him a bolt-hole, and when he has bolted, wade in and loot. This we discovered had been the argument: The *Sheikh* had carefully collected his boats on one side of the village only, and, after warning his enemy that our warships would soon appear and that he'd better get out, he had sat down and waited for us.

But the *Massoudieh* with her artillery and twenty-five soldiers put new life into the "Butterflies," and, with a brave glitter, they now spread their wings and dashed to the attack of the village. That there were only a few women remaining in it mattered not at all. With blood-curdling yells the boats were driven forward, while the warriors, balancing precariously in the swaying craft, discharged their Martinis at the sky until the air was blue with smoke. A few shots answered them from the village, but it was soon all over, bar shouting, and heavy columns of smoke rolled up into the blue sky as the reed huts were set alight.

Soon the victors began to return, in each boat the loot piled high: cows, sheep, jars of grain, clothes, brass pots, leather bandoliers—no one came away empty; but of the stolen rifles and ammunition no sign, for the enemy had had plenty of warning to get away with all such incriminating and valuable belongings.

The *Sheikh* came on board, grave and silent, and evidently well pleased with the day's work. He shook hands with each officer in turn, while he was complimented in flowery language by the Persian interpreter on the success of his army and the excellence of his staff work. After long and windy compliments had been made and returned, and he had been presented with an offering of tinned mackerel, Worcester sauce, and mixed pickles, with which he appeared delighted, the allied armies parted. The one, noisy with shouts and laughter, gay with many colours, flitted away over the marshes; the other, with puffs and snorts and clouds of noisome smoke, plodded off down the lily-covered creek to the open waters of the river.

Though this was certainly an amusing outing it had hardly effected what was intended, so that, the next time punishment was to be meted out to the local inhabitant, it was decided to do it without the help of any picturesque allies. There were plenty of gentry round about who were in need of a little correction, and about a week later the "Bellum Brigade" was given its first trial trip in an attack on another marsh village on the Euphrates. Unluckily, on this occasion again, the enemy was warned, and so able to remove looted rifles and ammunition; but that we should attack and pursue in boats was evidently unexpected and came as an unpleasant surprise.

Only an inexplicable order that there was to be no shooting—it was afterwards discovered to have been a mistake—prevented the boats making a big haul of prisoners as they escaped by their back door over the marshes; but, even so, our tactics were so unexpected that the enemy had no time to remove his heavy river-going boats and *mahelas*, all of which were captured and some destroyed, though most were held as hostages for good behaviour. This particular village had been a nest of snipers and had also taken part in the looting of the Shaiba convoys, so it was decided to make an example of it. All cattle and sheep were removed and the reed huts burnt down, a proceeding which is not so severe as it sounds, as a complete village can be rebuilt in a week.

It was interesting to be able to examine the dwelling-places of the Marsh Arab at close quarters, and one realised how really amphibious their existence is—man and beast alike. The village was surrounded by palms, but there was hardly any dry ground at all and no tracks whatever, creeks taking the place of roads. The houses were, of course, all of reeds, but very well built and apparently fairly dry, although standing only just above water-level on raised mounds of mud and palm branches. In several places we found floating islands of cut reeds—like huge floating haystacks—and on some of them were sheep and chickens. The village was full of livestock, cows, sheep, and fowls, and all of them seemed to be just as much at home in the water as on land.

Behind the village stretched the limitless expanse of open marsh,—the Khor Jezair, which extends to near Basra,—and over this most of the smaller boats of the village escaped, though a dozen or so big *mahelas* were stopped just as they were getting up sail, and, as these are by far the most valued possessions of the marsh villages, our *bellums* had been quite a success—indeed, without a fleet of boats it would have been impossible to get at the village at all.

But the great thing was that eight crews per regiment had been employed and had acquitted themselves so satisfactorily that it was considered possible that with further practice they would be fit for a more important role in the near future; and much-discussed rumours were soon confirmed.

A few days later, on 13th May, Sir John Nixon inspected the 17th Brigade—once more complete again—and told us definitely that we were to advance to Amara, first disposing of the enemy opposite to us. Nothing was said as to how this was to be accomplished, but as, with the exception of the enemy's positions, all the country was covered by the floods, it was obviously to be a watery business with plenty of work for the boats.

Preparations now went forward rapidly, and Kurna, once more promoted to the importance of being "the front," became the busy scene of concentration, slow and cumbrous, but very thorough. General Townshend, now in command of the VIth Division, had arrived with his Staff at the end of April, and in the same ship came the howitzer battery which was secretly at dead of night installed in Nahairat village as a surprise to the enemy.

The greatest activity prevailed in the boating world. Every ship arriving from Basra towed up a long line of *bellums*, complete with poles and paddles, which were distributed among the regiments until each possessed a large fleet; for, in spite of many birds of ill omen who croaked of impossibility, it was General Townshend's plan to transport the 17th Brigade in *bellums* across the floods and carry out a boat attack against the enemy's island positions.

All sorts of discouraging prophecies were made: that enough boats could never be collected, that the crews would never be able to handle them successfully, that crowded boats full of men would be wiped out by the enemy artillery, or that they could never disembark under close rifle-fire—in short, that the whole thing was unworkable, and that the casualties would be so high as not to make it worthwhile. It was certainly a bold scheme and unexpected, but for these very reasons it was entirely successful; and as it was an original undertaking it may perhaps be worthwhile to give a somewhat detailed account of its organisation and execution.

At this time the floods which separated us from the Turkish position were on an average not more than 3 feet deep; but in every direction ran channels and ditches, many of them 20 feet broad and 10 feet deep, yet of course indistinguishable from the surrounding shal-

General Townshend, K.C.B., D.S,O.

lower floods. This naturally made wading out of the question. There was very little open water, the floods being almost covered by grass and reeds which varied from 2 feet to 5 feet in height, and which, although not growing very thickly except in a few places, gave sufficient cover to make it difficult to distinguish a boat at 500 yards. Here and there were small patches of shallow, open water, and in the main channels a clear path had generally been made through the reeds by the natives' *mashoofs*; but these "roads," only broad enough for boats in single file, were completely shut in by walls of reeds, and so winding that it was impossible to be sure in what direction they eventually led, so that they were of no use for our purpose, and a direct advance across the marsh and through the reeds appeared the best way.

The distance to be covered, from the northern edge of the perimeter to Norfolk Hill, the first Turkish position, was 3500 yards; Tower Hill lay another 1500 yards farther north; and beyond again, 2000 yards north-west, lay Shrapnel Hill and Gun Hill. On the right bank these were the objectives which were if possible to be secured on the first day, and the distance over the marshes to the farthest point, Gun Hill, was 7500 yards (over four miles) in a straight line from Kurna. When it is remembered that the whole of this distance was without any cover from fire and with only rather uncertain cover from view,— that, theoretically, the crowded boats would be under shrapnel fire for the whole of their journey and close-range rifle fire from each position for at least 500 yards before the crews could disembark and wade through mud to the assault,—it may be said that the pessimists had some reason for their misgivings.

Four thousand yards beyond Gun Hill lay the main Turkish positions of Bahràn and Mazeebla—a curved island in the floods 5000 yards from north to south; 4000 yards farther north again another position was believed to exist at Sakricha; but advanced positions would have to be secured before these farther ones could be dealt with.

So much for the right bank. On the left bank, owing to the scarcity of "islands," there were only two positions: One small post on One Tree Hill, almost opposite Tower Hill, and one, a bigger one and a considerable camp, at Ratta. The first position was to be attacked simultaneously with Norfolk Hill, while Ratta was to be left for a second instalment. That is a catalogue of the Turkish positions, each commanded by the succeeding position, the ranges known exactly, the marshes and river mined; but it is no description of a country and a general situation which it is almost impossible to imagine without having seen. A careful study of the accompanying map, (page 151), may help towards the appreciation of the difficult problem which General Townshend had to solve. The forces which occupied these positions were estimated at three battalions of regulars, one of *gendarmes*, and an unknown quantity of Arab irregulars, with ten guns which were distributed as follows: one on Tower Hill, one in the marshes at Adar commanding the Al Huir creek, two on Gun Hill, four on Bahràn, and two at Ratta. The possibility of reinforcements was not known exactly, but it was unlikely that there was any force nearer than at Amara; so that the task would not have been difficult except for the conditions of attack and the manner in which we were forced to carry it out.

For the actual attack the 17th Brigade only was to be available, so that, as far as numbers were concerned, the defenders were at little disadvantage; but the 16th Brigade was to be brought up and to remain on the ships, ready to push through when needed, and a big concentration of artillery, superior in range and power to the Turkish guns, was to give us the necessary "pull" over his defence.

The three battalions at Kurna (Oxford and Bucks Light Infantry, 119th, and 103rd Mahratta Light Infantry) were to move across the marshes to a position west of Fort Snipe, and from there attack the positions on the right bank, while the 22nd Punjabis from Mazera were to act independently on the left bank against One Tree Hill—the whole Brigade moving by *bellums*.

For this an average of sixty-five boats per battalion was necessary. Each *bellum* was to carry ten men, two to pole, eight to fight, with their equipment, reserve ammunition, water, two picks, two shovels, 30 feet of rope, and caulking materials, two spare poles, and four paddles. In addition, boats had to be found for the Signal Company and for the field ambulance, and also for machine-gun sections and a battery of mountain guns. These latter were mounted on rafts, made from two *bellums* decked together, the guns protected by steel plates and the whole roofed over with reeds to make them more inconspicuous; while the field ambulance, besides medical *bellums*, evolved a wonderful craft which looked exactly like the Ark in picture-books—a *mahela* decked over with a large reed hut built on the deck.

Nearly every *bellum*—and there must have been quite 300—with its full equipment, had to be towed up from Basra, collected by the Brigade *Bellum* Officer, and then handed over to battalions. Each boat then had to draw and complete its equipment and be allotted to a crew of suitable weight—for no *bellum* was to draw more than 18

ARMOURED BELLUMS AT KURNA.

inches of water; and, in addition, the machine-gun and mountain-gun rafts had to be constructed on the spot. On 24th May, a week before the event, our boats were still incomplete, and we were hard at work distributing, caulking, and building rafts, reconnoitring the marsh to mark shallow water, and practising crews. The weather was frightfully hot, but there was so much work to be done that there was no idea of "knocking off" during the heat of the day—sun or no sun. As soon as the weather had warmed up at the beginning of May, sickness of various kinds had appeared, and now fever was in full blast. Men went down one after the other, and no sooner was a crew made out and working well together, than one or more would go sick and a general re-shuffling be necessary.

The armoured machine-gun rafts proving a success, it was decided that the *bellums* should also be armoured by placing two long strips of boiler-plating across the boats, bow and stern, protecting about 3 feet on either side and only just clearing the water: the idea being that, if held up by frontal fire, the men could jump out and, wading behind the projecting wings of armour, push their boat forward. "Expert" opinion was against the scheme, but the suggestion came from high quarters at Basra, and so had to be tried. After a lot of work some boats were fitted in this way, but proved a dismal failure, being very top-heavy and slow, as the projecting armour caught the reeds.

Finally, the same system was used on two boats joined by spars across the thwarts, and, though slow and cumbrous, it was decided to give each battalion twelve of these armoured double-boats. We knew they would be left behind or run aground, but the inventor, in his office at Basra, was persuaded otherwise.

Our greatest hopes lay in a surprise packet in the shape of aeroplanes. Many of us had never seen an aeroplane, and probably none of the enemy had, while, among the Arabs, such magic would have a great effect. Unfortunately, they had not arrived in time to carry out any reconnaissance, for which they would have been most useful, and there was some doubt whether they would be available in time for the show, as they were still at Abadan. It had been found that they were in need of much overhauling, owing, rumour said, to their having done the voyage from India packed beneath 4000 tons of "*bhoosa*." It is quite possible, as they love a good joke at Bombay.

The river now was full of life, and every ship in Mesopotamia seemed to be crowded into the reach opposite the town. A walk along the "front" gave one a pleasant feeling of confidence, for the Royal

THE DRESS REHEARSAL FOR THE REGATTA, 17TH BDE. STAFF

Col. Climo marked *.

Navy—always our very present help in trouble—was there in force, and one could stand and hopefully count the guns which were to support us. H.M. Sloops *Espiègle* and *Clio*, and the R.I.M.S. *Laurence* carried 4-inch guns, and the armed launches 12-pounders and 6-pounders; there were also two 4.7's mounted in horse-barges (known as H.M.S. *Nulli Secundus* and *Neverbudge*), together with two 4-inch and two 5-inch guns mounted on barges, and accompanied by an observation platform, balanced like a rickety Tower of Babel, on another barge—indeed, it was a very complete fleet of queer craft.

On Friday, 28th May, the preparations were completed by a "dress rehearsal." (On 23rd May Colonel Climo, 24th. Punjabis, took over command of the 17th Brigade, Brigadier-General Dobbie having gone sick with fever and being invalided to India.) The three battalions, which were to operate on the right bank, together with the mountain battery and machine-guns, pushed off in the evening and rendezvoused at the point west of Fort Snipe, whence the attack was to start on the following Monday.

The battalions moved across the floods from the perimeter in three long snake-like columns of boats, and then deployed at the rendezvous into a long line, two deep—a movement which came off quite successfully. We could see the enemy on Norfolk Hill crowding out of their trenches to look at us, and why the guns on Tower and Gun Hills left us alone is a mystery—we were well within range, and a fine fat target. However, there were no untoward incidents, and, but for the fact of the armoured *bellums* proving very slow and unwieldy, and the mountain-gun rafts being found to draw rather more than was expected, all was a success.

By Saturday evening the 16th Brigade had arrived and was lying out in the river, having come up from Basra in steamers that had lately arrived from India to reinforce our transport. There was no room for them ashore, so there they had to remain cooped up on the ships in the grilling heat. On shore it was about 112° in the shade, and we thought it bad enough, but on a crowded ship, iron decks, and only a thin awning, and surrounded by the glare of the water, the conditions must have been pretty trying.

On Sunday, General Townshend issued an order of the day to the troops, almost identical in wording with that of his ancestor before Quebec. The attack was to take place at 5.30 a.m. the next morning after half an hour's bombardment; the boats were to be in position at the rendezvous at 5 a.m.

Punting an Armoured Bellum

CHAPTER 12

May-June 1915

That night every man slept on the mud opposite his boat, ready to embark without confusion in the dark hours of the morning. It was a steamy night without a breath of wind; warm mist hung above the creek, and clouds of mosquitoes quivered over each sleeping form.

At 4 a.m. a *mashoof* with two officers and a cargo of red and white flags pushed out into the darkness to "flag" the course, as there were some shallow patches to be avoided. The flags were to be planted to mark the channels—red to be left on the right, white on the left, very much as a point-to-point course is flagged.

Soon afterwards the boats left their mooring-places and in long lines threaded their way through the darkness towards the rendezvous, led by a guide steering on a compass bearing. Before 5 a.m. the three battalions were in position west of Fort Snipe in two lines, the Oxford and Bucks Light Infantry on the right, the 103rd on the left, and the 119th in support, while the machine-guns and mountain battery took up their position on the left flank.

The waters of the marsh were turning from grey through all shades of intense blue, and on every side the vivid green of the reeds shaded the blue, till in the distance it appeared as a vast waving field of green stretching to the horizon. Overhead the sky was a very dark blue, but the last star had faded, the horizon grown pale, and already away to the east pink had changed to apricot colour, and then again to watery gold: soon the sun was due to rise.

An extraordinary stillness brooded over this scene of water and sky. High overhead flew a flock of pelicans, their white plumage tinged with pink, very like some huge blossoms drifting through the air; looking down the lane of boats one could see figures sitting motionless, helmet and *puggaree* silhouetted in black against the golden back-

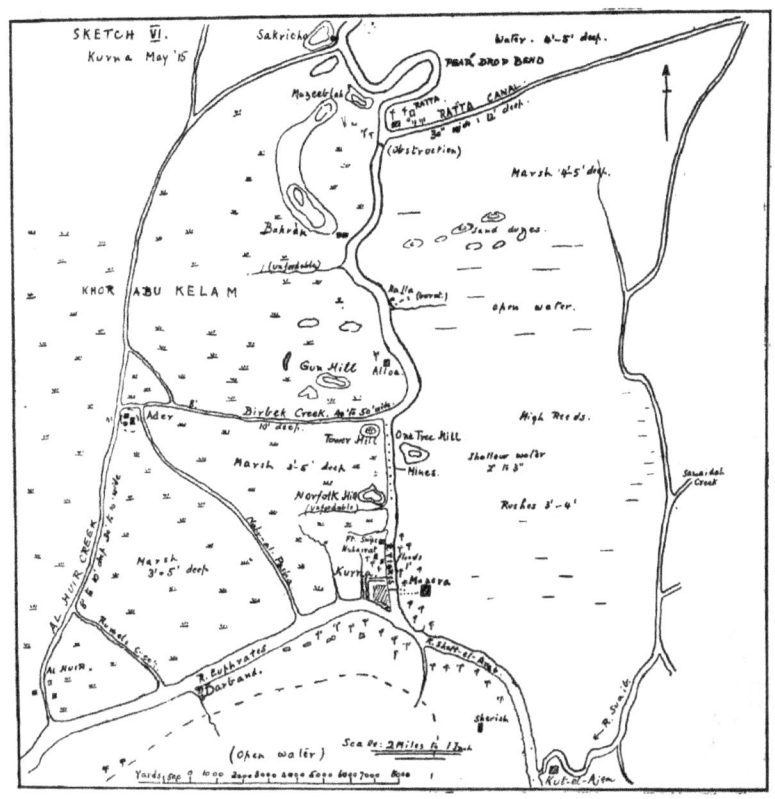

HRB sketch Kurna

ground of the sky. Now and then came the sound of half-whispered orders, or the rattle of a pole against a boat.

Then suddenly the sun shot up above the level horizon. The magic colours faded from the sky and the marsh turned to a hard, metallic blue, splashed with blatant green.

Just as suddenly the stillness was broken. Away to the right from the palms hiding Nahairat came four hollow booms in quick succession—the howitzer battery had opened the bombardment, and the day's work had really begun.

We had never seen a bombardment in Mesopotamia before, and now that about forty guns, from 5-inch to 10-pounders, were hard at it, we were suitably impressed. Norfolk and Gun Hills disappeared in a cloud of smoke and dust, which drifted like a dirty smudge across the clear blue of the sky. The bombardment continued for half an hour, then lifted off Norfolk Hill and concentrated on Tower Hill and Gun Hill, while the mountain battery took on Norfolk Hill and sprinkled it with shrapnel, while the boats began their slow advance. The Oxford and Bucks Light Infantry were to deal with the first two positions, while the 103rd, moving farther out to the left with the 119th in support, were directed on Shrapnel and Gun Hills.

There was no sign of the enemy till 6 a.m., when rifle fire from the other bank showed that the 22nd were at work against One Tree Hill—we heard later that it was captured with very little opposition soon after six. After the bombardment that Norfolk Hill had suffered, it seemed that nothing could have remained alive, but as the boats of the Oxfordshire Light Infantry approached, it was clear that somehow or other a good many of the garrison were still very much all there. A line of grey puffs broke out all along the position, and the boats came under a sharp rifle fire; at the same time the enemy guns opened fire—shooting very erratically—on the sloops in the river.

Norfolk Hill was carried with the bayonet soon after seven o'clock, at the cost of one officer killed and five men wounded—surprisingly light losses considering that the company concerned was under rifle fire at a range of 100 yards while they disembarked and waded up to the trenches. These, well sited and provided with overhead cover in places, were simply full of dead and wounded. As far as could be made out, the garrison had consisted of about one hundred men, mostly Kurds, and of these only about ten were unwounded by the time the hill was in our hands. A few probably got away towards Tower Hill, as a German was shot just as he was preparing to swim a creek at the far end of the island.

Tower Hill was next attacked and soon fell, together with about 100 prisoners, one gun, and much ammunition. The gun had been knocked out and the whole of the gun's crew killed, after which the garrison put up the white flag. Our losses here were again light, one officer and ten men wounded.

In the meantime, the 103rd and 119th had experienced some difficulty with Shrapnel and Gun Hills, which were surrounded with a very high growth of reeds through which our men could see nothing from the low level of the boats, though the enemy, in a more commanding position, could spot the punt-poles and, by "browning" into the reeds in their direction, make it very unpleasant. However, soon after eleven o'clock, our artillery fire was too much for the somewhat faint-hearted garrison—the guns on Gun Hill had ceased to reply, and presently several white flags fluttered up, and both hills were occupied, at the cost only of a few men wounded.

On Gun Hill one officer and 130 men were captured, together with both guns, and a very large quantity of shells, rifles, cartridges, and other material, including about a mile of 1-inch electric cable. Here the mystery was solved as to why the boats had never come under artillery fire during their slow approach across the marsh: we found the guns were so deeply dug in that they could not depress sufficiently to fire at anything much nearer than Fort Snipe. The Turk had never imagined we should attack, and consequently never considered that it was necessary to command the intervening marsh, or to be able to bring fire to bear on Norfolk and Tower Hills.

It was by now twelve o'clock and blazing hot, so a halt was called to reorganise and to clear up the ground—also the water; for an officer, investigating on his own a small island near Tower Hill, had found thereon a dug-out, in which was a powerful set of thirty-six batteries and a switchboard, with cables which disappeared mysteriously into the marsh. Beside the switch-board, with a key ready to his hand, stood a Turk; but luckily the turn of events had so confused him that he appeared to have forgotten what he and his apparatus were there for, so he was made a prisoner while the batteries were hastily disconnected. Later the cables were cut and dragged up, and twenty-four large mines discovered in the marshes and the river. Five of them were exploded by rifle fire, and those who saw one on Tower Hill "go up" felt very thankful that the man in the dug-out had been discovered in time.

It was now decided to leave Bahràn and Ratta for the next day, as they were both big positions and it was thought that we should meet with a stiff resistance. But, had we known it, the battle was over. We spent that afternoon in a temperature of over 112 degrees in the shade under the blazing sun and surrounded by the dazzling glare of the marshes; but on our little mud islands there was no shade whatever, and after a night of steamy haze and mosquitoes we realised what our friend the enemy must have had to bear during the last two months. Between our curses we found words to pity him.

Next morning, 1st June, the fleet set out again, and again, as dawn broke, the bombardment started and plastered Bahràn Hill till it disappeared in dust. But there was no reply. As we pushed on through the reeds we saw an aeroplane which had been circling high overhead, bank steeply, and turn towards Kurna. Soon afterwards the guns ceased fire. The aeroplane appeared again flying due north, and this time, as it passed beyond the farther end of Bahràn, we heard the rattle of heavy rifle fire coming in gusts on the breeze. But when finally, we landed on the western side of Bahràn, at 9 a.m., we found our birds had flown; the four gun emplacements were empty, and wheel-tracks down to the riverside showed what had happened: only three limbers and some tents and a general litter of hurried flight remained for us.

At 9.15 came a message from Divisional Headquarters to say that aeroplane reconnaissance reported all positions evacuated and the Turks in full retreat upriver in their ships. So, it looked like a stern chase, with every prospect of good hunting, as our sloops and armed launches certainly had the legs of their heavily-laden boats. But there was no time to be lost, for twenty miles upstream, just beyond Ezra's Tomb, the river narrows down and the sloops could go no farther; and already the enemy had five hours' start.

Now came the navy's turn; and the happy ending of the story, so satisfactorily begun by the army, is entirely due to the Senior Service. By ten o'clock the ships were anchored off Bahràn, while two armed launches swept for mines, and the demolition party, an efficient organisation led by an R.E. officer known as "the Anarchist," dealt with the obstruction in the river opposite Ratta. It was feared that this might cause some trouble, but the Turk, as usual, had only half-done the job, and a way through was very soon cleared.

At 2 p.m. H.M.S. *Espiègle* and *Clio* pushed on with the *Shaitan* in front, sweeping, and accompanied by the *Comet*, with General Townshend and his staff and Sir Percy Cox on board. By 3 p.m. they were past the obstruction and going hell-for-leather upriver after the Turks. The river in these reaches is extraordinarily difficult to navigate. It curls and winds in the most erratic way, while, at this season of the year, it is difficult to see where river ends and flood begins; in addition, it was probably being sown with mines by the fleeing enemy. But the ships pushed on, and in the evening the tail end of the enemy convoy came in sight. Fire was opened on it with such effect that a steamer dropped the two *mahelas* it was towing—full of men and stores—and scurried on alone. As the shells continued to molest them, more *mahelas* and more barges were dropped, and were duly captured by the pursuit; finally, the *Marmaris*, the Turkish gunboat, long marked down by the navy as their rightful prize, was sighted and hit at long range. The pursuit continued by moonlight, and, just before Ezra's Tomb was reached, the *Bulbul*, an armed launch, was sunk; and soon after a blaze appeared a mile or two upstream. It was the last of the *Marmaris*, crippled by the *Espiègle*, and run ashore and burnt by her crew.

The sloops could now go no farther, but the armed launches pressed on, though of the enemy fleet only the *Mosul* remained (a big Lynch steamer taken by the Turks on the outbreak of war)—the barges and *mahelas* were all sunk or captured, the *Bulbul* and *Marmaris* were burnt-out skeletons on the bank, and the *Kazimi*, a tug, was captured.

In the meanwhile, the army remained for the day in Bahràn, where it grilled upon the shadeless sand and suffered exceedingly. In the afternoon the 16th Brigade arrived on the ships, and was disembarked that evening, while the 17th Brigade, leaving their well-tried fleet of *bellums* to new masters, embarked in the 16th Brigade's place, ready to move upriver at dawn. Early next morning while it was still dark we left and started off upstream, not knowing exactly where we were bound for, though presumably we should go on as far as the enemy allowed us to; but the situation was "fluid"—no one knew yet how it would settle down.

Memories of that voyage will long remain. We were close-packed as sardines upon the *P. II.* (one of the new class of paddle-steamers brought out from Burma), on iron decks and under a single awning; there was not a breath of wind and the thermometer stood at about 114 degrees in the shade. We were still smothered with mud from our two days of playing about in the marshes, and in that heat, crowded as we were, it was very difficult to get ourselves, equipments, and rifles into some sort of order again.

Just after dawn we reached Pear-Drop Bend, an extraordinary kink

Gun captured on Gun Hill.

in the river which here describes almost a complete circle, and soon afterwards we passed Mazeebla and Sakricha, where a few derelict limbers on the bank and much litter bore witness to the enemy's hurried departure. We heard now that we were bound for Ezra's Tomb,—which sounded none too comfortable,—and, at 2 p.m., we came in sight of our destination. It appeared in the mirage which shimmered in the distance like a huge blue balloon suspended above a haze of green. A nearer view revealed the blue balloon as a gracefully-shaped blue dome showing above the tops of some surrounding palms, and, at 3.30, we were alongside and ready to disembark.

Accommodation, we found, was of the primitive order, and the thousands of pilgrims—Moslems as well as Jews—who are said to visit the tomb every year, must be very easily pleased. A courtyard about two hundred yards square encloses the tomb, and two sides of this court are formed by the *Khan*, with two storeys of little cell-like rooms, nearly all of which were in various stages of dilapidation. In one particular all the cells were alike—they were menageries of every loathsome insect imaginable, winged and legged; yet, even so, those with a roof to keep out the blasting sun found ready tenants determined to make the best of a bad job.

The outer walls of the courtyard are built of the yellow country brick, the northern and western sides forming the *Khan*, the east wall running along the river bank, while almost against the half-ruined southern wall is the tomb. The entrance to the yard, through an arch, frames rather a flattering picture of the interior, just showing three graceful palms and a bit of glittering blue dome; but, once through the arch, the romantic traveller is rather jarred by the sight, not to mention the smell, of a collection of old rags, broken brick, empty tins, dust and rubbish which strew the landscape.

So much our quest for billets revealed, and, that problem solved as best it might be, the tomb was examined. A wooden swing-door leads into a small white-washed chamber about 25 feet square, its walls decorated with inscriptions and arabesque in glaring colours, and the floor composed of coloured marble slabs. In the centre of the room, directly under the dome, is the actual tomb itself. All that can be seen is a wooden ark about 15 feet x 7 feet x 5 feet, covered with a green cloth suspended from four silver-topped posts at the four corners; and beneath this wooden ark, according to tradition, lie the mortal remains of Rabbi Azair—the Prophet Ezra.

The best of the tomb is certainly to be seen from outside: from

A MOUNTAIN GUN ON ITS RAFT STICKS FAST IN SHALLOWS.

an artistic point of view that is the only part worth looking at. Above the flat roof rises a tiled drum decorated with spirals of yellow, blue, and red, which end in a broad band of primrose; from this, springs the dome in perfect curves, a blend of every shade from sea-green, through lilac and mauve and blue, to a deep iridescent purple—the whole an indefinable ever-changing colour, a mirror to the blue sky above, to the swaying green tops of the palms, to the tawny flood of the river below.

Here the 17th Brigade remained in billets for three grilling days and nights, cursing their fate and wondering if heat and damp and mosquitoes and bugs had ever so afflicted mortal man before. Excitement and work had kept us all going during the previous week, but now that there was not much to do, the reaction set in. Fever laid its hand upon most, and they were the lucky ones, comparatively; for sun-stroke and heat-stroke were also common and far more serious, for most who went down with those complaints never got up again. On 3rd June we heard the news that Amara had been captured together with the garrison, complete and without casualties. This was rather surprising news, as the only force north of Ezra's Tomb was the gunboats, with General Townshend, Sir Percy Cox, and the Senior Naval Officer, which had disappeared into the night after the fleeing Turks on 1st June. The true story, as we afterwards heard it, may be told here.

On 3rd June, very early in the morning, the inhabitants of Amara had been surprised by the sudden appearance of the *Mosul* going for all she was worth upstream. She raced past the town and disappeared round the next bend. They were further surprised when, closely following her, appeared the *Shaitan*, which also steamed past the town, sprinkling a group of soldiers with her machine-gun, and then disappeared round the bend after the *Mosul*. Then came the *Comet* and *Samana*, with General Townshend and party, consisting in all of thirty officers and men, supported by two 6-pounders, four 3-pounders, and a machine-gun; and there ensued one of the best bits of bluff that has ever been tried—and succeeded.

A boat put ashore with an officer and a few bluejackets. Some were left as a guard upon the quay, while the remainder of the party marched to the Turkish barracks. There the officer inquired how many soldiers there were, and, on being told about 800, he said they'd better come out and pile their arms outside: they did so. In the meanwhile, General Townshend had interviewed the Turkish *commandant*, and, in-

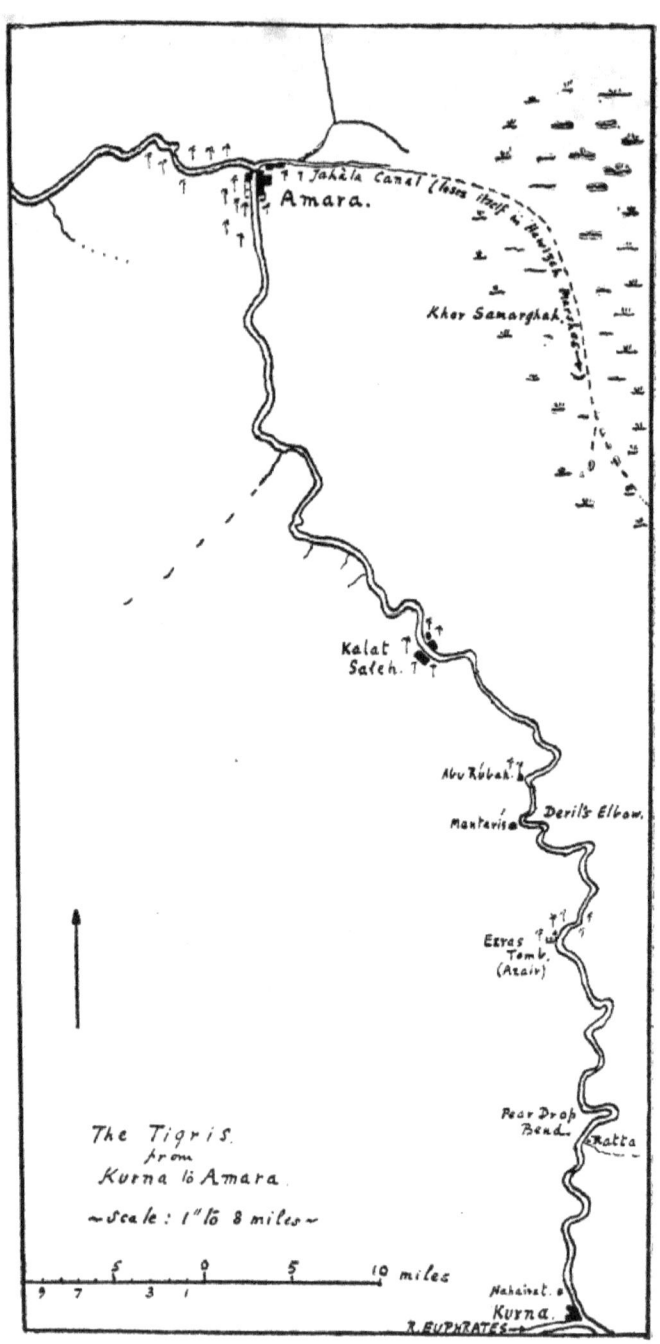

HRB SKETCH THE TIGRIS FROM KURNA TO AMARA

forming him that the British Army was just downstream, advised him to hand over the show without any unnecessary fuss: he did so.

And thus, it was that a town of 20,000 inhabitants, with forty officers and its garrison and military stores, surrendered to a general, a naval captain, a political officer, and about thirty men.

It was a wonderful bit of bluff, but it had to be kept up, and that was the difficulty—for the British Army, "just round the bend," was represented by a brigade still twenty-four hours' steaming distant! Somehow or other for a whole day those Turks were bamboozled; but they began to have a shrewd suspicion that their legs had been badly pulled, and it is no secret that the small band of conquerors breathed prayers of thanksgiving when the Norfolks (16th Brigade) arrived on the morning of 4th June, and Amara, and all it contained, was safely secured.

The 16th Brigade had passed us at Ezra's Tomb on its way upriver early on 3rd June, and on 5th June the 17th Brigade followed, having spent the intervening days in sorting and passing on prisoners and captured material. Dropping the 119th as garrison at Kalat Saleh we arrived at Amara after dark on 6th June; and disembarked next morning to find our various billets.

We had made an advance of 60 miles—by river, 90 miles—captured or destroyed the whole of the opposing enemy force, with guns and material and shipping, gained possession of Amara and the surrounding country. Our actual captures were nearly 2000 prisoners, 3000 rifles, seventeen guns, four steamers, several barges and *mahelas*, engineering stores, and a barge-full of explosives, together with a quantity of shells, fuses, charges, and small-arm ammunition. Our losses consisted of one officer and about ten men killed, three officers and about thirty men wounded, besides a few deaths and casualties from sickness.

So, the operations known as "Townshend's Regatta" came to an end, the unqualified success proving that the apparently impossible is sometimes quite simple, in spite of much wise and prudent argument to the contrary; provided that "the management" means business and is favoured with a reasonable amount of good luck.

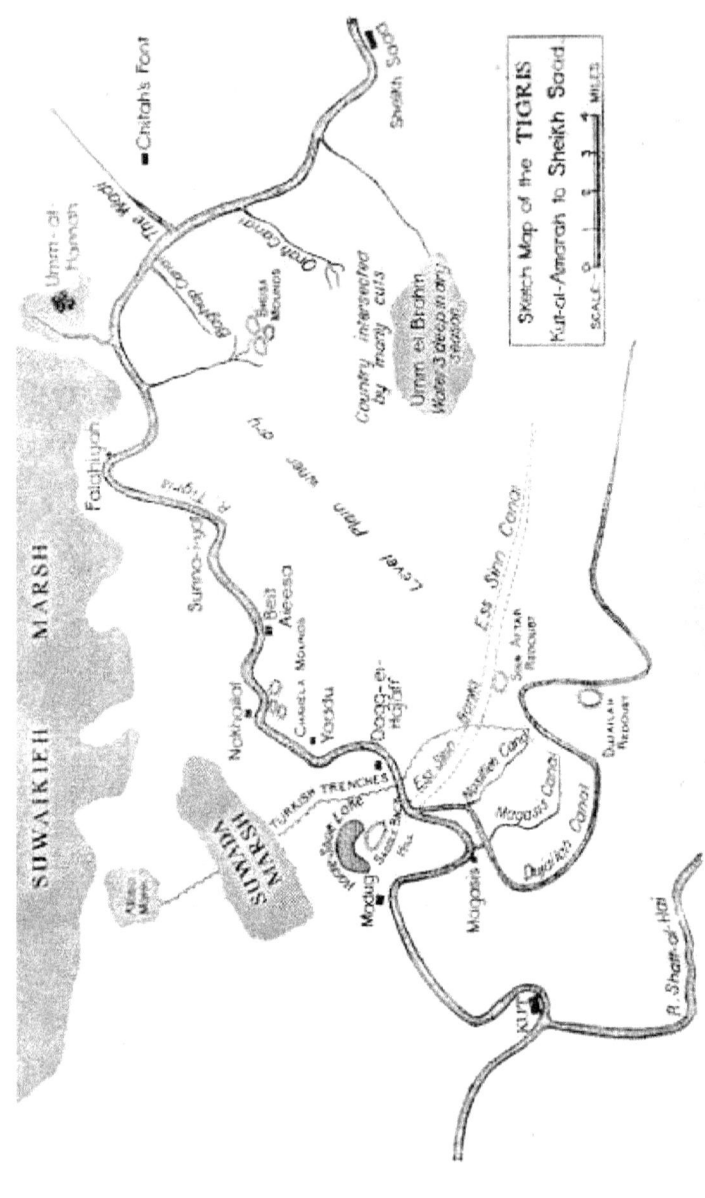

CHAPTER 13

Enemy Movement on the Tigris

While the VIth Division had been engaged in the "Regatta," the XIIth Division had also been active on the right flank of the advance carrying out operations which materially assisted the advance up the Tigris.

Ahwaz was in April confronted by eight battalions of Turks with eight guns and a large force of Arabs, estimated at 10,000, the whole under the command of Mahommed Daghestani. The object of this force was, while containing our brigade at Ahwaz, to move down across the Karun and get between Basra and the mouth of the river, and thus to interrupt our communications—the previous attempt, from the opposite flank, having been stopped by the Battle of Birjisiyeh. But this scheme also was nipped in the bud: before Daghestani was ready to move, General Gorringe with the remaining brigades of the XIIth Division and the 6th Cavalry Brigade arrived at Ahwaz.

By 24th April the Turks, their ambitious scheme withering before such odds, had retreated to the Kherkha River. Despite the increasing heat and every imaginable difficulty from lack of transport, General Gorringe followed in pursuit and crossed the river near Illah on 7th May. The stream is here 250 yards broad and very swift-flowing, but, despite a shortage of material, it was successfully bridged and troops passed across, whereupon the Turkish force retreated towards Amara.

We were now in the country of the Beni Taruf, a tribe with whom we had a long and heavy account to settle, for their part in the proceedings of 3rd March, when they had murdered wounded British officers and *sepoys*; for their treacherous murder of some officers and men of the 33rd Cavalry, and various other misdemeanours. Accordingly, a move was made down the Kherkha, Major-General Mellis commanding on the right bank, Brigadier-General Lean on the left,

"The Medical Mahela," a Direct Descendant of Noah's Ark.

and punishment was now meted out to this tribe. Their stronghold of Khafajiyah was attacked and destroyed. In this action a very gallant deed was performed by the *subahdar major* and twenty men of the 76th Punjabis, who swam the river under heavy fire and brought back a boat in which troops were ferried across to the attack.

But though the Turkish forces had retreated from the neighbourhood it was most important that they should not be available to reinforce the Tigris line, in view of our intended advance against these positions.

Sir John Nixon, therefore, instructed General Gorringe to keep in touch with the retreating enemy and to "demonstrate" from the region of Bisaitin against the troops between there and Amara. At this time the temperature was anything over 120 degrees in the tents—of which only a minimum could be carried, and those single-fly—and the troops suffered severely from the heat and also from shortage of water when once away from the rivers; for although the marshes lay upon every side, a shimmering expanse of tempting water, it was nearly all brackish and quite unfit to drink.

Sickness of all kinds, sun-stroke, heat-stroke, fever, and dysentery took a heavy toll, and many of the troops, particularly the less acclimatized, had to be sent back to Ahwaz, including the 1/4th Hants and the Gurkhas. But General Gorringe's energy and determination, combined with a certain amount of "bluff," carried the day. Among other ruses employed there was one that was most successful in increasing our prestige. It is said that about thirty transport carts, carrying stout poles and carefully covered up with tarpaulins, were drawn up in a line. Some influential Arab *Sheikhs* of doubtful loyalty were then invited to inspect the British Artillery—the guns, of course, had to be covered with tarpaulins in view of the damp climate! They departed much impressed, and the story was not long in reaching the Turks.

At any rate, this force was so successful in its demonstrations that the Turks were prevented from taking the shortest way home, and so delayed in their retreat that, not only were they unable to reinforce the Tigris line, but, when their advance guard marched into Amara they found General Townshend was there before them and were forced to surrender with the loss of two guns. Their commander, Daghestani, with some of the regulars, escaped to Kut, but most of the Arabs and Kurds dispersed into the marshes and disappeared.

There is no doubt that the "Regatta" was much helped by the XIIth Division's co-operation, and, furthermore, Persian Arabistan was

BELLUMS AND CREWS AS THEY TOOK PART IN THE REGATTA.

cleared of enemy, the pipe-line could be repaired and the oil-supply resumed. Casualties in action only amounted to about fifty, but during the seven weeks over which the operations extended, the temperature had hardly ever fallen below 120 degrees, tents were scarce and not sun-proof, shade non-existent, there was little water and that of poor quality, so it is little wonder that the troops suffered severely from sickness. As an exhibition of endurance and determination under the most trying conditions, this march from Ahwaz to Amara in the height of summer, a distance of over 100 miles, was a fine performance, and one which received very moderate recognition in comparison with more spectacular performances elsewhere.

On 13th June the advance guard of the column and 6th Cavalry Brigade arrived at Amara, and during the next few days the remainder marched in, having had just about as much as they could do with; the horses of the Cavalry Brigade had suffered severely.

By this time, we had settled down in our billets in various parts of the town—the weather was appallingly hot, our quarters were not luxurious, but, considering all things, we were probably better off at Amara than anywhere else.

The town is quite modern and built on the left bank of the river, with a frontage of rather fine brick houses. There is a good brick-roofed bazaar, and, beyond, the usual tangle of narrow streets, which get more disreputable and ruinous as one leaves the river. At the upper end of the town the river is crossed by an exceedingly rickety pontoon bridge, which the Turks had constructed, not so much for the convenience of the populace as on account of the tolls that could be squeezed from passing river-craft every time the bridge had to be opened. On the opposite right bank are a few houses, and some fine date plantations and lime orchards—indeed, Amara is conspicuous for the refreshing greenness of its trees and gardens.

The troops were quartered on both banks, with VIth Divisional Headquarters in a fine house on the river front; the Dorsets lower down on the left bank, the Oxford and Bucks Light Infantry in two big granaries on the Jahalah Canal, and the 104th and 48th Pioneers nearby. On the opposite bank were the 119th and 103rd, and the Field Ambulance and Transport, under canvas, the Cavalry Brigade; and also, an aerodrome, at this time still under construction.

The story of June in Amara would be but one long chronicle of hot days and breathless nights, of sickness and boredom, and shortage of most things which make hot weather bearable: indeed, summer in

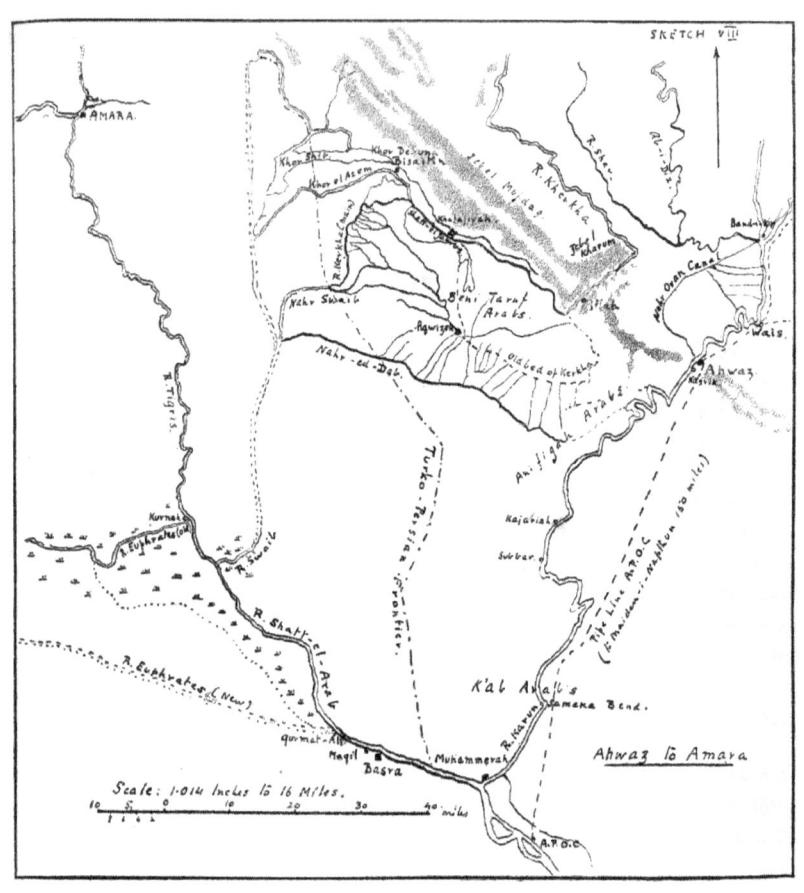

HRB SKETCH AHWAZ TO AMARA

Mesopotamia, at least in those days when transport was short and comforts rare, was a body-and-soul-destroying business—best forgotten.

General Townshend went down almost immediately with a very severe form of fever, from which it was at first feared he would not recover. He was invalided to India, and Major-General Fry was temporarily in command of the VIth Division.

As the weeks passed and the weather got hotter and hotter, sickness increased, not only sickness of body, but a worse and more insidious enemy—sickness of mind. It affected people in various ways—worry over trifles, restlessness, anxiety, and, often enough, shortness of temper were all symptoms; but the worst and commonest form was a sort of hopeless depression, when everything and everybody (including oneself) was utterly bad, and life unbearable. Terrors were in the way and the grasshopper had become a burden.

As to ills of the body and their causes, they were many and various. Vegetables were short, almost unobtainable; a much-boomed ice machine broke down after a fortnight's spasmodic activity, never to work again; there were no such luxuries as electric fans, and only one regiment possessed a soda-water machine. And as we grilled in the dust and heat we read in the *Times* that, according to the politicians, every effort was being made to make the troops in Mesopotamia comfortable: ice, and electric fans, and fresh vegetables, said the ready speaker at Westminster, were being regularly supplied. We smiled and wished that he lived among us!

The temperature during the day now varied between 115 degrees and 120 degrees, with very little fall during the short nights, as the "*Shimal*"—the north wind, which ought to blow at this time of year—had struck work. By 5 a.m. the sun was too hot to make further sleep upon the roof possible, and between 9 a.m. and 6 p.m., no one was allowed outside their billet, except on urgent duty. Sickness of all kinds became rife, sunstroke and heatstroke were common, fever and dysentery and para-typhoid—ample warning was given to those responsible of the difficulties to be expected if they should ever have to deal with the rush of a heavy casualty list.

Transport was still very short, material and personnel were scarce, for, from the beginning of the campaign, medical equipment and personnel had been inadequate. The VIth Division was sent from India with such medical organisation as is designed for frontier expeditions, when India, with her railways and resources, lies close at hand: distant Mesopotamia— a country of notoriously trying climate—was treated in the same way. But even this establishment was not complete, for the British General Hospital was short of personnel and equipment for fifty beds.

By April, I.E.F. "D" had been more than doubled, for the XIIth Division and the 6th Cavalry Brigade had been sent out; but except for the addition of seven sections of Field Ambulance, the Medical Establishment received no increase. That is to say, arrangements, at a most favourable estimate barely sufficient for one division, were, with only this small addition, considered adequate for a force more than twice as numerous.

Even so, there seemed no good reason why dying men should lie on the ground on a mat of rushes in a scarcely sun-proof tent; nor that the officers' hospital should consist of two small ill-ventilated rooms, without beds, and for long without *punkas*; nor that the doctor should come round and seriously prescribe a chicken or fish diet, when neither were available, and there was only one small stove and a native cook who could not even make soup. There were plenty of good houses in Amara occupied by rich Arabs who could have been turned out—or, failing that, the Divisional Headquarters would have made a fine hospital.

Even those who did not go sick were permanently on the borderline, and any extra exertion bowled them over. I remember very vividly a burial party. We started out for the cemetery, about a mile away, at 6 p.m. Before we had gone half the distance a man went down with heatstroke, and was carried back, limp and twitching, to hospital. As the corpse was lowered into the grave, one of the men on the ropes stumbled forward and fell limply into the grave on the top of the dead body, and, as we fell in to march back, another man went down. Luckily, we had brought a spare stretcher, and with one on this and the other on the stretcher on which the dead man had been carried to the grave, we returned. We had buried one man and lost three others over the job.

With things going in this way, every regiment was getting very short both of officers and men, and, towards the end of the month, drafts arrived; but many of them were half-trained, while for all it was a stiff test to be dumped down into such a climate, especially for those who came from France.

But downstream there was a new enterprise afoot, which raised hopes that we might be again employed and no longer have to stew in inactivity—for it is having nothing to do which is really trying in great heat.

The advance in the centre and on the right of our line had rather isolated our left flank, nor could it advance with safety until the country bordering the Euphrates had been cleared. The Turkish force which had been so thoroughly defeated at Shaiba (Birjisiyeh) had retreated as a disorganised rabble in the direction from which it had come; but that was two months ago, and there was reason to believe that the force had since been reorganised at Nasryeh and received reinforcements from Kut by way of the Hai Canal.

Any further advance up the Tigris, while this force remained in being on the Euphrates, would expose our communications to the danger of attack, by the Turks cutting in from Nasryeh in our rear. This enemy force therefore had to be cleared out, and their base at the junction of the Euphrates and the Hai Canal, leading from the Tigris at Kut, captured and permanently held, so as to prevent the enemy moving troops across our front.

As soon as the Kherkha operations were at an end, and the ships of our extremely limited transport had been brought down from the Karun, the XIIth Division was concentrated again with a view to a move against Nasryeh. There were considerable difficulties to be dealt with. Nasryeh is some 85 miles from Kurna, from which the approach to it is by the "Old" Euphrates and the Hamar Lake to Hakika, where a channel, the Gurmat Safha (or Hakika Channel) leads to the main-stream of the Euphrates, 20 miles below Nasryeh. In the middle of June, the Hamar Lake is 5 feet deep, and General Gorringe was able to employ steamers to transport his forces across the lake: further progress would have to be made by the Hakika Channel. But the Turk was quite aware that, after the middle of June, the water in the lake drops rapidly, till, by the end of July, it is mostly mud—and so Time was his most important ally.

Across the Hakika Channel had been built a very formidable "*bund*": This was commanded by guns and two Thorneycroft launches. General Gorringe had first to destroy the *bund* and pass his ships through the channel before coming to grips with the main Turkish forces. But evidently this was going to be a long job and not an easy one, and for some time no news was forthcoming as to how affairs were going on the Euphrates. In the meanwhile, we at Amara had to possess our souls in patience and find whatever work we could to distract our attention from heat and flies.

The defence of Amara and its surroundings was now organised in the shape of a chain of posts on either bank, occupying block-houses formerly built by the Turks as a protection against Arab raids. These indeed were about all we had to fear, but in case of more serious danger a mobile column was organised which was always to be ready to move at short notice. The bridge over the Tigris had been repaired and made passable for troops, while a pontoon bridge was built across the Jahalla Canal, and a few "test" alarms showed that the mobile column, with its guns and transport, could move out satisfactorily.

The next town, or rather village, of any importance above Amara was Ali-el-Gherbi, which had been reconnoitred and found innocent of enemy troops soon after the capture of Amara. But, since then, information reported that some Turkish officials had put in an appearance, and, as the telegraph line from there to Kut and Baghdad was still intact (the Turks in their hurried retreat had omitted to cut any telegraph wires), it was considered best to remove them.

A small party, escorted by a company and a machine-gun section, left Amara on 30th June and started upriver on the 90-mile voyage into, theoretically, enemy territory. All went well, despite the fact that near Kumait, 40 miles up, was encamped a huge collection of armed Arabs. These were under the leadership of a notorious villain—one Gazban (literally "the angry one"), a *Sheikh* of the Beni Taruf, but owning allegiance to no one, and a professional robber and highwayman of very thorough methods. His following was at this time supposed to number 20,000 fighting men—probably a gross exaggeration—of Beni Lam, Beni Taruf, and Albu Mohammad—all outlaws like himself, and as Gazban had been implicated in the 3rd of March attack near Ahwaz, there was reason to think he might be up to any tricks.

But at this time, he was undecided with which side to ally himself: he had received heavy payments from the Turks while being careful to give little in return, and at the same time had showed an inclination to come to terms with the British. He was very nearly won over, and, indeed, came into Amara to talk matters out with the authorities; then later he was visited in his camp (his tent was decorated with a Union Jack!) and a direct offer made—so much down, so much after six months, if he behaved; but in the meantime, his young son must live in Amara—as the general's guest. Gazban, in spite of his bad reputation, had one or two virtues—he was not so full of words as most of the local Arabs, and knew his own mind. As soon as he heard the condition, he shook his head emphatically, got up, and left the Political Officer's launch—only stopping to ask for the favour of a dozen of soda, as he "had a bad stomach." That was the end of our "conversations" with Gazban: evidently we might expect no help, and probably we were well out of such uncertain allies.

The Turkish officials were found intact at Ali-el-Gherbi—indeed, they said they had returned, as they were most anxious to be made prisoners by the British. Their desire was granted, and they returned to Amara *en route* for Basra and India.

At this time the only possible form of exercise in Amara was parade—for an hour at 6 a.m. in the morning and 6 p.m. in the evening—or rides in the desert in early morning or evening; for the rest of the day one lay in as few clothes as possible, or for choice in a large towel only, while the sweat poured off one. Sleep, with the myriads of flies, was out of the question. But the rides and walks, as long as a start was made early or late enough, were good fun, particularly if one called in on the Arab camps which now were beginning to appear along the river bank—for, with the hot weather, the pasture farther afield is burnt up and the tribes and their flocks migrate to the rivers. We always found a friendly welcome awaiting us—whether it was genuine friendliness or merely diplomacy I do not know. As soon as we rode into a camp a rush would be made for our ponies' heads, and a free fight would ensue for the honour of assisting us to dismount, when we were led to the *Sheikh's* tent and the ponies to a feed of barley.

Arrived at the *Sheikh's* tent, we were led to one end where a carpet and pillows were spread on the ground; here we would sit while the *Sheikh* and his brothers and cousins made polite conversation, examined all our belongings, and inquired the exact price of each. Presently the farther end of the tent would fill with the *Sheikh's* relations, the ladies keeping in the background, but evidently very curious, while we breakfasted off a huge bowl of milk or "*leben*," sour curds (probably the same as that "butter in a lordly dish" which Jael gave to Sisera), *chupatties*, sweet cucumbers, topped up with coffee, served very sweet and thick in tiny cups by a huge negro. One is limited by etiquette to three cups of this, though it is so excellent that we always wanted more—and one is expected to tip the negro who hands it round.

Conversation was rather a difficulty, as our small stock of Arabic was of the town variety—also we had learnt it from a Jew, and the Jews use rather a strange dialect very unlike that of the Desert Arab; however, we got on somehow or other, and our visits to the tents were a great success.

The children were most attractive, and generally not at all shy. I remember one fat little baby of about three, the son of a *Sheikh* we were visiting, who was brought in to see us; his father told him to show us how he could be a soldier, whereupon he marched up and down the carpet in front, and gravely saluted each of us in turn—his uniform was one small handkerchief. The children are absolutely unafraid of horses, and used to pull our ponies' tails and dodge in and out between their legs, liberties not always appreciated by Indian and Waler polo-ponies; but a small fox-terrier which always accompanied us was an object unknown and fearful, from which they ran wailing to their mothers—which was bad luck on poor "Sally," who was most anxious to play with them. But the dogs about the Arab camps are savage, unfriendly beasts, while the ponies live with the family in the same tent and grow up with the children, who are always playing with them. It is an extraordinarily pretty sight to watch them riding the ponies down to water—many of them almost babies. They will charge right into the river, and there proceed to have a regular romp, ducking the ponies' heads, pulling their tails, and diving under them—no one appears to get hurt or frightened.

In July, in spite of every doctor being overworked, a Civil Hospital was opened for the treatment of the local Arabs. Used to Turkish ways, they could not understand this at all, and their attitude was amusing to watch. At first a few old men came and looked and went away; then one or two of the bravest spirits brought their old and helpless male relations for treatment as an experiment. This proving satisfactory, men came regularly. Then one or two brought their women but stood guard jealously while the doctor prescribed; and then gradually the male escort was dispensed with, and every morning a crowd of women and little children could be seen waiting to interview the doctor. Exactly the same thing happened at Kut later on, and to stand by and watch the absolute confidence with which these natives submitted to being examined and, if necessary, operated on by our doctors, was about the finest tribute to the British ways of "conquest" that can be imagined.

Indeed, it is something to have seen Great Britain stepping into a new country, and to have watched the ways of our soldiers with a strange people; I never saw a case of ill-treatment of man, woman, or child, of roughness or of injustice. Even in those early days hospitals were opened, sanitary measures introduced, and justice dispensed in the military governor's courts, so that even the poorest could get a fair hearing; and since then the whole country has changed—the desert is being made to bloom as the rose, and the squabbling tribes gradually turned into paths of prosperity.

But it was the beginning of it all, the sowing of the British seed, that was so fascinating to watch, and one longed to have at hand some of those whom one remembered as the fluent decriers of their own country, who (before the war) had sat in their arm-chairs, sniffing their horrid insinuations. Those men, many of them clever and apparently sincere, who, through some strange kink in their brains, can take pleasure in believing that our Imperialism is a thing of pitiless blood and iron, that the Indian is our much down-trodden Aryan brother, and that we systematically ruin all helpless natives with gin and then exploit their countries when they are in a state of advanced alcoholism! There were some who really talked like that, and who seemed to prefer to believe it all (for had they not seen it in print?) rather than go and look for themselves. Perhaps many since the war began have looked for themselves and understood, so that henceforth their speech will be changed. Anyhow, we will hope so.

We also paid calls in Amara on the Chaldaean priest, who wore a patent leather hat, spoke queer French, and plied us with terrible drinks, which from politeness we swallowed somehow or other. He showed us over his church, a dark and dingy little hole decorated with tinsel and oleographs. Fear of having again to swallow his drinks prevented further visits. But there was also a mission run by the Sisters of the Sacred Heart, and, after much debate, we summoned up courage to call on them. The Sisters were perfectly charming, and we soon became regular visitors. They lived in a large house, comprising courtyard, chapel, and school at the lower end of the town.

The staff consisted of three wonderful women—an old Sister of over seventy, who had come out from France more than thirty years before, had never been home since, and had scarcely seen a European all those years; another Sister, fat and cheerful, a native of Baghdad; and a young Mother Superior. She had come out from France, from near Paris, only just before the war, and for eight months had had no letters from home and no word of her three brothers who were fighting. Before our arrival there these women had lived alone among a fanatical and hostile population, still carrying on their work of teaching and nursing. The Turkish authorities, they said, had more or less left them alone, but during the war the attitude of the townspeople had often been threatening, and on some occasions, they were hustled as they went about the streets, and insulted. As soon as the news of Birjisiyeh reached Amara this attitude was changed, and directly General Townshend had arrived, the worst offenders became most civil, even leaving presents at the convent gate. They had seen no Germans, though they knew there had been several in the town.

We often went round in the evenings to talk with them and tell them the war news—having heard nothing but the Turkish and Arab versions of what had been going on, they were longing to hear the real story, and much appreciated the Reuters in the *Basra Times*. They would say little about their work in Amara except that they taught the girls and nursed the women and held services in a beautiful little chapel which we were shown. They said that they never converted Moslems to Christianity; but I have since heard that a good many of the women are secret converts, though it is never spoken of, as their lives, and probably the nuns' lives, would end suddenly if it became known.

If they enjoyed our visits half as much as we did, we may feel that we did something to relieve the monotonous exile of three women for whom we felt the deepest admiration. We were sampling one hot season in Amara, with plenty of cheerful friends round us: they had spent many years there, far from any friends or countrymen. I once said to the Mother Superior that it must be awful to live permanently in Amara, and that I hoped she would be relieved soon, to return to France. She answered, "No, *Monsieur*, I will never leave this place. I have been sent here. We have our orders and must do our duty, just as you soldiers do: I may die here, just as many of you have died here."

Amara society cannot be dismissed without mention of a strange sect, some members of which lived in the town. This sect, the Sabians, was represented in Amara by a few families living near the Jahalla Canal, who worked as silversmiths; their speciality was the inlaying of antimony on silver by a secret process said to be very old and believed by some to date from Babylonian times. I often went round to watch one old man working. Certain conventional designs gave an appearance of roughness to his work, but he was really a very exact and finished workman and a good draughtsman. He would copy any design submitted to him—even making excellent drawings from photographs; these were deeply cut on the silver with a graver, with extraordinary accuracy. So far one could sit by and watch. But the inlaying of the antimony was not done in public, and I never managed to witness the course of operations beyond the heating of small lumps of antimony on an exceedingly primitive stone forge. This stage reached, he would pointedly suggest a cup of coffee—outside—which his talkative and very amusing old wife had prepared.

The Sabians, or as they call themselves "the Christians of St. John," are no doubt a very ancient sect, though their history is rather obscure. Sir Henry Layard estimated their numbers in 1840 as only 300 or 400 families and bore witness to their persecution by the Turks. They were then distributed between Shustar and various spots on the Karun and Shatt-el-Arab, where they plied their trade as silversmiths. Formerly their headquarters were at Hawizeh but owing to a change in the course of the Kherkha River which left Hawizeh high and dry, they were forced to leave; for running water is a necessity for their religious ablutions. They have their own sacred books, said to be very ancient, written in an obsolete Semitic language, and they also use a peculiar Semitic dialect, though this is now dying out.

Queen Victoria took an interest in them and did a good deal by gifts of money and diplomatic representations to the *Sultan* to improve their state and put an end to their persecution.

******

The news from the Euphrates was not very reassuring. Though Suk-es-Sheyuk had been occupied without opposition, considerable difficulty and delay had been experienced before the Hakika Channel could be passed. In the meanwhile, the water in the Hamar Lake was sinking, our troops were suffering from the appalling heat, and the Turks were reinforcing from Kut by way of the Hai Canal. At the same time, they had pushed forward detachments downstream on the Tigris and seemed to be trying the same gradual and tentative approach to Amara which they had practised at Kurna: they had again occupied Ali-el-Gherbi, and by the beginning of July had a force of infantry and guns at Fillaifillah.

In order to prevent further reinforcements leaving Kut for Nasryeh it was decided that we at Amara should make a demonstration upstream. On 11th July, 200 of the Dorsets, with the two 4.7's in horse-boats and two 18-pounders, set out to have a look at the enemy at Fillaifillah; but the position, some mounds and trenches commanding a loop in the river, was found to be too strong for such a small force, which accordingly retired. It was to be reinforced by the remainder of the division and some guns, the advanced troops being ordered to embark at 4.30 p.m. on the 15th; this was later postponed to 4 a.m. on the 16th. But at 3 a.m. the move was declared off, and the Norfolks and every available gun, instead of going upriver, steamed off down to Kurna *en route* for the Euphrates, where reinforcements were suddenly and urgently needed.

There followed a silence from that quarter until 20th July, when an urgent wire arrived asking the respective strengths of the two remaining British battalions—the Dorsets and the Oxfordshire Light Infantry; both were under strength, presumably so much so that they were considered unavailable, for they were not sent. It looked as if matters were not going at all well on the Euphrates, and everyone naturally felt rather anxious, and great was the relief when a wire arrived reporting the capture of the Turkish advanced positions at 1.30 on 23rd July, soon followed by a wire on the evening of the 24th reporting Nasryeh captured and the complete victory of the XIIth Division.

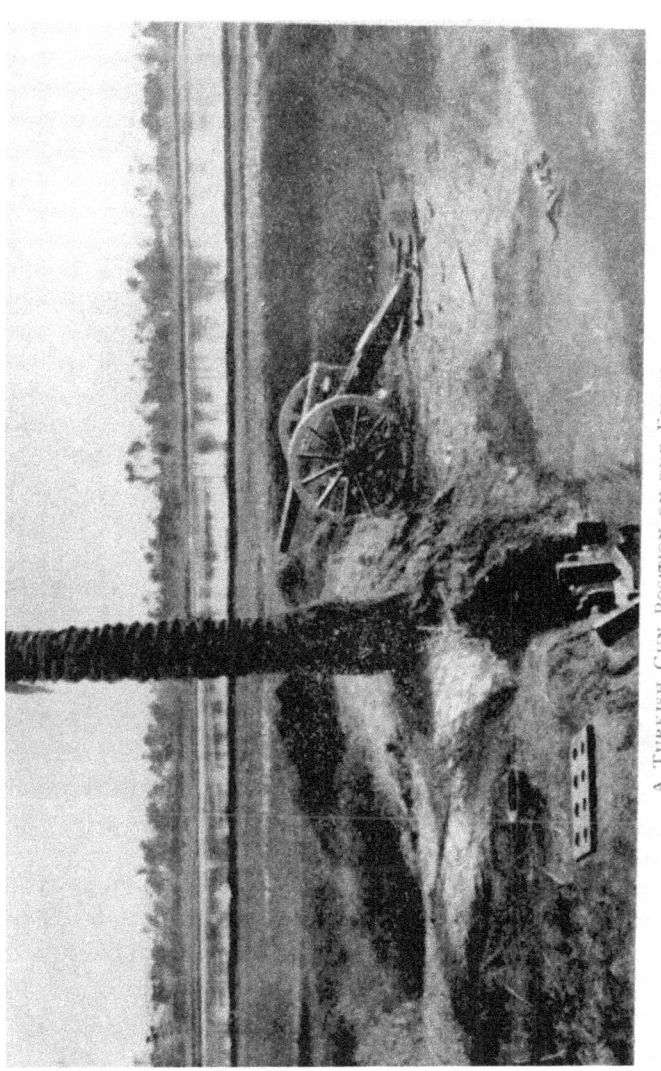

A Turkish Gun Position on the Euphrates.

CHAPTER 14

July and August 1915

For the story of the Nasryeh operations we must go back to the end of June, when the XIIth Division and the navy (represented by the armed launches *Samana, Shushan,* and *Massoudieh*) had crossed the Hamar Lake, in which there was then 5 feet of water, so that the steamers had no difficulty. The first difficulty appeared in the shape of the very solid "*bund*" which had been built across the Hakika Channel, the only way into the Euphrates and to Nasryeh. This *bund* had, however, been built solely for irrigation purposes, and only by chance achieved fame as a military obstacle.

Charges were successfully laid and exploded on 28th June, and a breach, 4 feet deep and 50 yards broad, was blown in the obstruction, through which the dammed-up water of the Euphrates rushed like a cataract into the lake. The current was far too strong to allow of the ships going through under their own steam alone, but, by using tow-ropes, they were slowly and laboriously hauled through, and, by 4th July, all were past the obstruction and collected about 2½ miles below the junction of the Gurmat Safha (or Hakika) Channel with the Euphrates.

On 5th July an attack was made on the Turkish position of Gurmat Safha, which lay on the right bank of the Euphrates, commanding the exit of the channel, and a mine-field which had been laid by the enemy about a mile down the channel. The position was carried by the 30th Brigade under Major-General Mellis soon after midday, the 24th Punjabis and the 30th Mountain Battery using *bellums* to effect a most successful turning movement. As soon as the right bank was cleared, the mine-field was swept by the navy (ably assisted by a captured Turkish officer), and the exit of the channel could be made. Our casualties were 26 killed and 80 wounded, while our captures included 4 guns and 132 prisoners; the enemy suffered heavy losses.

But this was only an advanced position which had to be cleared before we could pass through the narrow exit of the channel, only 200 feet broad. The main Turkish positions were at Medjenineh, four miles below Nasryeh, astride the Euphrates, their flanks resting on marshes and their front protected by deep creeks.

General Gorringe moved up to Asani, some two miles below the enemy's advanced defences, where the force dug in, as after a reconnaissance on 7th July it was decided that reinforcements would be needed to attack these positions.

The Euphrates above its junction with the Hakika Channel is about 200 feet broad, and on both banks, except for narrow strips of dry land, the country was at this time of year completely under water: but even the narrow strips of dry land were intersected by numerous irrigation channels forming difficult obstacles.

Life in the trenches with the thermometer at 120 degrees in the shade and an exceedingly damp atmosphere, was absolute purgatory; but the delay was perhaps unavoidable as there were by now only 3 feet of water in the lake, so that only the smallest steamers, lightly laden, could pass—and reinforcements and stores took very long in coming up. Dysentery and heat-stroke were rife in the airless, crowded trenches, and day and night Turkish snipers, well-concealed, and excellent shots, took toll of those unwise enough to show themselves. But at last preparations were complete for an attack, and on the night 13th-14th of July a move was made on both banks, the 12th Brigade attacking on the left bank, the 30th Brigade on the right.

It was only partially successful. On the right bank the 30th Brigade secured an entrenched position 400 yards from the Turkish trenches, but an attempt by the 24th Punjabis and the 30th Mountain Battery to capture some sand-hills, though most gallantly pressed, ended in disaster. The sand-hills were almost won when the regiment was fiercely attacked in rear by Arabs—advertised as "friendly." The men were, at the time, wading waist-deep in water (for this, too, was a "*bellum*" operation), and few of them got back to their boats. Nearly every wounded man was drowned, and the regiment lost heavily in British officers, all except the commanding officer and one subaltern being killed; only by the splendid support given by the 30th Mountain Battery was the remainder of the force able to withdraw. So much for "friendly" Arabs in the rear.

Further progress was considered impracticable without more guns

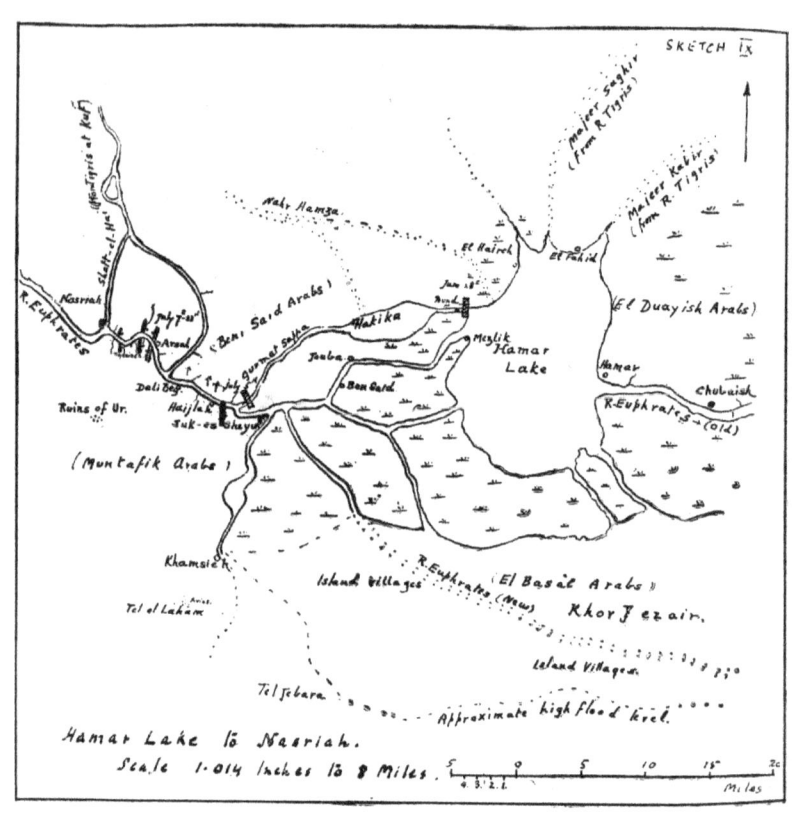

HRB sketch Hamar Lake to Nasriah

and reinforcements, and so there was another long wait in the grilling inferno of the trenches while these were collected and brought slowly across the shallow waters of the lake. In the meantime, every available man was kept busy digging and sapping forward, while the Turks sniped and bombarded the working parties incessantly. At last, at 5 a.m. on 24th July, the attack was launched, 12th Brigade on the left bank, 30th on the right. By 7.30 the 12th had occupied the enemy's advanced trenches, while the 30th went ahead until brought to a stop by the Medjenineh Creek, just in front of the enemy's position. It was too deep to wade, far too broad to jump; but the troops had to get across, and that quickly.

The navy came to the rescue. The *Samana* (Lieutenant Harris), carrying bridging material, steamed into and up the creek right in front of the Turkish trenches and under a storm of rifle and gunfire, to which she replied with her 12-pounder. Though hit over and over again she got where she wanted to, and the 17th Company of Sappers and Miners, under Captain Lord, R.E., threw a bridge across the creek. The 30th Brigade passed over successfully and captured the advanced trenches of the position at 9.30. The attack continued on both banks, meeting with strong resistance, and by noon the main position was captured. Here the enemy stuck gamely to his trenches, and some 500 were killed, mostly with the bayonet, the 2/7th Gurkhas doing great execution.

After reorganisation the troops pushed forward to the enemy's final line of defence at Sadanawiyah, which was soon captured, mainly by the senior naval officer, Captain Nunn, who ran the old *Shushan* alongside the enemy trenches on the river bank and pumped all available lead into them at close range. By the evening the enemy were in full flight, and our troops bivouacked on the ground they had won. Our captures included 1000 prisoners, 17 guns, about 1600 rifles with much ammunition, also two Thorneycroft launches and the pompoms with which they were armed.

For some reason the navy was not permitted to press on to Nasryeh the same night, though it appeared they could easily have done so. The delay allowed the garrison a whole night's law, of which they wisely availed themselves. About 2000 escaped upriver and into the Hai marshes, whence in course of time they worked up to Kut and were incorporated in Nur-ed-Din's army, which later concentrated here.

The town was occupied without opposition on 25th July, and the

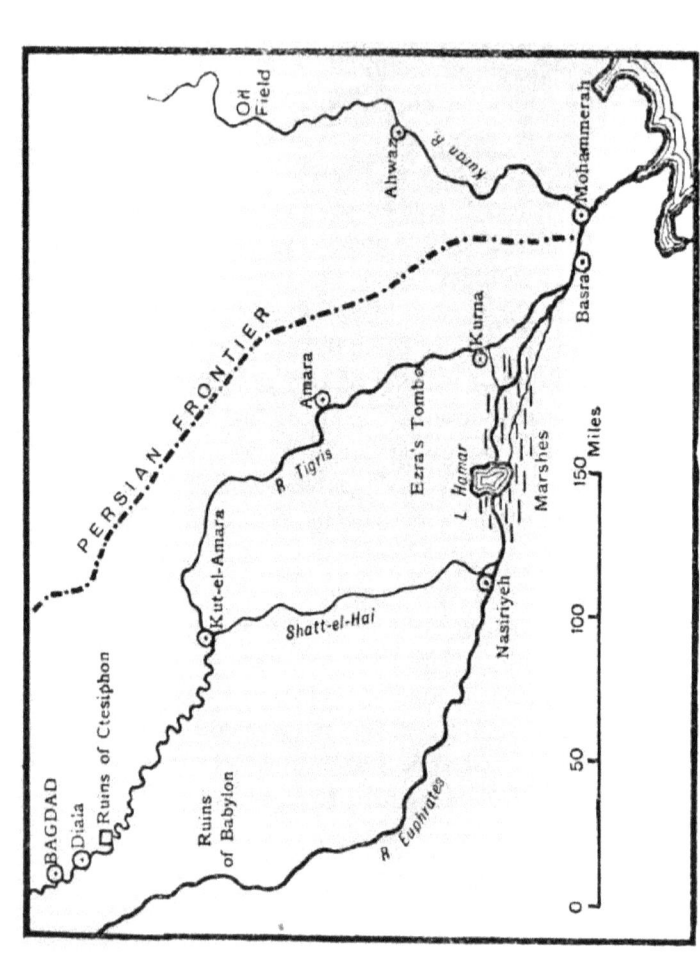

The Mesopotamian Campaign.

operations, after a long period of suspense and anxiety, were at last brought to a termination.

Though the geographic and climatic conditions were certainly unavoidable, it may perhaps be questioned whether the operations before Nasryeh were not unduly extended, and whether the delays experienced were indeed unavoidable. Difficulties of transport were certainly very great, owing to the shallowness of the Hamar Lake and shortage of suitable ships; but compared with General Townshend's operations from Kurna to Amara there appears to have been considerable less energy and "push" shown on the Euphrates. However, that may be, the troops of the XIIth Division have to their credit in the capture of Nasryeh a victory gained by hard fighting against a resolute enemy in strong positions, under the most appalling conditions of climate and discomfort that can well be imagined.

Our casualties in action were about 150 killed, including 15 British officers, and 600 wounded, including 30 British officers, not at all heavy considering the nature of the fighting and what we had accomplished; but casualties from sickness amounted to about 2000.

Probably seldom before have British, or, for that matter native, troops been required to fight under such terrible conditions of weather and climate, in a difficult country, against a resolute enemy. Let anyone try to imagine trench warfare among marshes in a temperature of 120 degrees—the trenches crowded and full of dysentery cases—and they will get some sort of idea of what the XIIth Division suffered in that blazing month. Furthermore, communications were exceedingly uncertain and slow, so that it took long to get up necessary reinforcements and stores—towards the end of July everything had to be punted in *bellums*, and the unfortunate sick and wounded had to be evacuated by the same means.

By the capture of Nasryeh and the defeat and dispersal of the enemy force there, our left flank was now freed from any immediate danger from that direction, as, during the low-water season, the Hai Canal is not navigable. Furthermore, British control had been established up to the westward limit of the Basra Vilayet, and Nasryeh, an important centre of the Arabs, was henceforward in our hands.

But northward of the line Nasryeh-Amara the Basra Vilayet still remained beyond our control, and information pointed to the concentration at Kut of considerable Turkish forces under Nur-ed-Din. These had already shown themselves at Fillaifillah, 30 miles from Amara.

As soon, therefore, as the Euphrates operations had ended, General

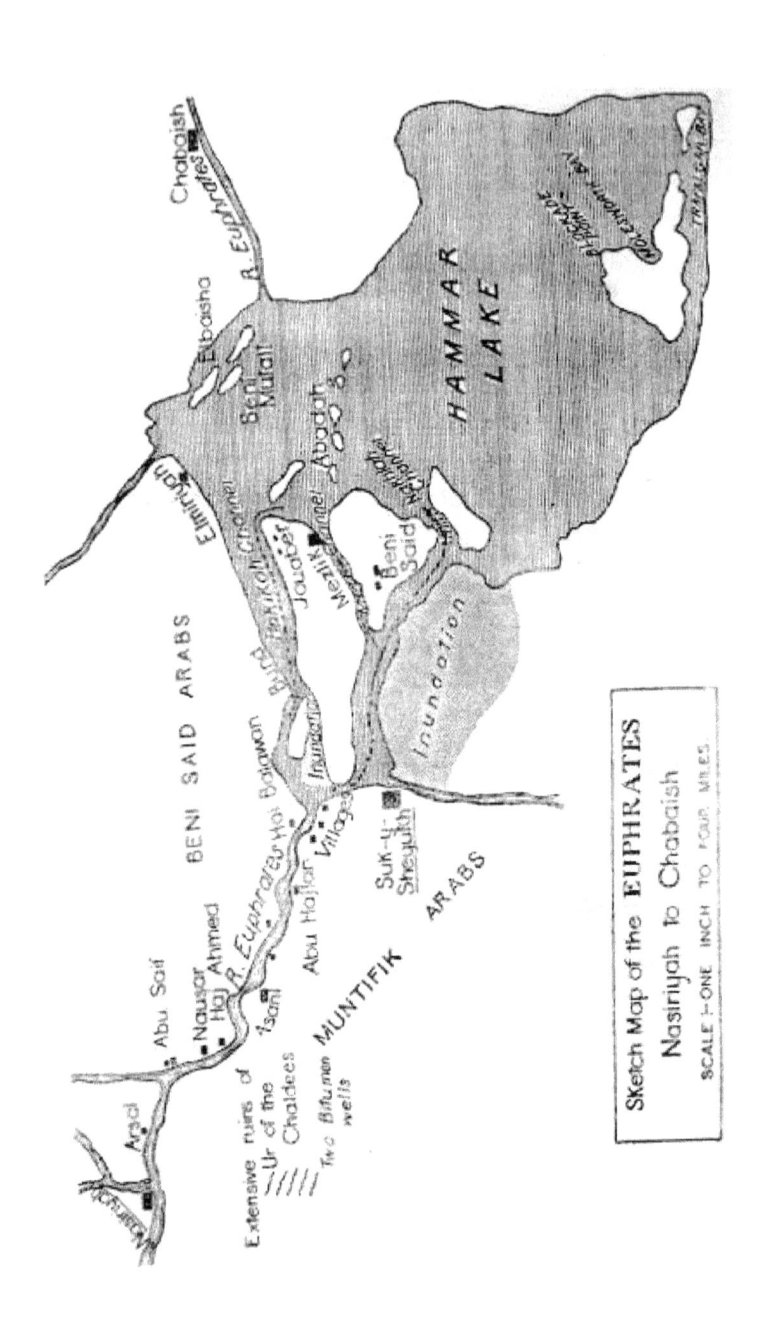

Nixon had to turn his attention once more to the Tigris.

A glance at the map of Mesopotamia, will show the strategic importance of Kut, and that he who holds it, if he can also command the two rivers with his ships, virtually controls Lower Mesopotamia; while the position of a force at Amara cannot be considered strategically sound in face of an enemy operating from the north.

General Nixon had been ordered by Simla to submit plans for efficient control of the "Basra Vilayet," a triangle of territory extending from Fao westward to Nasryeh and northward to within a few miles of Kut. To effect such control was difficult without occupying Nasryeh and Kut, which though administratively in the Baghdad Vilayet, is geographically the most important gate of the Basra Vilayet.

Accordingly, an advance against Kut was decided on—in intention it was a defensive, and not an offensive, operation.

In the meantime, a sort of game of hide-and-seek had been going on upriver. Gazban's large force of Arabs were still encamped near Kumait, and, in order to keep an eye on him and also to give confidence to the Sheikh of Kumait, a friendly Arab, a "River Column" was formed to patrol the stream in these reaches. It consisted of the 22nd Punjabis on two ships with a section of field guns, and left Amara on 17th July.

The Sheikh of Kumait professed himself exceedingly friendly and also exceedingly frightened of the Turks, and so in need of protection. A camp was formed at Kumait by the 22nd as a *pied à terre* from which they could carry out their river patrols, as it was impossible in the exceedingly hot weather to keep the men cooped up on board; also, their presence seemed to give the *Sheikh* confidence, though everything seemed quiet enough and the nearest Turk was a good 25 miles away. Relations continued on a most friendly footing (in spite of an officer shooting the *Sheikh's* tame and much-prized gazelle in mistake for a wild buck) until, on the evening of the 23rd, the force re-embarked for another patrol trip.

The *Sheikh* was not informed of their intended departure, and it appears that this was just as well; for that night the place was surrounded by Turks.

It is true that the *Sheikh* himself was carried off, but the less charitable are inclined to believe that this was merely an "extra" in order to save his face, and had our men been there *they* would have been carried off while the *Sheikh* smiled. However, that may be, the *Sheikh* was returned intact to his mud palace, where he was found later bitterly complaining of the way in which he had been left to his fate; but he never could quite explain how it was that his captors had so soon grown weary of his presence! So, the mysterious little comedy must remain mysterious.

But all such small matters were brushed aside by larger movements now in prospect. On 30th July, General Delamain with the 16th Brigade and artillery left Amara to push the Turks from their Fillaifillah position. This was reached at dawn on 1st August, but the Turks, though strongly entrenched, contented themselves with a few long shots from their guns before legging it away upriver for all they were worth. They made no stop at Ali-el-Gherbi, which was occupied by the 16th Brigade from this date.

The movement forward had begun, but the concentration of the VIth Division for the march on Kut was to be a long and laborious process, and we had to bear with Amara for some time yet.

It seemed only lately that we had been bewailing the watery condition of the world, when swamp and marsh and rivers were all too generous for our comfort. We were yet to meet with marsh, but henceforward the scarcity, and not the abundance, of water was to be our trouble.

The Tigris was dropping; and we depended on the Tigris for everything—to carry us, our guns, our ammunition, our food, and to keep us in touch with the world without: it was by the ships upon the river that we lived and had our being.

River transport had never been abundant—in fact, ever since the advance from Basra it had been short, so that each operation had to be finally concluded before the concentration for the next could be started. Shaiba had to be done with before the Karun operations were started; the ships had to be brought back from the Karun before the advance to Amara could be made; then back again down the Tigris before troops could fight at Nasryeh. A long interval—in other words, a rest for the enemy—could not be avoided between each operation; but the ships and their staffs never got a rest.

So far it had been very inconvenient, scarcely dangerous: there had been no disastrous consequences. But what if in addition to shortage of ships there was to be a shortage of water in the river, if we were to find that only half our small fleet was available? Already we heard ominous stories of the ships which had arrived from Burma in May—seven paddle-boats, four tugs, and four launches. The paddlers made terrible trouble at the sharp bends of "the narrows," as they had not

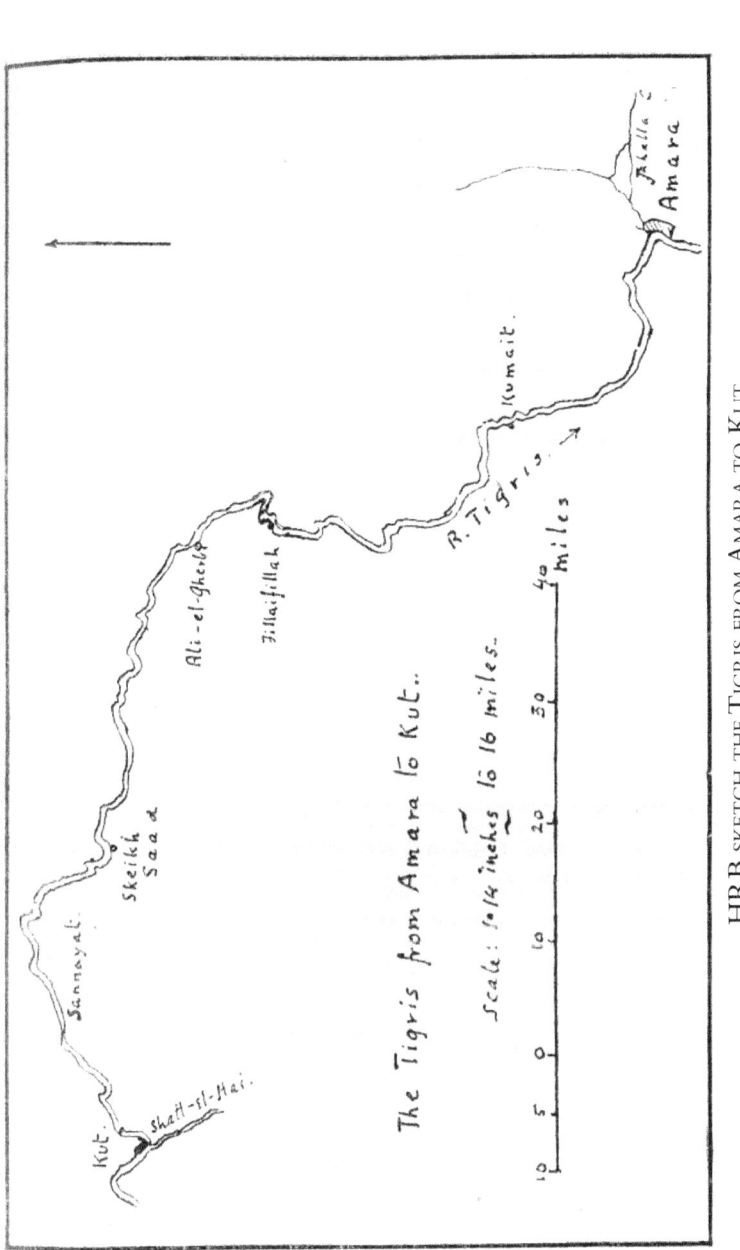

HRB SKETCH THE TIGRIS FROM AMARA TO KUT

got independent paddles, and both they and the tugs were of far too deep draught and were considered unreliable for use above Kurna. And they'd got to go to Kut! It looked as if it might be very awkward, but still one hoped for the best—indeed, in view of subsequent events, it may be said that a rather facile optimism was the cause of disaster. But the river was unusually high this year—a fact not appreciated till too late—and so the deep-draught boats maintained a fairly regular service, though, even so, there were not the boats in the country to carry more than five battalions with artillery (but without horses) at any one time; so our concentration was going to be a lengthy business.

In the meantime, life at Amara cannot be said to have improved very much. The heat of the day began later and ended earlier, but it was still very hot and conditions had otherwise not changed for the better, except that there was certainly an improvement in the health of the troops as soon as July was passed. What we particularly needed was fresh vegetables: onions we could get, and a horrible growth known as "Ladies' fingers," but these had long since palled, so that our joy was great when we heard that a barge-load of potatoes had been sent up from Basra. In time they arrived—and we knew they had come, for the stench of them filled Amara. Every one was rotten; and what wonder, when the genius responsible at the Base had sent them up on five days' voyage in the well of a barge, and packed artillery horses on a plank deck above them!

It was now cool enough in the mornings until 9 a.m., so parades could be held more regularly, and brigade exercises were indulged in on a small scale. They were badly needed as, since Shaiba, the brigades had not worked together—at least on land. But when I say "cool" it must be understood to mean comparatively cool for summer in Mesopotamia—it would be considered scorchingly hot anywhere else, and, by the time we had finished these morning outings, we were generally done to a turn.

On 7th August the Norfolks and some of the Field Artillery which had been engaged at Nasryeh returned to Amara, the first sign of the preparatory concentration which was now proceeding prior to the intended advance. The XIIth Division were for the most part to be left at Nasryeh (they remained there till 1916), so that only the artillery, Norfolks, and army troops had to be transferred from the Euphrates. The shipping was now employed at full pressure on the Tigris in bringing up stores and material from Basra to Amara: we were again "the front," and Ahwaz and Nasryeh were side-tracked.

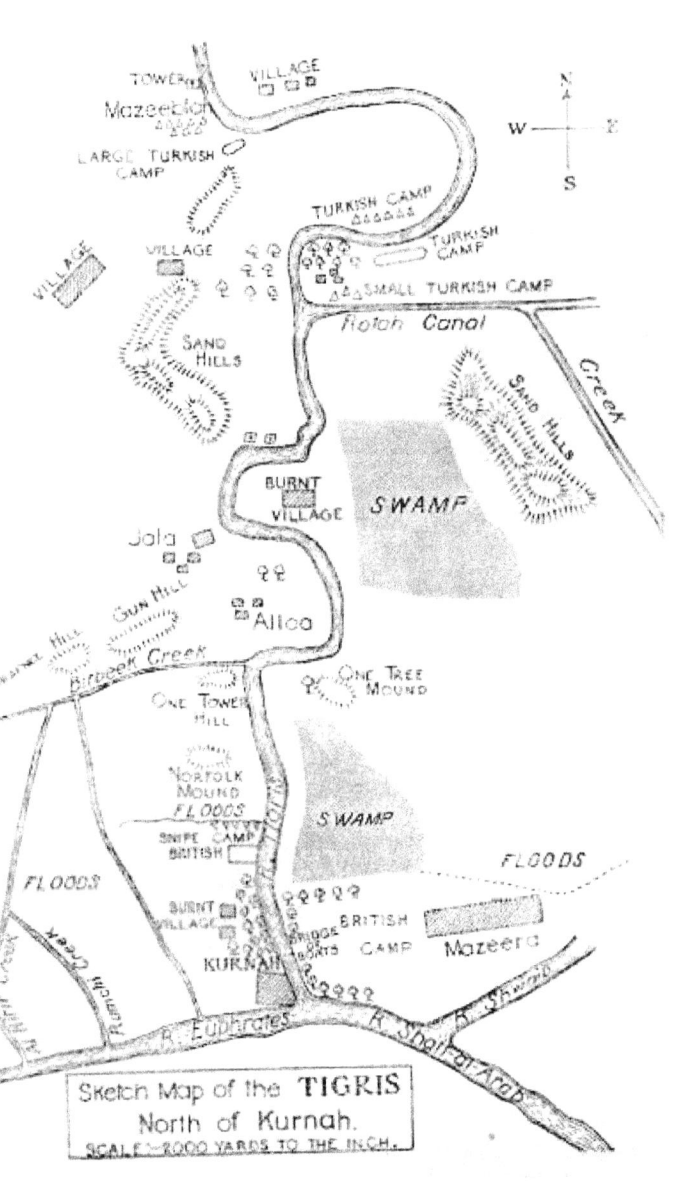

As is usual when an advance is imminent, the air was thick with rumours. It was said that the Turks had begun to evacuate Kut, and were retiring on Ctesiphon, only twenty-three miles from Baghdad; also, that they had received reinforcements of German artillery—two batteries with German gunners.

The story about the evacuation of Kut was obviously unlikely, as, though our intelligence was experiencing a good deal of difficulty in getting exact information of the Turks' position there, it was known to be a very strong one, held by probably ten battalions of regulars with about twenty guns, while at Sheikh Saad, twenty miles downstream, two hundred enemy and four guns were reported. One Yusuf Nur-ed-Din, ex-chief of police for the Basra Vilayet, was making his presence inconveniently felt, by catching and hanging our "agents." He was apparently one too many even for the wily Arab, and quite successful in catching and dealing with suspected characters.

Another rumour, still premature but good to hear, was that General Townshend was expected back immediately; at least we had definite information that he had recovered and was going to return to us in time to command the division in the advance, which all ranks were very glad to hear. Already we had tremendous confidence in him.

The aeroplanes were now much in evidence every morning, flying over the right bank and practising fire-control by signals of smoke balls.

The Flying Corps had started life in Mesopotamia in May with two Maurice Farmans of an obsolete type, one of which was constantly out of commission through engine-trouble and was finally lost, causing the death of both pilot and observer, during the Nasryeh operations.

In July two Caudrons, also very antiquated, had arrived, but they, too, were unsatisfactory and needed constant repairs, which were exceedingly difficult to effect in the country. The establishment, both of flying officers, mechanics, and spares, was terribly limited, and, considering the difficulties, they had already performed wonders. In those early days, practically nothing was known about flying in tropical climates, and there was little experience available to show the effect of heat and sun and dust on engines and fabric.

Towards the end of August, the Flying Corps received its first modern aeroplanes: six Martinsyde Scouts—considered fairly fast machines in those days—with pilots and mechanics, though only a minimum of personnel was sent. These machines and pilots were to prove themselves invaluable in the coming operations.

27th August was a memorable day, for two reasons: first, because General Townshend arrived back from India, which was felt to be a sign that we should soon move on; and secondly, because, for the first time for five months, we saw some clouds. Clouds do not sound very interesting nor exciting; but only those who have endured the full glare of a Mesopotamian summer, and learnt, with good cause, to hate the sight of the blue sky, will understand our feelings. One can get very tired of waking up to a cloudless sky, and I now understand the sentiments of that old colonel whom the subaltern greeted at breakfast with "Another nice fine day, sir!"

But, on the other hand, the cloudless nights of the summer are, for their beauty, hard to describe. In that country of flat horizon and vast views, where, in the desert, nothing exists, neither hill, nor tree, nor building, to encroach upon the wide expanse of the sky, the night is something to fill one with wonder and a sense of immensity not felt by day.

It seems that the distant horizon on every side must be the limit of the dark earth over which hangs this vast blue dome, flashing with million upon million of stars of every conceivable colour. The black silent earth seems dead, but this boundless glittering world above full of mysterious movement and restless life.

And if it be a night when the full moon rises, large and brilliant over the desert, one may watch her stately passage across the open sky and understand why the Oriental finds in her a perfection to which he may compare the face of his mistress, or the pure light of a jewel, or the graceful shape of a blossom; the moon is to him a type of perfect beauty. What wonder that in this land they worshipped her? Before the dawn of history, the men of Sumer and Akkad knew her and built their vast temples and towers to Sin, the great goddess.

But to come down to earth again. We heard definitely on 29th August that the advance on Kut had been authorised by the Government, and that now we could go ahead: we should start upriver immediately. The plan was to effect a preliminary concentration at Ali-el-Gherbi, whence the force would move to Sheikh Saad (at present held by the Turks). There the final preparations would be completed, and the advance against the Es Sinn position, the Turkish lines protecting Kut, begun.

On 2nd September we embarked on *P. I.*, and were off by 8.30 a.m. It was a perfectly fiendish day, with a scorching hurricane blowing downstream, and the air thick with dust; the ship and the two barges on either side were cram full. That night a halt was called at 7.30 p.m., and we tied up by the bank, having accomplished about 40 miles. We started next morning at 5.30. The same burning north-west wind was blowing again, with a breath like the blast from a furnace door—it has to be experienced to be believed—and the air was so thick with dust that often the farther bank was invisible. The river was noticeably low—far lower than we had expected—and soon our troubles began.

At 9.30 the starboard barge ran aground, and we had to heave to, with the result that the whole outfit was blown on to the bank and there we remained. Another regiment of the brigade passed us by, like the priest, on the other side, taking no pity on our plight—in which they were probably wise, as their ship would only have joined us. We remained high and dry for over four hours, while our eyes and ears and throats gradually filled up with sand, and tempers became edgy; but at last a compassionate tug towed us off, and we finally arrived at our destination at 5 p.m.

We found Ali-el-Gherbi a sun-scorched, wind-swept little town of mud houses upon the right bank, with no arrangements for disembarking save exceedingly steep and rickety gangways to the bank, which made unloading a long and difficult process. That night we spent bivouacked on the beach below the town, and no one is likely to forget it: the overpowering stench of mud and garbage, combined with swarms of active sand-flies, made sleep out of the question, though we were spared the customary sniping. Next morning, we shifted our quarters into a big walled garden, and spent the day pitching tents and getting stores ashore. Troops were constantly arriving, and the place was a scene of giddy activity.

On the right bank beyond the town, the featureless brown of the desert stretched inimitably, but on the opposite bank, across the familiar prospect of boggy marsh, a new sight greeted us. About thirty miles away rise the foothills of the Pusht-i-Kuh, a purple and grey jumble of rocks, broken by the deep violet clefts of narrow valleys; and to eyes weary with the eternal uninteresting flatness of Mesopotamia, as we knew it, such a change was indeed welcome. In that clear atmosphere distances are reduced, and often one could see distinctly the winding valleys, and here and there green patches of meadow, which from our oven below looked refreshingly cool.

In the early morning and just before sunset, the higher peaks beyond took on the most gorgeous colours, and fantastic shapes appeared and vanished as light and shade chased each other across the broken slopes.

The hot weather, we discovered, was not by any means at an end yet, and often enough 119 degrees was registered in the tents, while, outside, the sun was perfectly grilling in the middle of the day. The Turks upstream at Sheikh Saad had been making a nuisance of themselves by sending down snipers almost nightly, and there were also patrols of their cavalry hanging about, so on 6th September a small column of all arms went out to see if they could catch anything. They sighted a body of the enemy, mostly Arab cavalry, but these, as their custom is, lost no time in fading into the landscape, and beyond a little shelling of stragglers nothing could be done; but on the march back the infantry suffered very severely from heat and thirst, the 20th Punjabis losing two men dead from heat-stroke and several sick. The climate was still an enemy with whom one could take no liberties.

But Ali-el-Gherbi had anyhow one attraction—the sand-grouse shooting was particularly good. The birds would start coming in from the desert for their evening drink at about 4 p.m., and for an hour and a half the air would be positively thick with them. Every evening we used to go about a mile upstream on the left bank and get really good sport. Guns and, even more, cartridges, were scarce, but we got fifty-two brace one evening, and forty-eight on another occasion, though, owing to the heat which was still considerable at four o'clock, one had constantly to cease fire and let one's barrels cool down.

On the evening of the 7th we heard definitely that we were to start from Ali-el-Gherbi the following Sunday, the 11th—the 16th and 17th Brigades, the Cavalry Brigade, and the guns by route march across the desert, the 18th Brigade by ship. Our destination was to be Sheikh Saad, which would be occupied with or without a fight—it depended on the Turk—and there we should halt for about a week to complete our concentration before moving against the Es Sinn position. But the usual problem cropped up: transport. I.E.F. "D" was fitted out (we were told) on the supposition that the campaign in Mesopotamia was to be a "river war"—that is to say, that it was to depend on the rivers and rely on river-transport.

We have seen that there was nothing like enough shipping supplied, particularly when the river was low, so that now when it was necessary to move a whole division with divisional troops and stores at one time, two brigades and the guns had to walk. That was no particu

A Creek on the "Old" Euphrates, with a Marsh Arab Village.

lar hardship; but this being a river-war, why provide land transport?

There is no polite answer to such a question, but the problem had to be solved. The 30th Mule Corps and the detachments of Imperial Service Transport were there, but they were nothing like enough for the work, and besides, they were much reduced in personnel and mules. The only thing to do was to go out into the highways and hedges and look for transport. Accordingly, a general round-up of every four-footed beast for miles round was instituted—camels for choice, but donkeys and cows accepted. As soon as the Arabs heard of this scheme they began to make tracks for the desert for all they were worth; but somehow or other some were circumvented and induced at a heavy price to hire out their camels.

These arrived in camp on the 10th—about 500 of them—and a more mixed assortment was never seen. They were not baggage camels at all, and most of them had never carried a load before, so that the Transport Sections spent a gay and giddy time trying to induce them to accept loads of blankets. To add to the difficulties there was only one driver to every twenty camels—ragged, shrivelled Bedouin, who alone could persuade the beasts to do anything but gurgle and bite, and they spoke a strange lingo which no one could interpret. There also arrived droves of tiny donkeys, most of them less than three feet high, and several cows, which obliged by carrying entrenching tools and anything else which the camels particularly objected to.

The two brigades moved out at 5 a.m. on the 11th, and marched till 9 a.m., most of the time through a dust-storm; it was by then too hot to go farther, so a halt was made by the river bank. Neither brigade had done any marching for a year, except for a few very brief field-days at Amara, and the troops' consequent unfitness combined with the heat—which now suddenly stoked up again for our benefit—caused a good many losses: the Dorsets lost two dead that morning, the Oxfordshire Light Infantry about twenty sick, and the Indian regiments very much the same. A certain number of ships and barges had been told off as "parent ships" to the troops marching, and carried reserve ammunition, stores, cooks, and tents. As soon as these arrived, camp was pitched and a meal served out.

The next morning, we left at 4.15 and marched till eight, which brought us just short of Sheikh Saad. That afternoon General Townshend made a personal reconnaissance upstream in the *Comet*, and found Sheikh Saad evacuated, except by a few cavalry who retired hastily before the launches' machine-guns. We reached Sheikh Saad at

8 a.m. on the 13th—a memorable morning, for, instead of being able to pitch camp as soon as we got in, we found that the parent ships had all run aground, so that there were no tents and no food; the sun was blistering, and, to make matters worse, a tremendous wind and sandstorm was blowing.

There was no vestige of shade or shelter, and sun and dust had to be endured all day, with a consequence that a lot of men went down. Aeroplane reconnaissance now reported the Turks to be evacuating Es Sinn, so that, instead of halting at Sheikh Saad for a week as originally intended, General Townshend determined to push on immediately to a position whence he could watch the enemy more easily. Accordingly, we set off again at 3.43 next morning, the 14th, and, after two more marches, arrived on the 15th at Sannayat, 12 miles from the Es Sinn position. Towards the end of the march the Cavalry Brigade gained touch with enemy patrols.

Here news, good and bad, greeted us. The Turks, far from retiring, were holding their position in strength, and there was no sign of evacuation; but one of the new Martinsyde planes had been shot down just in front of their trenches that morning, and pilot and observer made prisoners. This was serious, as we were short of aeroplanes—the remaining Maurice Farman had been badly smashed at Ali-el-Gherbi, and two of the Martinsydes were in dock already; with another captured, we were left with only three reliable machines. No one was sorry that the march was finished—the men had sore feet, the mules, sore backs, and the mixed transport had given endless trouble, and it was a wonder that it had arrived at all.

While we were marching, the whole desert in rear seemed covered with wandering beasts—camels and their calves sauntering along, unled and unsecured, browsing where they liked, apparently (but not really) quite uncontrolled by their handful of ragged drivers. As one looked back on the march and saw this huge unwieldy crowd of camels and donkeys and cows, which no escort could possibly guard, one could not help feeling what fun a few enterprising cavalry could have had. But at last this comic cavalcade, more like Lord George Sanger's outfit than an army's transport, was safely shepherded into camp, and we settled down for a week's final preparation before "the business" started.

Chapter 15
September 1915

Sannayat needs no description, as it is just a name on the river bank (meaning, I believe, "a winding path"), with a prospect of blistering desert on one side and marsh on the other. The camp was pitched, but no perimeter built and no defences constructed, with the exception of a few very shallow trenches for the outpost line, and a small post which was to be garrisoned when we marched on; for "the offensive spirit was to be fostered." In other words, it was hoped that the Turks might be fools enough to move out from the Es Sinn lines to attack us, in the event of which we should fall upon them in the open; but the Turks refused to oblige.

However, we had quite a lot of false alarms and excitement, and, on the 19th, the guns opened up a furious bombardment and it looked like business. The order came for the whole force to "Stand to," followed by an order to fall out but not remove equipment. We remained with our loins girded for about an hour, when again the guns started up and the order came to fall in immediately; we then marched out of camp about a mile to the north, but, after an hour pleasantly spent in admiring the scenery, we returned again to continue our interrupted Sunday breakfasts. The explanation of it all afterwards appeared to be that a large flock of sheep had been mistaken for enemy cavalry and thoroughly shelled by the heavy guns—it was said, very effectively—so we hoped, in vain, for fresh mutton for dinner.

Such mistakes were constantly occurring owing to the difficulties of observation, for, in addition to mirages, there was nearly always a sand-storm blowing which made it almost impossible to see any distance. Observation posts were established at both ends of the camp, and an officer and two signallers always on duty at each, in two-hour reliefs—it was impossible to remain on duty longer, for the suffocating dust and the strain of looking through glasses over the glaring desert made it most trying work. In addition to observation posts, the cavalry were constantly patrolling to the west and south, but met with no organised resistance, though, on one or two occasions, they suffered heavily in bickers with mounted Arabs.

The Indian cavalry on their big Walers with heavy equipment were always at a disadvantage against the extremely mobile Arabs, mounted on nippy little ponies and carrying nothing but a rifle and bandolier. But, in spite of constant observation and patrolling, the enemy cavalry, we discovered later, had evaded us, and, marching wide round our left flank, were able to bring off a tip-and-run raid against our communications at Sheikh Saad while we were engaged at Es Sinn.

The last reinforcements were now arriving, and the VIth Division was strengthened by the 30th Brigade of the XIIth Division, less one battalion (24th Punjabis). The R.F.C., suffering from lack of machines and pilots, received a welcome addition in two seaplanes of the R.N.A.S., which looked very large and imposing as they buzzed up and down the river, though, unfortunately, their wireless proved too heavy and had to be dismantled.

There was also one decidedly humorous addition. Since before we had left Amara each regiment had been promised an extra section of machine-guns—that is, four guns per regiment instead of two, as it was known that the Turks were well supplied in this very important arm. So extra gun-teams had been carefully trained and extra mules drawn—we counted in pleasurable anticipation our four gun establishments and only waited for the guns. By the time we had reached Sannayat we had long ago given up all hope, so were much surprised to hear that the guns had arrived.

But one look was enough—the much-advertised machine-guns were strange and uncouth monsters, mounted on pram wheels and looking more like mangles than anything else: they told us that you fed them through a hopper—gently—and that they had been quite the thing in the early eighties! We shed tears and left them. Later, after a long search and many inquiries through all the force, one man was at last discovered who knew how to work them. He was an old white-haired *sepoy*—a reservist—who remembered in his youth how they had instructed him in the ways of such guns. So, he and a few old friends and the strange weapons were told off for duty on the "L. of C."—and that was the result of asking India for more machine-guns!

The aeroplanes were busy carrying out daily reconnaissances of the enemy position and doing their best to photograph the trenches and redoubts, a matter of some difficulty, as none of the machines were fitted for photography, so that the observer had to lean half out with the camera in his hands and chance a "snap" over the edge of the lower plane—not a very satisfactory way of doing an important job. On the 18th, a reconnaissance had been carried out on the left bank (the river had been bridged by pontoons) by the 7th Lancers and the 20th Punjabis, who made their way nearly up to the Turks' front line and captured a hostile patrol of one officer and four men, besides gaining some useful information as to the nature of the ground.

By September 21st the first maps of the Es Sinn position were issued. These were afterwards added to and corrected, but the first version was quite enough to show that we had a big job on hand—about twelve miles of trenches astride the river, strengthened by many redoubts, with plenty of wire, and a perfect maze of communication trenches in rear. In front of some of the redoubts appeared, on the map, strange marks—straight lines ending in a sort of broad arrow—and these were a subject of much speculation: no one could interpret them, not even the makers of the map.

They appeared in the photograph and that was all that could be said. Then someone very inconveniently suggested that they were saps leading to gas-apparatus, and for lack of any better theory this was considered quite possible, for it was known that some Germans had lately arrived. There was no kind of chance of making any sort of gas-masks, so the outlook was particularly pleasant. But as it was, only "the day" itself could prove what those queer lines really stood for.

By the 25th everything was completed, and that evening tents and kits, in fact all our belongings except one blanket each, were put on board the ships, and the force moved out from camp at 5 a.m. on Sunday, 26th September, the 16th and 17th Brigades and the Cavalry Brigade on the right bank, the 18th Brigade on the left. At Sannayat were left men unfit to march, and one gun of the Volunteer Battery: the next post on the L. of C. was at Ali-el-Gherbi, fifty miles away.

A march of about two hours brought us on the right bank to Chahéla Mounds, about 7000 yards from the enemy's position on the right bank. The march was unopposed and without incident, except for the explosion of two small mines on the road, which unfortunately caused some casualties. On the left bank the 18th Brigade marched to Nakhailat village, meeting with very little opposition. As the battle may really be said to have been begun from the time we occupied the

Chahéla Mounds on the morning of the 26th, some more detailed account is necessary of the Turkish position and of General Townshend's daring and most successful plan for dealing with it.

The troops at his disposal were the VIth Division, the 6th Cavalry Brigade (less "S" Battery R.H.A., and itself much under strength), two battalions from 30th Brigade XIIth Division, and the Maxim Battery (army troops); three batteries R.F.A., Hampshire Howitzer Battery, one section 86th and one section 104th Batteries R.G.A. (heavy), and a battery of 4.7-inches mounted in horse-barges and comparatively ineffective. All regiments were below strength, and the infantry did not number more than 10,000 all told, while the Cavalry Brigade was only about 700 strong; all artillery, with the exception of the Field Batteries, was obsolete and inaccurate.

The Turks had in position two divisions, with a reserve in rear, estimated at 10,000 to 12,000 infantry with about thirty guns (all, but two batteries of Krupp field guns, more or less obsolete); their cavalry was an unknown quantity, but believed to number between 600 and 1000 regulars, without Arab auxiliaries.

These troops were entrenched on both banks, one division on each, with a reserve on the left bank near a bridge about three miles in rear of the front lines.

The defences themselves had been most thoroughly constructed, were exceedingly difficult to locate, and, in all cases, commanded a perfectly open field of fire. There was no cover whatever for the attacking force.

On the right bank redoubts and trenches, protected by sunken wire, extended from the river bank into the desert south-east for about five miles, ending, on the extreme right, in a strong redoubt. Immediately behind this line there were the ruined banks of a high-level canal about 30 feet high and 50 feet apart. The forward bank was entrenched; on the reverse of the rear bank were emplacements for heavy guns, and down below were dug-outs, shelter trenches, and horse-lines. The fire trenches were supplied with water by an aqueduct leading from a pumping station, three miles in rear, while covered ways also led down to the river. The river itself was blocked just downstream of the trenches by an obstruction which was commanded by rifle and gun fire. The ground in front of the redoubts nearest the river was mined.

On the left bank the defences were not continuous but, if anything, stronger. The front of seven miles here was broken by three marshes—marked in the sketch Marsh I., II., and III.—and the intervening ground was strongly entrenched. The position was thus divided into three sections.

Section 1, a redoubt and trenches, had its right flank on the river, commanding the obstruction and the approaches on the opposite bank; its left flank was securely protected by Marsh I.

Section 2, a series of fire trenches and gun emplacements, very strongly protected by wire, spiked pits, and mines, completely closed the gap between Marsh I. and Marsh II.

Section 3, the largest group of all, consisting of four redoubts, fire trenches, and gun emplacements, stood between Marsh II. and Marsh III.; the left flank of this section was turned back due north-west by the addition of a new redoubt shortly before our attack.

North-east of Marsh III., and almost, perhaps quite, joining it, lay the great Suwechi Marsh, stretching for miles to the north-west and south-east, down to the river near Sannayat.

Gun positions were well hidden, but there appeared to be twenty guns on the left bank, and only six on the right, four of which were probably 4-inch howitzers.

A first glance at the map, taking into account the strength and extent of the defences and the lie of the land, would probably suggest that the easiest, in fact the only likely, solution to the problem, was to turn the enemy's right flank: the positions were apparently weaker, there were no marshes, and the right flank rested only on a redoubt.

These obvious arguments were probably just what Nur-ed-Din was counting on; but they failed to tempt General Townshend.

If it were possible, there was one great advantage to turning the enemy's left flank—it was his strategic flank, and his line of retreat lay along this left bank; trouble there would interfere with his withdrawal to Baghdad. In spite of the difficulties and the great strength of such impassable obstacles as the marshes, there was one weak spot—and in that lay the possibility. The gap between Marshes II. and III. was designed to be closed by Section 3 of the defences. But aeroplane reconnaissances and reports from Arabs showed that Marsh III. was drying up—the water-line was receding northwards, and consequently there was a gap, small, but daily widening, between the northern (left) flank of the defences and the protecting marsh.

On the 24th September this gap was only 300 yards across, but General Townshend decided that it was the key to the position—the Turks would no doubt dig to span the gap, but the marsh would prob

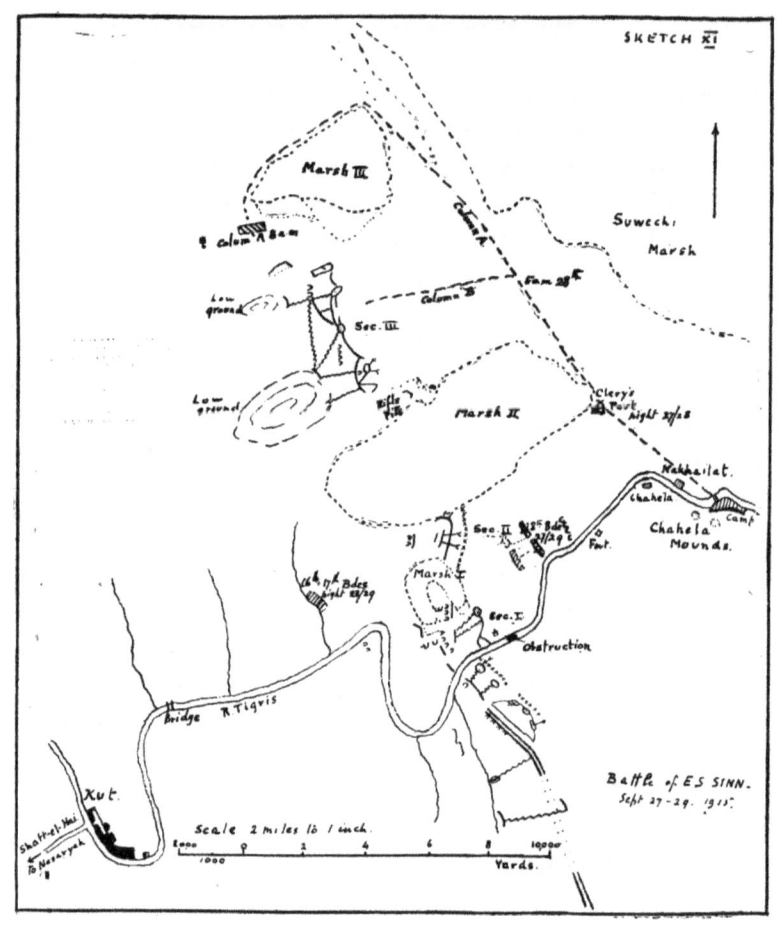

HRB sketch Battle of Es Sinn

ably recede too quickly for them.

We were to force our way through this narrow defile and turn the enemy's left.

But, till the last moment, Nur-ed-Din was to be allowed to think that we were obligingly going to fall in with his plans, and with that object a concentration and feint were to be made on the right bank, before the main force was transferred to the left bank for the decisive attack.

To return to the morning of the 26th and the Chahéla Mounds. As soon as we arrived at 7 a.m., camp was pitched—every available tent was put up, so as to make a big show and persuade the enemy that we had really "come to stay" on the right bank. We had not long to wait before they showed that they had seen us, for shells soon began to burst about camp. However, there were plenty of ditches and little damage was done, though they made rather good practice at the navy, H.M.S. *Comet, Shaitan*, and *Santana*, lying near the right bank, which were forced to withdraw downstream.

During the day another of the few remaining aeroplanes was unfortunately put out of action by capsizing on landing and smashing its lower plane.

By the evening of the 26th the final maps were issued, and we knew the plan of operations.

That night the 104th Rifles and a squadron of cavalry moved across the enemy's front on the left bank under cover of darkness, and took up position at Clery's Post on the south-east corner of Marsh II.; two days' rations for two brigades accompanied them.

On the morning of the 27th a feint was to be made up the right bank, while the 18th Brigade on the left bank advanced and dug in within 3000 yards of Section I. defences.

That night the pontoon bridge was to be thrown across the river after dark, and the 16th and 17th Brigades and Field Artillery and Cavalry were to cross and move on Clery's Post, and, divided into two columns under General Delamain, they were to march across the enemy's front to be in position to attack at dawn on the 28th. Column "B"—the Dorsets, the 117th, and the 22nd Company Sappers and Miners—was to attack the centre of Section III. frontally. Column "A"—the 17th Brigade and the remainder of the 16th—was to force its way through the gap and turn the left.

At the same time the 18th Brigade was to pin the enemy to their positions in Section 1 and Section 2, and as soon as the flank attack farther north had taken effect, press in with a frontal attack. Their at

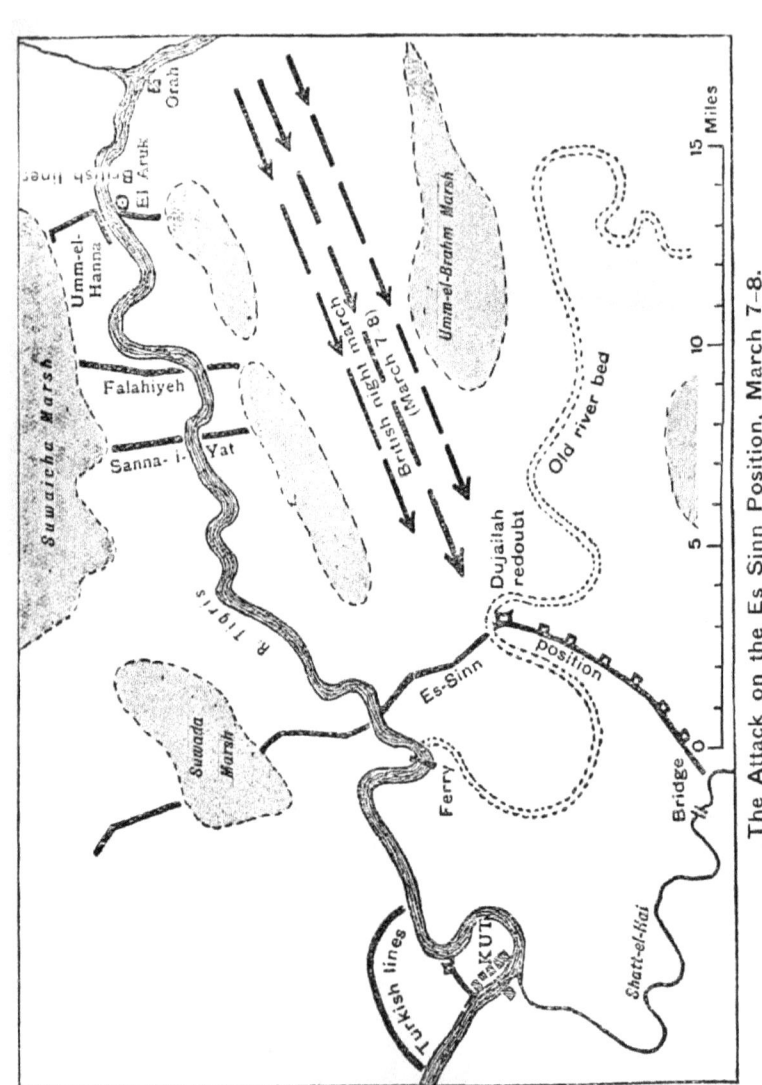

The Attack on the Es Sinn Position, March 7–8.

tack was to be covered by the heavy guns which were to be landed from their barges and dug in in rear during the night of the 27th. The Turkish bridge at Magasis was, if possible, to be bombed by a seaplane, so as to prevent the enemy shifting troops from one bank to the other. On the right bank was to remain only the two battalions of the 30th Brigade under Colonel Climo, to hold on to the bridgehead, supported by the 4.7s on the river, and the fire of the 18th Brigade on the opposite bank.

It was decidedly a daring plan. It entailed a movement by nearly the whole force right across the enemy's front at a distance in places of only 5000 yards, and over ground which it had been impossible to reconnoitre beforehand. In the event of accidents, retreat down the left bank was cut off by the Suwechi Marsh, and the only way back to the right bank was by one bridge defended against the possible attack of at least a division by only two weak battalions. One mistake that night—a noise, a light, a spy in the camp, or a chance enemy patrol—would mean failure and probably worse than failure; on the other hand, success meant a big victory and the saving of many casualties.

At 4 a.m. on September 27th, the Oxford and Bucks Light Infantry, the 119th, one section of guns and one squadron of cavalry (the whole under Lieutenant-Colonel Darley, 119th) moved out from camp, and, by the time it was light, were deployed some 4000 yards from the high-level canal. By 6 a.m. heavy rifle fire could be heard from the left bank as the 18th Brigade advanced, and soon the guns of both sides were hard at it.

It was a cloudless morning with a certain amount of mist over the river and the most extraordinary mirage effects, which made it exceedingly difficult to make out what was happening; it was impossible to spot the enemy guns.

On the right bank the banks of the canal showed up like lofty cliffs, broken and crumbling, and apparently miles away, while beneath them shimmered a boundless sea strangely dotted here and there with huge trees and crossed at intervals by squads of men with immensely long legs, who appeared to be walking on the water. We knew, of course, that there was no such wide expanse of water, no such trees—the men (though not their elongated legs!) were probably real, though it was impossible to say.

While the 18th Brigade, covered by the heavy guns on their barges, was digging in on the left bank within 3000 yards of the enemy, the small force on the right bank was told to make much of itself; but, in spite of the thorough self-advertisement of everybody—including an officer who sat on an ant-heap, reading the *Times* most obtrusively— no notice was taken. Never a shell came their way, and they returned to camp by 1.15 p.m.

Meanwhile, the 18th Brigade, though well shelled, had got where it wanted to, and was dug in with its left on the river. At 4 p.m. a further feint was made on the right bank by the Dorsets and the 20th Punjabis, who advanced along the river and started to dig trenches where the Turks could see them. As soon as it grew dark they knocked off and returned to camp.

All day working parties had been employed in building roads and cutting a ramp down to the river, and as soon as darkness fell the pontoon bridge, till then kept out of sight, was swung across and made fast. It was covered with mud and camel-thorn to deaden the sound of marching. The large camp pitched the day before was left standing, the tents tenantless, to impose upon the Turks. Evidently the desired effect was secured, as it was heavily shelled most of the night. Only the Gurkhas and half the 67th under Colonel Climo remained, in an entrenched position guarding the approaches to the bridge.

By 6.30 p.m. the Artillery, the Cavalry Brigade, and the 16th and 17th Infantry Brigades were fallen in, and we shuffled off through the darkness, down the ramp and on to the bridge. Absolute silence was of the greatest importance, and this was impressed on all ranks—no talking, and not a light to be shown.

There were some hitches in the passage of the bridge, as the ramps were a bit steep for the transport carts, but at last we got over successfully and out on to the open desert beyond on our way to Clery's Post. For the next two miles, though marching across the enemy's front, there was little risk, as the 18th Brigade was between us and them. This was just as well, for, though dead silence was the order of the day—or rather night—there seemed to be a terrible amount of noise: every wheel in the transport seemed to screech and scream, while the "*drabis*" (native drivers) were, of course, seized with a fit of coughing. Anyone who knows the *drabis'* cough will realise what this means— he has a good rake round and suppresses nothing!

To finally "put the lid on it," some of the transport got out of place and bumped along between the column and the Turkish line, while the drivers carried on frenzied arguments with their friends 100 yards away. Knowing the importance of silence and the way in which sound carries over the desert at night, this was simply agonising. One felt a savage longing to knock every gibbering native on the head!

By 9.30 p.m. we reached Clery's Post, where we found the 104th and the squadron of cavalry who had been there since the night of the 26th. As far as they knew they had been unobserved.

The two brigades formed a square with horses and mules picketed in the middle, and those few unoccupied by outpost duties and care of the horses, lay down to have a sleep while they could; but the less fortunate had to take the animals to the marsh for a drink, though, when they got there, the mules would not touch the water.

During the halt food was served out; water was scarce, for as much as possible had to be kept for the next day, and the marsh, reported drinkable, was found to be horribly brackish, though probably the Arabs who had reported on it were in the habit of drinking it. Water bottles and company "*packals*" (water tanks carried on mules) had been filled before we left camp, and all carried a haversack ration: these supplies lasted us till the 29th.

At 1 a.m. on the 28th, Column A and Column B formed up, B leading, and we started out on the last lap. The two columns marched together at first until opposite B's objective. Second line transport and brigade reserve ammunition was left at the post.

Now began the most difficult part of our march and the most dangerous, as we had nothing between our flank and the enemy. Owing to the marshes and the necessity of the two columns deploying in exactly the right place and at the right moment, the greatest accuracy as to distance and direction was needed, both exceedingly difficult to secure, as the route had only been reconnoitred by aeroplane. So, it was not surprising that a mistake was made—perhaps a fortunate mistake as things turned out.

Till 5 a.m. we plugged on in suffocating dust through the darkness. The atmosphere was damp and heavy, like clammy cotton-wool, and at every halt the men would fall asleep at once, some of them as they stood, overcome by the closeness of the air. They were still none too fit, and, since leaving Sannayat, sleep had been scarce and work plenty.

Shortly after 5 a.m. Column B, with General Delamain and two batteries, left the column, wheeling south-west for their frontal attack. Column A, the 17th Brigade, and the 104th and 20th Punjabis of the 16th Brigade, with cavalry and guns continued north-west in order to arrive at the base of Marsh III. before turning in to round the Turkish left.

CHAPTER 16

Kut and Its Conquerors

When the maps on which we were working were issued, there had been no, or scarcely any, gap between Marsh III. and the Suwechi Marsh; the only possibility of turning the enemy's position had been to force the gap between his flank and Marsh III. It was for that gap that we were marching.

But, somehow or other, there was a miscalculation. After General Delamain and Column B left us we expected to march only another thousand yards or so before wheeling left towards the gap; but we kept on and on and, when about 6 a.m. the sun rose, we saw that there were marshes on either side of us—there was no gap to the south-west! What had happened was, that, since the last reconnaissance, Marsh III. and the Suwechi Marsh had both receded, leaving a defile of dry land between, up which we were now marching; at the same time Marsh III., the gap which was our objective, and Section III. of the Turkish line, were all farther to the south than shown on the map. Consequently, the column was considerably too far north before it attempted to turn west and found Marsh III. in the way. So, the only thing was to go round by the north of the marsh—a much, longer march than originally intended—and this the column did. About 6.30 we opened into artillery formation as we began to round the northern end of the marsh, and, soon afterwards, the cavalry who from the left flank had now moved out ahead, were fired on by patrols. These were soon disposed of by machine-gun fire.

It was not until seven o'clock that we were clear of the marsh and found that, in consequence of our mistake, we were almost behind the enemy's left flank, in an exceedingly favourable position: furthermore, a newly-constructed redoubt beyond the enemy's original left showed that we should have had a hot time if we had tried to come in south

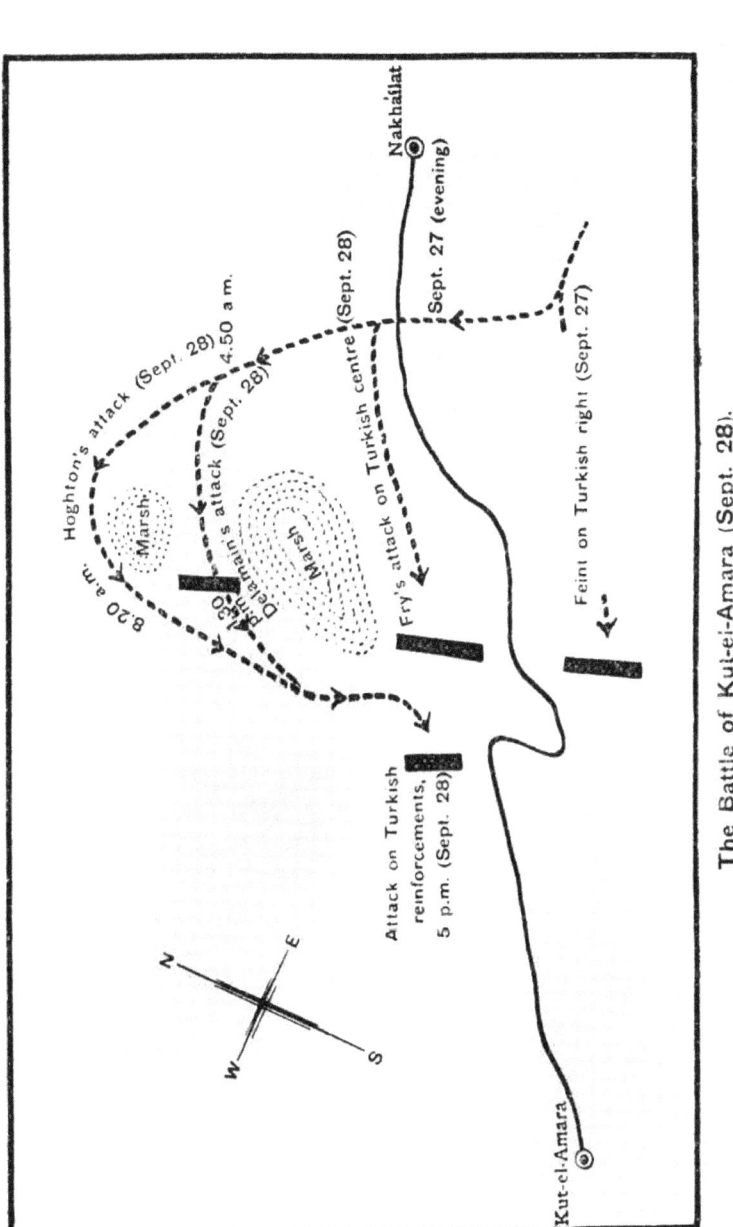

The Battle of Kut-el-Amara (Sept. 28).

of the marsh.

But for Column B our failure to be on the spot up to time was serious, as their frontal attack against a very strong redoubt had to be pushed without our help on the flank as arranged: consequently, they were held up for some time. Before we could move to help the frontal attack, the new redoubt on the extreme left had to be cleared, and this was done by the 17th Brigade machine-guns with the 20th and 104th at 8 a.m., and immediately the flank attack on Section 3 was launched; the cavalry meanwhile moving out to the right accompanied by an armoured car. The works here were found more formidable even than was expected, several supposed communication trenches proving to be enfilading fire trenches.

However, the 17th Brigade pushed hard and enabled the frontal attack to get on, the Dorsets, 117th, and 22nd Company of Sappers and Miners carrying the opposing trenches by assault at nine o'clock, while, soon after, the Oxfordshire Light Infantry captured the next redoubt to the south. Two counter-attacks had been launched from the south-west in the meantime, but the 22nd Punjabis, supported by the 76th Battery, effectually squashed these, and freed our right flank from what at one moment appeared rather a nasty position.

By 2 p.m. the whole of Section 3 of the defences was in our hands, together with a battery of guns and many prisoners. The 119th were left behind to garrison the captured works. But the development of further counterattacks from the south-west (the direction of the bridge) necessitated the 17th Brigade, under General Hoghton, moving out west of Marsh II., while General Delamain, with the 16th Brigade, moved south. The 17th Brigade, supported by 76th and 82nd Batteries, were successful in forcing a retirement, though the enemy's artillery—particularly the "german" (*i.e.* modern q.f.) guns—inflicted a good many casualties. But the 16th Brigade were held up, and about 3 p.m. General Delamain ordered the 17th Brigade to rejoin him; accordingly, it retired to the western edge of Marsh II., where the two brigades were again concentrated at 4 p.m.

During this movement, the brigade ammunition carts and a battery limbered up, were caught under a severe artillery fire, and a good deal of damage was done, particularly among the horses—every horse of the gun-team was hit. But the Turk gunners, as usual, were erratic; having got plump on to their target, right away, they proceeded to look for other game elsewhere, and—luckily for us—only half did the job. This was always a very noticeable feature of the enemy's artillery—they did not seem to know when they were well off.

Everyone by now was pretty well beat, and most horribly thirsty. All day there had been a blazing sun and a hot wind laden with dust—most water-bottles were empty, and the mules with the water-tanks, after the transport had been bombarded, had kicked up their heels and gone off anywhere. The remaining mules were nearly mad with thirst, and dashed at the marsh, pulling men after them, where they immediately got bogged in the mud, and were sniped as they lay. Some men tried to drink the water, but it was pure Epsom salts—both in taste and effect. In the meanwhile, no news had been received from General Fry and the 18th Brigade, who, "according to plan," were to have shoved in a frontal attack down by the river as soon as our flank attack took effect; so, a halt was called while the two brigades were re-forming, and news was awaited from him.

At 5 p.m. an aeroplane arrived with a message from General Fry, to say that the 18th Brigade was held up and could not get on unless we could put in a flank attack. So, the 16th and 17th Brigades moved off at once towards the south-east to see what could be done.

We had gone hardly a mile before suddenly a heavy fire was opened on us from the south-west. The two brigades immediately wheeled to face it, and the two field batteries and the howitzer battery unlimbered and came into action. It was hard to see exactly where or what our enemy was, for we were moving through long grass straight into the eye of the setting sun; all that could be seen were the flashes from a battery they had brought into action, while the sound of the bullets showed that there were plenty of them. The attacking waves went forward. An hour before, the men had been dead-beat with thirst, tired out, dropping, and lying where they dropped, with little thought of anything but water; now, as if a new lease of life had been granted them, they swept on in an attack at a pace which in the peaceful days of manoeuvres would assuredly have been criticized as "impossible under real conditions."

The guns had to cease fore for want of light, but the infantry went on unsupported over the flat ground with never a halt, straight into the blinding streak of sunset; a thousand yards, a charge nearly all the way, brought them into their enemy, and, with a cheer, they were at them. Some got away, some were bayoneted, and the rest, together with a battery of guns and two machine-guns, were captured; and then the night shut down suddenly like a black curtain.

No one knew exactly where we were. It was thought at first that

AN ARMOURED CAR AND CREW

the bank of the river had been reached and that we could get water; but no such luck—we found that we were only in a dry *wadi* and the river must be somewhere out in front—but where and how far it was not known.

Patrols might have been sent out to clear up the situation; but, unfortunately, it was impossible, for, as soon as the *wadi* had been cleared, reaction set in. The men were so dead-beat that they literally could not understand an order: thirst and exhaustion had produced a stupefying effect.

A few volunteers went back to try and find the wounded—a very difficult job—as most were lying in long grass and spread over a wide area; but at all costs they had to be found, for it was known that Arabs were on the prowl in our rear. What medical arrangements there were had proved most ineffective. With the exception of two motor-ambulances lately arrived, there was not, nor had there been since the commencement of the campaign, any provision for the transport of sick and wounded by land, while any form of hospital ship was equally lacking for river-work. The wounded had to be transported by the ordinary iron A.T. carts across the desert, and shipped on to river steamers "converted" (but very moderately so) for their accommodation. The collecting stations and field ambulances had early been lost, and all day one had met wounded men and stretcher-bearers wandering about asking where on earth these could be found.

Some of these small bodies wandered about for hours before they found help; others, lying wounded alone, were robbed and murdered by the Arabs and, in some cases, horribly mutilated; others died from exhaustion and cold, whose lives could have been saved if only they had been found sooner.

In the meantime, the *wadi* was, as far as possible, put into a state of defence, and a careful look-out kept for possible counter-attacks. Beyond, in the darkness, one heard the groans of some of the Turkish wounded, who were gradually collected and brought in; otherwise there was not a sound.

That night (28th-29th) the temperature dropped 50 degrees, and it was bitterly cold, so that what with thirst and hunger, we were not sorry to see the dawn. Our scarecrow appearance might have provoked a smile, but that nearly everyone's lips were cracked and black, and facial contortions, under the circumstances, were exceedingly painful! In front of us we could see no sign of the river, but only open desert dotted with bundles and boxes and mule-loads—signs of the Turks' rapid departure the previous evening; about a mile away was a low jungle of scrub, beyond which we judged the river must lie.

Presently an aeroplane arrived with a message, to say that we were to press on to the river immediately—the enemy was in full retreat; but what this really meant no one realised till later.

The river was reached without opposition, and none of us are ever likely to forget those first mouthfuls of muddy Tigris—champagne wasn't in it—nor an exhibition of discipline which, though expected at the time, is rather remarkable when one looks back on it. There was only a limited space of bank where the river was shallow enough for the men to wade in and drink, so that regiments had to take turns: someone had to go first while the others stood fast and watched their pals lapping—and that is a hard test when your lips are blackening with thirst and your tongue feels like a wad of hot cardboard! Here it was that we heard the full story and learnt that the whole position had been evacuated.

The enemy on the right bank had begun to leave during the afternoon of the previous day (28th), but, owing to mirage and difficulty of observation, had not been spotted. They had been streaming away to the river and their ships all the evening and through the night and had managed to get away all their guns—including heavies—from that side. How they managed it is rather a mystery, but the Turk had always proved a quick mover, and this was a particularly fine performance.

On the left bank, too, they had played the same game. During the night the troops in Sections 1 and 2, opposite the 18th Brigade, had withdrawn; leaving only light covering detachments in their trenches, and, profiting by the gap between the 16th and 17th Brigades and the river, had slipped through without a sound, and got clear away under our noses. If only we had known our whereabouts and been able to push on that night, we should have been across their line of retreat and might have caught the lot.

It was reported that Kut was already evacuated and the enemy in full retreat up the left bank with their ships some way ahead of them.

However, we had turned Nur-ed-din out of a position which he had boasted he could hold for six months, captured 1153 prisoners and 14 guns, besides inflicting heavy losses, estimated at over 3000, on the enemy, at a cost to ourselves of 1233 killed and wounded. Kut—a position of the greatest strategic importance, the capture of which was the object of our advance—was now ours.

Though perhaps not the perfect victory he would have chosen and had hoped for, the battle of Kut was a great success, and proved once more the qualities of our commander's generalship. It was planned and fought under great difficulties in the initial stages, from the lack of transport and very extended line of communications, necessitating improvisation and makeshift; in the latter stages, from the difficulties of adequate reconnaissance and communication.

The actual positions to be attacked were exceedingly strong, the flanks (apparently) secure, the approaches over dead flat ground without a vestige of cover. Throughout the actual day of the battle, dust and mirage made visibility as bad as possible, and observation was so difficult that the artillery had constantly to cease fire as they could not distinguish friend from foe, real from unreal, in the bewildering mirage. Consequently, the infantry had often to advance without any artillery support whatever.

Communication throughout was difficult; the operations extended over a wide front and the columns were at times far separated; aeroplanes were scarce, and every telephone wire was cut almost as soon as laid, by Arabs who slunk about in rear.

As soon as it had been established that the enemy were in retreat, pursuit was organised. Already, early in the morning of the 29th, the cavalry had made their way into Kut, and, finding it unoccupied, had pushed on along the caravan road which runs along the left bank of the river from here to Baghdad. They overtook the Turks in full retreat along this road, but, finding them withdrawing as a still intact and organised army, covered by a strong rear-guard with artillery, our weak squadrons unaccompanied by guns ("S" Battery could not be brought upriver in time for the battle) were obliged to hold off until reinforcements could take up the pursuit.

The 18th Brigade was at once detailed for this, and, embarking on the ships, started off upstream in the afternoon, the 16th Brigade being sent to occupy Kut, as there was not enough transport to send this brigade after the Turks as well, while the 17th Brigade was to go into camp on the left bank, some way upstream of Section I., and from there clean up the battlefield. There were a good many unburied dead, both ours and the enemy's, still lying out, and a great deal of material to be salved.

Just before the 17th Brigade moved off down the bank towards its new camp, H.M.S. *Comet* steamed past, scarred and battered almost past recognition. It was then that we heard the story of a very gallant exploit.

On the evening of the 28th, as soon as General Townshend knew that the flank attack from the north had been so successful, he ordered the flotilla to attempt to push upstream past the obstruction in order to get at the Turks' bridge at Magasis.

The obstruction was found to consist of two iron barges aground on either bank, from which ran heavy cables to a sunken *mahela* in midstream. The whole of that reach of the river was commanded by the Turkish guns, while the obstruction itself was under a point-blank fire from guns and rifles. Lieutenant Commander Cookson, R.N., in the *Comet*, acting S.N.O., led his ships upstream under cover of darkness, but was immediately spotted by the Turks, who opened an exceedingly heavy fire. The *Comet* went on, and, though now under a point-blank fire at a range of a few yards only, attempted to break the cables by ramming: they held fast.

Nearly all the crew were wounded and her guns were out of action, but Commander Cookson laid his ship alongside the *mahela* to see what could be done. He decided that the only thing was to board and try and cut the cables, but, since it was plainly practically certain death for any man to attempt it under that hail of bullets, he, to borrow the words of General Townshend's dispatch, "took an axe and went himself." No sooner had he started to climb from the *Comet* to the *mahela* than he fell, hit in a score of places: his body was recovered from the river immediately, but he was found to be dead.

The *Comet* had by now hardly a sound man on board, and, as nothing further could be done with the obstruction, a withdrawal was ordered and the flotilla returned downstream. Commander Cookson was awarded a posthumous V.C. for this splendidly gallant action.

The 17th Brigade received with very mixed feelings the tidings that they were to remain behind to clear up—a peculiarly unpleasant job in a hot climate; but it was not possible to push on any more troops than the 18th Brigade in pursuit, as there was a shortage of coal and oil fuel for the ships. This, we learnt, was due to a whole convoy of *mahelas* having been successfully attacked and sunk near Sheikh Saad by a body of Turkish cavalry, with four guns. They had, it appeared, moved far round our left flank, marching wide in the desert, and slipping past us at Sannayat had chipped in in rear: this accounted for the very few cavalry the enemy had put in during the battle. At Sheikh Saad they had done their job very thoroughly, sinking and burning every ship of the convoy and capturing the small escort, besides a telegraph launch and repair party. However, it was rather a flea-bite, all things considered, and it was in no way due to this that the pursuit failed.

In the evening, there were many heartening rumours, to the effect that some of the Turks had been overtaken and 2000 prisoners made, besides a gunboat, the *Pioneer*, which was said to have stuck in the mud: it was considered likely that the whole Turkish Army would be captured. But rumour lied, and all our fond hopes were destined to be rudely shattered, for, in riding into Kut next day, the 30th, we found that the 18th Brigade's ships were still in sight, only a few miles upriver: it was we, not they, who were stuck in the mud. It became plain that the enemy had made good their escape, and that no hope of catching them now remained.

But Kut was distinctly interesting as a newly captured town, only entered by its captors the previous day. To see the crowded bazaars, the shops doing a roaring trade, and the exceedingly affable population, one would never have guessed that we were such newcomers among a technically hostile population. There was no sign of any nervousness or doubt as to our intentions— rather the opposite; it was even said that directly the cavalry arrived they were presented by an Arab with a claim for compensation, as somebody had ridden over his lucerne! The late Turkish commander of the place had been encouraging the inhabitants' loyalty by shooting and hanging the too-obviously lukewarm, which may have accounted for their effusive attitude.

Kut, as a town, is a poor place, smaller and dirtier than Amara, but possesses—or possessed in those days—rather a good mosque with a leaning minaret, and extensive bazaars, though they are so hidden away that one is apt not to discover them. A few brick houses on the river front and on the streets leading to it are the only civilized dwellings in the place, and one of these it was discovered had been turned into an arsenal. In it we captured a large store of shells varying from 4.8 to pom-poms, and a tremendous quantity of small-arm ammunition: the Turks had neglected to burn or destroy anything.

"Clearing-up" a battlefield is a peculiarly unpleasant duty, but in this case it was certainly interesting, as one was able to examine at leisure, and in comparative safety, the whole of the long line of defences—comparative safety, because there were mines and unexploded grenades lying about everywhere. Some of the mines were contact affairs, but the larger ones were arranged in front of the wire to be fired by keys operated from the trenches: In no case did the Turk responsible keep his head sufficiently to press the button at the right moment! These mines were the explanation of the strange broad-arrow-like marks on the map. The soil turned up in burying the charges and the cables had been moister than the surface of the desert, and though the excavations had, of course, been carefully filled in, the moist earth had shown up to the observers in the planes as dark lines.

Walking round the defences on the left bank, one realised what extraordinarily few casualties we had had, considering their strength and siting. Except where there was wire, the works were quite indistinguishable at 100 yards distance, the 9-inch command of the parapets being so gradually sloped, and the trenches so cleverly sited that they were impossible to spot. The wire, though, was bad stuff and weak, and in several redoubts the headcover had been faced with concrete which had dried white and so showed up very clearly. All trenches were beautifully dug, deep and narrow, the fire trenches very solidly traversed—provided with huge jars of water in recesses every fifty yards; the communication trenches ran about a mile back in rear of the redoubts, 10 to 12 feet deep, and provided with signboards at all junctions.

Most redoubts were provided with overhead cover of poles, brushwood, and earth, and there was generally one large dug-out about 40 feet square in the middle—perhaps for officers: two redoubts in Section 3 boasted wells. Section 2, besides mines in front of the wire, had a second course of most grisly pits, about 9 feet deep and 4 feet across, tapering to 3 feet at the bottom, which was decorated with a 3-feet sharpened stake: not at all nice. On the whole we found very little worth salving, though the Arabs must have gathered literally hundreds of rifles and a good deal of ammunition—a bad business, as the Arab is not to be trusted with such things.

As soon as the left bank was finished, we crossed by the bridge, in order to clear the position on the right. Whether the Turks ever contemplated using this bridge to transfer troops from one bank to the other it is hard to say, but, judging from its condition, they cannot have done so during the battle, and large landing-stages and ramps on both banks just below, made it appear that they had relied on the ferry. We found the bridge in the last stages of disrepair, so wobbly that it was impossible to bring a field gun across, and an attempt to pass a mule cart over ended in its going through, and the untimely death of one mule.

From what could be seen of it, the right bank seemed hardly as strong as the left, but for all that it was pretty thoroughly done. The redoubts nearest the river were provided with sunken wire, perfectly concealed, and the approaches were heavily mined. In rear of the first line of redoubts and trenches the high parallel banks of the canal would have proved bad to get at, while any troops in rear were under cover from anything but very high-angle fire, and completely sheltered from view. The water supply was most thoroughly arranged for by an aqueduct leading from a pumping station direct to the trenches, and also by covered ways down to the river. We found that, here again, the Arabs had been too soon for us, and nothing remained—not even the wire, though we successfully retrieved two guns. But, to be honest, it must be said that these were antediluvian weapons: 7-pounder brass cannon, bearing the date, in Persian, 1181 (*A.H.*)—which is equivalent to *A.D.* 1802! And, to be still more honest, it must be owned that of our total capture of fourteen guns, eight were these brass muzzle-loaders, and the remaining six semi-obsolete Krupps: all the q.f. guns were got away.

But the Turk who decided to use these museum pieces must have been possessed with a certain sense of humour, though an officer in the 18th Brigade, who was hit by a 3-lb. iron ball, at its third bounce, could not see the fun of it. He said he would have to take his meals standing up for three weeks, and that Mesopotamia was bad enough without that!

We hung about for some time on the right bank, digging for treasure-trove in the shape of the enemy's heavy guns, which the Arabs said had been buried. They showed us many spots to dig, and, when we had got nicely down to it, they faded into the landscape. No doubt they enjoyed such harmless little jokes.

Finally, we gave it up as a bad job, and, with our two brass cannons towed by mules, we recrossed the bridge and, on 4th October, joined the remainder of the 16th and 17th Brigades in camp on the outskirts of Kut.

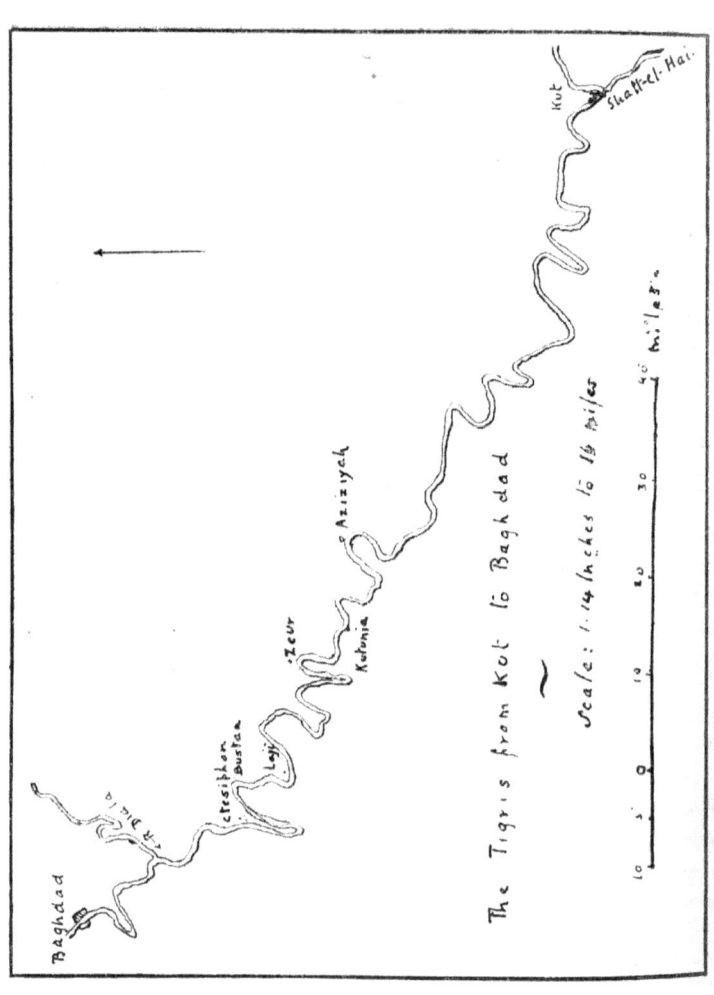

HRB sketch the Tigris from Kut to Baghdad

Chapter 17

On the March

Kut, or rather the desert just outside the town, afforded quite decent quarters at this time of the year, for the sun even at midday was not too hot for the double-fly tents which by now had been issued: the only unpleasantness was caused by the dust-laden wind which blew at intervals.

North of the town there was a certain amount of cultivation among the palms—plots of lucerne and vegetables and a few fruit trees, though the gardens here were poor affairs compared to those at Amara; all beyond was open desert, though much intersected by dry canals. Only the ruins of these remained, but the height of the banks and their extent, stretching away as they did into the distance, gave one a good idea of how immense must once have been this system of canals. Now only the broken dry skeletons remain scattered over the face of the desert like the bones of some prehistoric monsters.

Just upstream of the town on the opposite (right) bank can be seen the mouth of the Shatt-el-Hai, which, running south-east to Nasryeh, connects the Tigris with the Euphrates.

In very early days the Shatt-el-Hai was perhaps an artificial canal, one of the system which spread all over the country. Then, later, the Tigris adopted it as its regular channel for some centuries, only to change again later back to its present one.

The country here between the Tigris and the Euphrates on either side of the Shatt-el-Hai is full of interest to the archaeologist, for it is thick with the remains of the oldest civilizations of Mesopotamia and the site of many of the most famous cities, the remains of which lie beneath countless mounds which cover the face of the desert. Comparatively few of these have been excavated, and even where the archaeologist has had a chance there still remains much to be done.

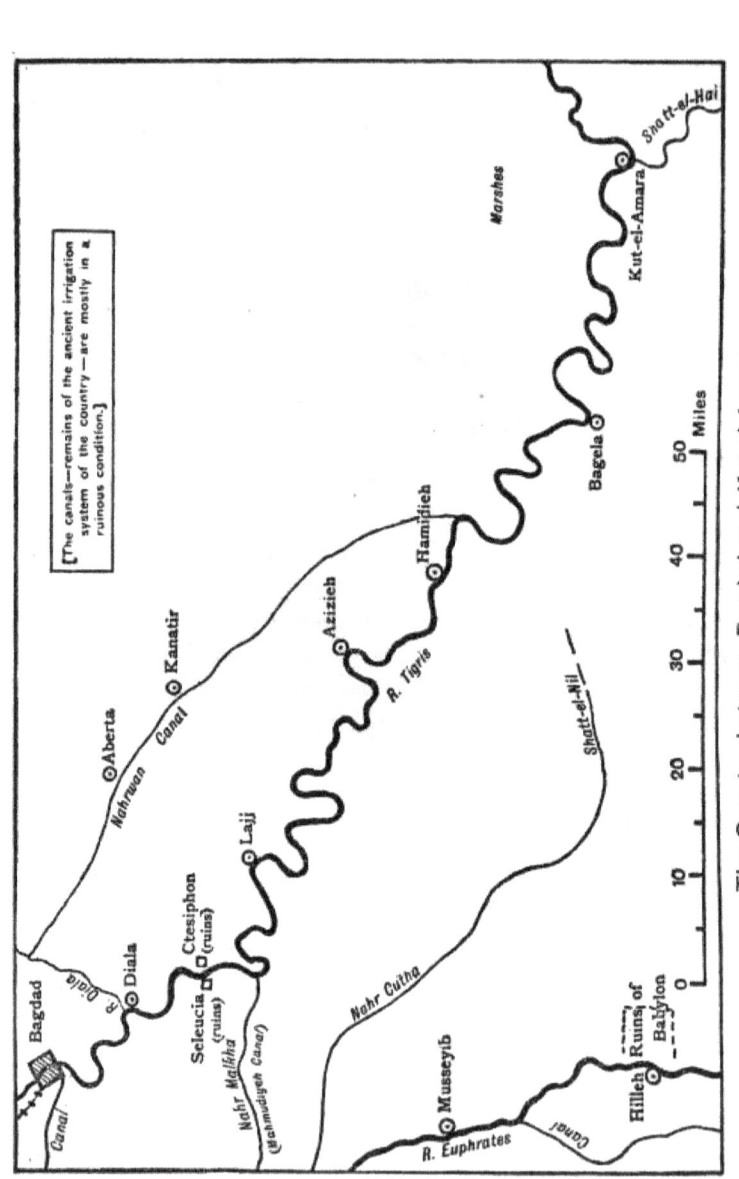

The Country between Bagdad and Kut-el-Amara.

Erech, Lagash, Ur, Eridu, Tel Lo, Nippur—these are only a few of the cities where immense ruins have been laid bare, the signs of a civilization we can as yet only partially reconstruct. But there remains much wonderful and fascinating history still locked up in these hummocks of the wilderness; there are still cities and palaces and temples whose names even are unknown, secrets and mysteries which cannot be solved until the desert mounds are probed.

We know comparatively little of this land of Shinar—of whence the Akkadians came, or who exactly the Sumerians were, that strange race of round-headed, smooth-faced men who inhabited the delta. But we know at least that they were great keepers of records and that they wrote on a more enduring medium than the Egyptians—on clay tablets. There is every prospect that enough material will be found to have survived underground to give us the history and the customs of Shinar; and when peace rules in the land it should not be a matter of great difficulty to recover it.

In later days Wasit was founded by Hajjaj in 702 on the left bank of the Shatt-el-Hai, which was then the Tigris, from which time dates the falling of Basra from its importance. Wasit itself was later cut out by the building of Baghdad by the Caliph Mansur in $A.D.$ 766.

But though all this land may be holy ground to the archaeologist it is of peculiarly small interest to the less instructed, consisting as it does of an immense area of dry-mud desert, sparsely covered with camel-thorn and partially flooded in the high-water season. It is inhabited by the nomadic sections of the Muntafik, while the Shammar generally move into it from across the Euphrates during the winter.

Directly on our arrival in camp at Kut, we heard that General Townshend and the 18th Brigade had been definitely outstripped by the Turks, who had succeeded in withdrawing to their strong position at Ctesiphon, 20 miles from Baghdad. The 18th Brigade and Divisional Headquarters had reached Aziziyeh, 50 miles from Baghdad, and were there encamped on the left bank of the river.

But the position of such a small force, with a difficult line of communications in their rear and no reinforcements handy, was more than usually precarious; so, the 16th Brigade and all available artillery were to march immediately to join them.

At this time there was naturally much speculation in the force as to whether we were going on to Baghdad or should be content with what we had got. Rumours were constantly contradictory—but they were of course only rumours and we knew nothing of the official view. Unofficially, among ourselves, we were naturally all for going on, as we had wiped the floor with the Turks every time and, optimistically, saw every reason why we should do so again. Although everyone was pretty tired and none too fit after a year of Mesopotamian conditions, the same must apply to the Turkish forces in front of us, who were old friends: chances of their reinforcement by fresh troops seemed scarcely worth considering.

On 7th October the 16th Brigade left Kut to march up to Aziziyeh; the next day the 17th Brigade was unexpectedly ordered to follow them as soon as possible, leaving the weak 30th Brigade of the XIIth Division to garrison Kut.

Our march was unfortunate from the start, for the hot weather, to which we thought we had said goodbye, gave a last kick to assert itself, and we suffered accordingly. The first day, as there seemed no particular hurry, only twelve miles were done, but as we did not arrive at our halting-place on the river bank till 1 p.m. the sun was a good deal too hot for comfort. But that afternoon a message was received directing the brigade to press on. Owing to the winding course of the river it was necessary to cut across the bends, and, if we were to press on, we should have to cut across without touching the river and make a march of twenty miles without water. This does not sound much, but it must be remembered that the sun was still horribly hot in the open from ten till four, and there was a hot, dust-laden wind; in addition, no one was fit for much exertion.

Next morning, we marched from 5.30 a.m. till 10 a.m. and then knocked off for three hours for a rest, finding the sun even hotter than we had expected as we lay out in the desert. We started again at 1 and expected to strike the river again at 5 p.m. where we were to halt for the night. But unfortunately, the column somehow lost direction, and, at 6 p.m., we were still marching, looking in vain for the river and getting extraordinarily thirsty. We plugged on, occasionally cheered for a moment by a glimmer in the distance which appeared to be the river, but always we found that it was only a white salt deposit shining in the moonlight. This happened time and again, so that at last even the cheeriest gave up trying to start the choruses of "Here we are again," it became so obvious that we weren't.

It had been a very hot day with a dust-storm most of the time, and water-bottles, full at dawn, had proved a short ration. By now everyone was getting very far through, and at about seven o'clock men began to fall out—most of them complaining of a terrible stiffness and numbness in their legs. The problem was to know what could be done with them, for we had practically no wheeled transport, as we were relying on our "parent" ships for everything, and we might still be miles from the river.

Those who could sit on were put up on any ponies and mules available, while those who were too bad were collected as far as possible into groups with one or two sound men as guards and instructed to light flares of camel-thorn at intervals to show their position. The danger, of course, was from the Arabs, who no doubt were a-prowl close by.

So, we continued, leaving an ever-increasing trail of cripples behind, and at last, at 9 p.m., we reached the river—only to find that food and blankets were not forthcoming, as our "parent" ship had gone aground some miles downstream! Beat as we were, we had the energy to find a few expressions befitting the occasion.

By 11 p.m., however, the ship and food arrived, which put a rather more cheerful complexion on matters, and by this time most of the sick had managed to crawl in and could be put on board: about half a dozen remained out all night but were not molested. We were also cheered by the news that the force at Aziziyeh was going to attack the Turks, who had moved down towards them. The attack would be postponed until the arrival of the 17th Brigade, if possible—but the brigade must be at Aziziyeh by the next evening.

So, we should have to put our best foot foremost again and march quite 25 miles without the river; but there seemed an excellent reason now for getting a move on.

Very much the same thing happened next day, for, though due at Aziziyeh at 5 p.m., we again lost our bearings and did not arrive till night; but just as we were getting very far through we were met by a convoy of water-carts sent out from camp, so that the last six miles were bearable, though again a lot of men were obliged to fall out. However, when on our arrival we asked if we should be in time for the attack, we were told that there was no idea of attacking at present: it was gathered that the story had been by way of encouraging us on our long march! It had certainly done so, and made us step out, though we felt rather sore in spirit, as well as feet, when we learnt the truth!

Aziziyeh is the usual village of ruinous mud huts and, just below it on the left bank, the division was now encamped. The river here describes a narrow loop, and a small garrison in an entrenched post on the opposite bank was holding the neck of the loop. The prospect was depressingly featureless and bare, blue sky and brown earth, with only the yellow river, running between steep earthen cliffs, to vary the monotony; a dust-laden wind seemed to blow almost continuously, until earth and sky and river became a monochrome in khaki. Not a tree was visible in any direction; here and there the bare skeletons of the old canals broke the level horizon, and over on the right bank there was a scrubby jungle of liquorice—that is all in the way of scenery that Aziziyeh could boast of.

And yet such unpromising material as this could appear beautiful: dawn and sunset even here worked their wonderful alchemy and changed the dingy monochrome of sky and desert into a picture glowing with tints of pink and gold and blue, half revealed and softened by veils of purple mist.

The enemy had lost no time in sending down a detachment from Ctesiphon to watch what we were up to, and already a body of them—mostly cavalry—with four guns, was reported at Zeur, about 15 miles upstream. The same night as the 17th Brigade arrived, the post on the opposite bank, held by the 110th, was heavily attacked by Arabs, who managed to get through the wire and killed a few men, and got away with a good many rifles: they were heavily fired on, but showed considerable determination. Evidently the enemy meant to keep us busy, for a few days later a force of all arms moved down from Zeur and occupied El Kutuniah, only six miles from camp. This was considered to be rather too close for our comfort, and it was determined to oust them. But the evening before we were to move, aeroplane reconnaissance reported that Kutuniah was evacuated and the force marching back to Zeur: So, it was a case of "as you were."

I think it was the next day that we were definitely and officially informed of future plans. The information was to the effect that no further advance was going to be made at present, but that as soon as two divisions arrived from France we should go up to annex Baghdad; however, it would be at least two months before these troops could arrive. We were in the meantime to get up all our tents, heavy kit, and stores, and "make ourselves comfortable" at Aziziyeh, while those who were in need of a change or required the attentions of a dentist might go off to Basra on leave.

This was not rumour or any kind of camp-gossip, but definite and official instructions given personally from high quarters.

It was rather a relief to hear we were not to move on at once, for the division was in a pretty bad way as regards health. The mysterious complaint which had attacked the 17th Brigade during its march up from Kut had spread with alarming rapidity at Aziziyeh among the three British regiments and the gunners, and more men were going down every day and a considerable number of deaths occurring. After a lot of uncertainty, it was diagnosed as *beri-beri*—but what had caused it, unless it were lack of vegetables, it was hard to say. Scarcely any cases occurred among the Indian troops.

In addition to this plague which had settled upon us, the cold nights were now bringing out a lot of fever, and it became increasingly plain that most men were pretty well worn-out and quite unfit for any exertion for the present, so that a rest would be very welcome.

Besides, although the troops were concentrated at Aziziyeh, the move on from Kut had been rapid, and there was a lot of stuff which still had to be brought upstream: the river was terribly low and we now had only six ships of any size which could work above Kut with any degree of reliability.

★★★★★★

These were the *Julnar, Blosse Lynch, Medjedieh, Malamir, Mosul,* and *Salimi*; there were also the small stern-wheelers (about 30 tons) *Massoudieh* and *Shushan*.

For the reaches below Kut were available the seven "P" boats (though these were not reliable), the *Bhamashir, Karun,* and *Kazimir* and the "T" class of tugs—these last, too, were really of too deep draught, and frequently ran ashore.

The navy was represented by H.M.S. *Comet, Shaitan,* and *Samana*, armed launches.

★★★★★★

So, all things considered, a rest was very welcome, although Aziziyeh was certainly not the place one would have chosen, but there was a certain amount of game about—bustard and black partridge—and the camp was soon moved to a better site, behind the village and some distance from the river, and everyone settled down to make themselves as comfortable as possible under the circumstances, while the few lucky ones went off on leave to Basra.

It was very pleasant to sit at ease upon the deck of a ship and watch those miles of baked desert, over which we had so lately footed it, slip past without effort. If any excitement was needed to vary the monotony of the voyage it was always on tap, for certain Arabs, Shammar it was believed, had been lately indulging in their favourite sport.

This is to lie up on a high bit of bank overlooking the river and wait till a ship is passing; our Arabian humourist can then just peep over the edge and take pot-shots right down on to the deck of the passing steamer beneath—"every time a cocoanut," and no risk!

This game is best played at a loop in the river; after the first innings a sprint across country brings the sportsman into position for another go, while the ship is steaming round the bend, and so he can have his fun all over again! As the deck of the ship is well below the level of the bank, those on board are hopelessly handicapped, as, of course, the sniper shows practically nothing but the end of his rifle; but a machine-gun mounted on a high platform rather altered the betting.

The journey down, except for such excitements as this, and the continual dodging of sandbanks which showed their brown banks above the water in all directions, was featureless and peaceful and not too hot: the continual monotonous chant of the leadsman induced slumber. The "leadsman" was a man who squatted in the bows, armed with a long, graduated pole, which he plunged regularly into the water, reading the depth as he withdrew it.

The regular swing of his arm and the monotonous cry "*Arba, arba, arba w'nuss*"—four, four, four and a half—had a strangely hypnotic effect. They are great men, these sailors on the river boats, and so different from the local riverside inhabitants that one is at once struck by their appearance. It appears that they are nearly all Chaldaean Christians from Mosul way, and are employed on these ships as they are first-rate watermen, and, besides being hefty fellows, are very reliable; some of them were quite fair and had that peculiarly hawklike type of countenance noticeable among Kurds—perhaps they have Kurdish blood in their veins.

As soon as Amara was past, a new country came into view— new, because, when last we had seen it, it was under water, a wide expanse of shimmering floods as far as the eye could see. But now, though the reeds still grew in places, there was dry land on either bank, and pasture where sheep and ponies were grazing. We noticed that all the ponies were swathed in rugs and sacking, carefully secured under their bellies, and as it was still very hot at midday, one rather wondered why. However, the reason was soon apparent, in the shape of swarms of the most voracious kind of horse-fly—a big, grey brute—that bit most horribly and attacked us even on the ship. Wherever it got home it drew blood and was distinctly painful.

The Narrows, just above Ezra's Tomb, when we had passed them at the beginning of June, had not been noticeable, owing to the floodwater out on either side; but now, with the river dead low, one realised what a difficulty to navigation they are, and why it is necessary to have a very particular type of steamer and barge on the Tigris. For the river here, besides being very narrow—in one place only 85 feet—describes the most acute bends, the worst of which is known as the "Devil's Elbow." So narrow is the river and so sharp the turns that it is very difficult to get the ships round at all, even those with independent paddles. When coming downstream before the current, with a barge either side, it looks like sudden death—the terrified passenger stands trembling on deck and wonders if he's in for a shipwreck.

Then the fun starts. The bows appear to head straight for an elbow of bank, there is a thud and a bump and a heave, and the ship rebounds from *terra firma* with a crash, and bounces into the stream again; while the barge (if the hawsers hold) merely skids up on to the bank, and travels by land—they are used to it and it's the custom of the country. This goes on at intervals of half an hour until the twenty-eight miles of the Narrows are past. There is never a serious accident apparently, though it is only ships and barges (and perhaps passengers) that have been specially built for the game that will stand it.

After such a nerve-racking performance, the sight of Ezra's Tomb at evening, its shimmering blue dome and gracefully slanting palms, seen against a deep golden sky, has a wonderfully soothing effect; think of a peculiarly distressing cab accident, and then visualize a scene from Kismet, and you will "get there."

North of Kurna we looked interestedly for the battlefield over which we had pushed our boats during the "Regatta"—but everything was changed. In place of the miles of water and the little sandhills, was one vast expanse of waving crops that stretched as far as one could see: it might have been a different country. On either bank rose the level ranks of a wonderful crop of *"jowari"* quite 13 feet high, where only four months before there had been nothing but water and reeds. So, in that short time the floods had subsided, the rushes and reeds died down, the seed been planted, and now the crop was ready to cut—quick work, and a proof, if one were needed, of what the soil will do. In spite of the hellish climate one is almost tempted to believe that this may really have been the site of the Garden of Eden!

Basra, in October 1915, to any newcomer would no doubt have appeared primitive enough; but to those of us who had seen it in 1914 there were great changes visible. Even in the early morning light, as we lay off Ashar Creek, the town looked swept and cared for, as if someone had gone round the streets the night before, and given even the houses a hasty rub down—which is very much what had really happened; only the broom and duster, and many other aids to cleanliness, had been hard at work for a year to produce this effect.

The port itself appeared little changed except for the big timber landing-stages, though there were signs that other work was in hand; but the streets and lanes and houses all bore witness to a new order, very different from that of the Turk. The date groves were drained, and the tracks through them, once horrid bogs meandering among the pools, were now roads on solid causeways above the flood-level, with a good surface; along them, on scarlet-painted bicycles, sped small Arab telegraph-boys, hugely filled with their own importance.

The "strand"—fronting Ashar Creek—was now a level street with at least three big shops (branches lately opened by firms from India) and a fine bridge over the creek in place of the rickety affair of earlier days. On the bridge was an armed Arab policeman, controlling the traffic, who slapped his rifle and "eyesright"-ed with most military precision whenever an officer passed. All public buildings, offices and stores, hospital and messes, were lit by electric light and cooled by electric fans, and ice could be had for the asking—in fact, it was all very nice, and seemed a great change after the sandy wilds of Aziziyeh.

Basra itself seemed little changed, though of course the bazaars were far busier than in 1914, and the crowds of slowly-processing idlers seemed endless. The manners of the native here had certainly not improved—they thought nothing of shouldering one into the gutter and jostling one at the shops. Undesirable as is any cringing and servility on the part of a native population, the other extreme can also be reached, as it was here. It is not good for our prestige for an Arab to be able to push a British soldier into the gutter; for though the soldier probably doesn't notice, or good-naturedly does not mind, the Arabs among themselves know it, and intend it, to be an insult. There is little question of such incidents being due to an oversight or "not meant," for in such things the Oriental has a very meticulous code of manners.

In the days of the Turkish regime things were very different, and an Armenian resident told me that if a Turkish officer was crossing the Ashar bridge no Arab would even venture on to it at the same time, much less pass him; if he had . . . my Armenian friend threw up his hands in horror! He himself had suffered from the Turk. As a small boy of eight he had seen the whole of his family, father, mother, brothers, and sisters, murdered before his eyes by Turkish soldiers. Somehow or other he had avoided their fate and escaped from Basra to Baghdad, whence he wandered all over the world. He worked as a lad in Paris, then in London, and later was in business in New York, where he was most successful; but when he came to set up for himself he chose to live in Basra and to do his business in an office not 100 yards from the place where he had seen his family murdered forty years before! But his strange choice did not seem to depress him—perhaps he was content to spoil the Egyptians.

Basra, in spite of cheerful evenings at the club, and days enlivened by the dentist's small-talk, is not a place one lingers in longer than necessary; so, although there was no rumour or whisper of any incident from the front, a week in the metropolis seemed enough. Two more days of hectic shopping for friends upstream—anything from bootlaces to huge sacks of sugar—and the smuggling of them on to an already heavily laden ship, and then, on 30th October, we said goodbye to Basra and started off upstream on the long trail back to Aziziyeh.

The voyage was uneventful as far as Amara, but there, from a chance meeting with a friend on the river-front, we heard most unexpected news: an advance was to be made against the Turks at Ctesiphon almost immediately, and we were all to get back to our regiments as soon as possible, or rather sooner! After the very explicit information we had had only three weeks before, this news came as a complete surprise. There had been no whisper of it in Basra, and nothing noticeable on the river, except some drafts going up; but these had been considered merely the ordinary scale of reinforcements to make good the Kut casualties and losses from sickness. However, a few inquiries showed that the news was perfectly correct: we were going for Baghdad.

CHAPTER 18

The Battlefield

The decision to advance on Baghdad altered the character of the campaign in Mesopotamia. Hitherto, from its inception, it had been governed by a defensive policy, and the various advances had all been guided by motives of protection—either to protect the pipe-line of the oil-supply, or to prevent concentrations of the enemy. The capture of Amara and Kut, though tactically offensive operations, had been strategically defensive measures: the advance on Baghdad was both tactically and strategically offensive.

But, apart from such considerations, this advance brought other changes to the campaign. They can be best summed up by the one word "Baghdad." That name alone was a moral factor, the power of which was felt by both armies; though, no doubt, most strongly by our enemies.

It must be considered that the swamps and deserts of Lower Mesopotamia are distant from Constantinople a matter of 2000 miles. The country, to the Turk of Anatolia, is as strange and as unknown as Scinde is to the men of Kent, the Two Rivers as mythical as Abana and Pharpar. There can be little question that the Turk knew or cared next to nothing of this distant corner of his empire, and would have been inclined to let it "go hang" had not the German bid him stick to it—for Germany.

Even so, it was not a job to waste good troops over, and consequently its defence had been left to a scratch collection, got together from anywhere—from Stamboul, Aleppo, Smyrna, Van, Mosul, with some sweepings from the Kurdish and Arab tribes—and these had been pitched into Mesopotamia anyhow and told to do their best. They had done their best, but their hearts were not in it; their homes were far away, and this was a strange country. As an Anatolian sergeant

A 5-INCH GUN AT KURNA.

said, captured at Kut, "What are we fighting for in this far country?"

And then—Baghdad. It was quite a different story now. They were no longer fighting in an unknown land, defending dreary miles of bog and desert: Baghdad was known through all the Moslem world—a city of great fame and holiness. Though Enver and his Young Turks had proved that they cared little for their religion, and the new official had broken loose with a cynical disregard for the old traditions, they could not go too far: Islam was still a power, and Baghdad was a name among those old traditions, a city of the great Caliphs from whom the Ottoman so anxiously, and so vainly, claims descent. The modern *befezzed* gentlemen in Constantinople had to recognise an older power than theirs and take measures accordingly.

But to look at the other side of the medal. To estimate the effect these considerations had upon the Indian Mahommedan troops is a difficult and intricate problem, with many cross-currents to consider—religion and sect, race and loyalty. At best their position must have been made very difficult and their loyalty hardly tried; certainly, they cannot have been encouraged by the prospect of the task in front of them. Islam, in spite of its reproaches, commands a very real feeling of religious fervour in the East, and a devotion which, to the modern Occidental, would appear scarcely respectable. And yet, all honour to these men, there were wonderfully few "conscientious objectors" among them.

But, on the British regiments, the effect was very different: Baghdad, to the enemy, was a great stake to be defended, and, to us, a great prize to win. And the other arguments follow, conversely. For a year we had been fighting in a country practically unknown to us and to our friends at home; we had marched over nameless deserts and marshes, fought battles in dust and heat and thirst which, compared to the great battles in the West, were mere skirmishes of no importance; we had captured miles of country and villages and towns—but all of them unmarked on any map; we had travelled far under this blazing sun but had arrived nowhere: for we had not got a name.

And then—Baghdad. So, we felt at last that we were going to do something, that we had a real objective with a real name which all knew and had known almost since we could remember.

Besides, the word had more significance even than the "blessed" Mesopotamia; no one can say it without conjuring up scenes from the *Thousand and One Nights*, with all their glitter and music and fragrance; without seeing Haroun al-Raschid move, in his disguise, about the lamplit bazaars; without remembering the strange adventures of the Kalandars or the story of the Barmecides. And there is a background to such memories: flickering firelight and a quiet room and a gentle voice reading of old Baghdad. After that, who would not fight to get there and really see it?

But even now we were on the edge of a country of great and famous names, the late-comers, perhaps the last, of a procession of armies of many ages and many nations which had met upon these reaches of the Tigris. Asshur had fought and burnt and plundered here three thousand years ago, Cyrus the Great and his Persians had passed by on their way to Babylon, and, after him, Alexander with the men of Javan—ever an unending procession of new conquerors, new armies, new people, whose dust was mingled with the old ruins upon the Tigris banks, and whose ghosts, perhaps, remain watching for the newcomers who shall join them.

Nearby, over two thousand years ago, Cyrus the Younger, with his Greeks, had met the Persian army in his bid for the throne. In November 401 B.C. he was defeated and killed at Cunaxa, and there began that great retreat of the Ten Thousand—the handful of foreigners in a strange land who fought and marched a thousand miles back from the Country of the Two Rivers to their homes. The most famous retreat in history, but—*absit omen.*

After the death of Alexander at Babylon in 323 B.C., and the subsequent partition of his huge dominions, the Seleucids reigned beside the Tigris in their great capital of Seleucia, whence Hellenism, its philosophy, society, and architecture, spread through the East.

Seleucia (though not its influence) was destroyed about 130 B.C. by the new power—Parthia, whose Arsacid kings now became the masters of the great city which they had destroyed.

Ctesiphon—so soon again to be the scene of battle—had a wonderful history. For seven hundred years it was a great city, the prize of Parthian, Armenian, Roman, and Sasanid, the centre of vast powers, fought for in turn by each, besieged and captured and freed again. From *A.D.* 116, when Trajan first appeared before its walls, Ctesiphon and the surrounding country was for five hundred years a battleground of Rome and Persia until *A.D.* 627, when the Byzantine Emperor Heraclius defeated the Sasanian Khosrau and pushed on down the Tigris. But then the end was near. Already, far to the south-west, the great power of Islam was kindled and blazing—and the flame soon reached to the Two Rivers and swept across them. In 641 the

Arabs stormed Ctesiphon and left of the Sasanian Power only a heap of smouldering ruins.

But the greatest monument of the great city they could not destroy. The palace, which had housed the King of kings, the magnificence of which, with its enamelled halls, its golden ceilings, its fountains, its columns of gems, was famous through all the East, defied their attempts at destruction; though it was robbed and looted, the palace remained, and still the audience hall, "the Throne of Khosrau," stands up above the empty desert over the ruins of a forgotten world.

★★★★★★

"It was a superb palace, 90 cubits in length and 70 cubits wide, built of marble and red cornelian. In the centre was a fountain filled with rose-water and purest musk; and there was an emerald column and on its summit a hawk of burnished gold; its eyes were topazes and its beak of jasper. . . . The whole palace was full of perfumes and the ceilings glittered with gold and silver. It was the wonder of the period, the miracle of the age."— El-Asma'ee, *Romance of Antar.*

★★★★★★

It was here, before the very palace doors, that we were to fight; the right to the Country of the Two Rivers was to be disputed on familiar ground by yet another army and a new people.

CHAPTER 19

First Sight of the Arch

For the advance against Baghdad practically the same troops were available as had fought at Kut—that is to say, the VIth Division with the 30th Brigade XIIth Division, the 6th Cavalry Brigade, the 10th Brigade R.F.A., the 1st Heavy Brigade, R.G.A. (less one section 86th Battery), 48th Pioneers, two Companies Sappers and Miners, and Medical and Transport units.

The VIth Division had received drafts since the beginning of October which, to some extent, had made good the Kut losses, and "S" Battery, R.H.A., had rejoined the 6th Cavalry Brigade; but the sickness at Aziziyeh had caused losses in quality as well as quantity, and our numbers were no criterion of our fighting strength. For instance, the medical officer of one British regiment considered 150 of his men unfit to march, but on re-examination by a higher authority all but a dozen of these men were pronounced fit; consequently, many of the force who marched out of Aziziyeh did not take part in the battle, and out of a good 13,000 (our estimated strength) not more than 10,000 were actually in action at Ctesiphon.

The navy had been reinforced by the first of the new "fly" class of monitors—H.M.S. *Firefly*—mounting one 4-inch gun, one 6-pounder, and a machine-gun; of the armed gunboats—H.M.S. *Comet, Shaitan, Samana* and *Shushan*—only the last could navigate with any degree of certainty above Kut.

Of the fleet of transports, as before mentioned, only six were of use above Kut, and the land transport was to be of the same mixed quality as had been employed on our advance from Ali-el-Gherbi in September.

The XIIth Division, less the 30th Brigade, with two batteries of mountain guns and the Volunteer Battery (converted 15-pounders) were finding garrisons for Basra, Ahwaz, Kurna, Amara, Nasryeh, and Kut, and a few small posts along our very extended lines of communication. The distances over which this division was distributed are interesting. Basra to Kut, by way of the Tigris, is 350 miles; Kut to Aziziyeh, 100 miles; Basra to Kurna, 45 miles, and on to Nasryeh, by way of the Euphrates, another 90 miles; Basra to Ahwaz, by the Karun River, 110 miles. Owing to the shortage of river transport, communication between each centre was slow and uncertain; and though the country (except for the Euphrates above Samawa) was clear of Turks, the surrounding Arab tribes were untrustworthy in the event of a setback to our arms.

The VIth Division had before it in position at Ctesiphon, 11,000-13,000 Turks, with about thirty-eight guns. More than half of the enemy force consisted of troops who had been defeated at Kut and whose moral was exceedingly low; but, as we discovered too late, they had received heavy reinforcements just before the battle. Rumours were, indeed, now rife that the enemy's reinforcements were close at hand, and, though we had learnt that such rumours were generally to be mistrusted, it seemed as if there was something in this yarn—judging by the "hush-hush" attitude of those who ought to know. Suspicions were further aroused when one fine morning—the 10th or 11th—we were informed that an aeroplane had been dispatched to cut the telegraph wire beyond Baghdad!

But why risk an aeroplane, pilot, and observer on a job any Arab would do for five "chips"? was the natural question. And, when it was learnt that the 'plane had gone laden with guncotton and dynamite; that it was an old bus which could carry scarcely enough petrol for the journey (but was very slow, and could be landed easily pretty well anywhere); that its chances of making the return journey were very thin: well, then some put two and two together and guessed that this was by way of a "forlorn hope," to destroy not the telegraph wire, but the railway line, beyond Baghdad. However, that may be (and it was only a guess), the aeroplane failed to accomplish its mission, and was eventually forced to descend in the desert, where it was destroyed; pilot and observer were made prisoners by the Arabs.

******

El Kutunia, occupied again by the Turks since their withdrawal from it in the middle of October, was again evacuated by them before a reconnaissance in force carried out by the 16th and 17th Brigades on 7th November. On 11th November the Cavalry Brigade and the

THE ARCH OF CTESIPHON

16th Brigade occupied Kutunia, while the 17th and 30th Brigades were to join them there as soon as possible; transport difficulties prevented the whole division moving together.

These two brigades were originally ordered to march on 14th November—the barges carrying oil fuel for their ships making an earlier start out of the question; but, on the 13th, these barges were spotted, by an aeroplane, hard aground forty miles downstream—consequently our departure was postponed till the 16th.

Having struck camp and packed our modest kits, we waited in a blinding sand-storm for the word "go"; but, instead, we were bidden to stay, as the barges were not yet in sight. We sighed, and gazing at sundry neat loads and bundles, all that remained of our happy home, resigned ourselves to Fate. The 17th saw us still at Aziziyeh, with the barges still far away and no prospect of leaving for another day. However, Fate, in the guise of a summons from upstream, was kind, and, after orders and counterorders (and their sequel), we marched out of Aziziyeh, leaving behind us in an entrenched camp a garrison of men considered unfit to march, and two 4-inch guns—these latter very unwillingly, and only because there were not enough bullocks to draw them. But whether the old barges still remained cuddling their mud bank we knew not—nor cared, as long as we could get on to join the rest; and this was accomplished by our arriving at El Kutunia that night.

On the 18th, the 17th Brigade (less 119th) moved a short way upstream and crossed by the pontoon bridge over on to the right bank; the remainder of the force remained on the left, and the next morning the advance was to be continued in this order against the Turks, advanced position at Zeur.

But, in the end, the 17th Brigade were left behind to enjoy a little paroxysm of excitement all on their own. About 7 p.m., just as we were thinking of supper and bed, came a message to say that aeroplane reconnaissance reported a large body of enemy moving down the right bank from Zeur. Particulars as to exactly at what point they were seen and at what time, were not forthcoming.

Two battalions were immediately sent forward into the dark, and ordered to send out patrols to watch the narrow neck of land here formed by a bend in the river, while the remaining battalion was held in reserve, ready to move at once.

We waited all night but nothing happened. As soon as it grew light the neck of the loop was at once occupied by all three battalions, which began to entrench with feverish haste: if we were to be attacked there was no time to be lost.

In the meanwhile, the remainder of the force had left us and continued their march up the left bank on Zeur, in order to cut in behind the enemy on the right bank, for whose entertainment we were preparing in front. Anxiously we waited news of their whereabouts.

Digging hard from 5 a.m. till 2.30 p.m. we had managed to excavate some very nice trenches and had just knocked off for a rest and feed—the first the men had had—when a bitter blow fell: The brigade major arrived with orders for the brigade to move at once—there were no enemy on the right bank. The observer who had reported them the previous evening had made a mistake—it was only cattle he'd seen, after all!

So, cramming the remains of our meal into mouths and pockets, we hastily "packed up" and were away by 3.30, leaving our trenches, fashioned at cost of much honest toil, for "an habitation of jackals and an abode of owls."

We had a considerable grudge against that observer: for we had lost a night's sleep and laboured meatless through the day, and now had to march far and fast to join the rest. All that afternoon we plugged along the river bank with scarcely a halt till the sun set; and on again through the pitch dark night, tumbling into *wadis*, losing our way and crashing blindly through head-high liquorice (bane of our childhood now tormenting us in old age!), till at length by the light of a brilliant moon we found the silver-blue waters of the river once more and regained the bank. Then another two hours through soft sand a foot deep, wondrous heavy to weary legs, and we saw the lights of the ships upstream. Sometime after midnight we stumbled on to the shore at Zeur—and slept drunkenly.

Next morning, we learnt that the enemy had made no stand the previous day against our advance, and that the cavalry had driven them out of this potentially strong position with few casualties. Now the whole of our force was concentrated here, on the left bank, except the 17th Brigade, which still had to cross over.

This was done on the morning of the 20th, and transport was redistributed among that strange menagerie—camels carrying forty blankets each (in two rolls of twenty), or their equivalent weight in tents or stores, cows were saddled with more stores, and in some cases ammunition, and the little donkeys with picks and shovels. Much sympathy is due to the transport officers.

The *Mosul* and *Blosse Lynch*, though still doing duty as transports, were being hastily converted into hospital ships—that is to say, canvas wind-screens were rigged along the sides and medical equipment put aboard. However, as our probable casualties were estimated at only 500, no extensive preparations were necessary. The badly wounded could be moved to the ships in A.T. carts (as there was no medical land transport), while, for the slightly injured, there were extra riding mules.

On the afternoon of the 20th, the division continued its advance, and marched to Lajj, just over ten miles from the Turkish positions. No opposition was encountered, and we spent a quiet night, unmolested by snipers. The Turkish position at Ctesiphon was as at Kut, astride the river, which originally described a deep loop here, almost due north and south, eight miles deep. The neck of this loop had, however, been cut through, and the old bed though dry formed a considerable obstacle. At the upper end of the loop, on the left bank, stand the ruins of Ctesiphon and the immense arch—the remains of the Khosrau's Palace.

Here, on the left bank, the Turkish lines ran from the river, just downstream of the arch, in a north-easterly direction for six miles. They consisted of fire trenches supported by redoubts at close intervals, the left flank resting on some high ground defended by a large redoubt and strong system of trenches: there appeared to be nineteen gun-emplacements in rear of the first line, ten of them towards the extreme left. This flank redoubt and high ground was known by us as "V.P." (Vital Point).

Behind the first line on the left bank was a second line, some two miles in rear, supported by thirteen guns, parallel to the first line for three miles, after which it was turned back due northward, thus refusing the left flank. A mile in rear of this second line a bridge of boats spanned the Tigris. A third line was formed by the Diala River, the bridge and ford over which were commanded by fire trenches on the farther bank. In the Diala the enemy had a difficult obstacle in their rear, and their line of retreat (for the road to Baghdad follows this left bank) was narrowed here to a defile—the one bridge over the river. (A second bridge over the Diala, was constructed just before the battle.) The ford was reported by Arabs to be impassable.

On the right bank, the position extended in rear and beyond the original river-bed for about three miles to the south-west. In front, and beyond the line to the south, the ground was broken by the channel and ruined canals, and by an expanse of dried-up marsh, so fissured and cracked that it was impassable for any troops. The guns immediately in rear of the first line appeared to be thirteen in number and commanded both the Lajj and Bustan reaches of the river.

About five miles in rear a series of high-level canals and watercourses were entrenched to form a second line, and another nine miles in rear again there was a similar system about four miles upstream of the junction of the Diala.

In this position it was now estimated that there were 13,000 Turks. There were rumours current that heavy reinforcements were on the point of arrival, though aeroplane reconnaissance had not reported any sign of them.

General Townshend's plan here was very much the same as at Kut. The defences on the right bank, though apparently suspiciously weak, were known, owing to the impossible state of the approaches, to be exceedingly formidable. As against this, though the lines on the left bank were strong, they could be turned without leaving the river (and water), and behind them the enemy had the Diala with its one bridge. The left was the Turk's strategic flank, and its security essential for any orderly retreat on Baghdad: this flank once turned there was every prospect of a big haul before the enemy could make good the passage of the defile in their rear. The main attack, therefore, was to be pushed in against "V.P."—the mounds and redoubts on the left flank.

The 18th Brigade (Brigadier-General Hamilton) on the right flank of the main attack was to move directly against the outer flank of the Turkish second line, while the Cavalry Brigade and half the 76th Punjabis (the latter in carts) on the extreme right were to make a rapid movement in order to get behind the enemy. If the attack on "V.P." proved a success and their line fell back, this mobile force was to push on to the Diala bridge. At the same time a "holding attack" was to be developed against the right centre. The defences on the right bank were to be engaged by the navy and the guns mounted on barges, otherwise they were to be left alone.

To the 16th and half the 30th Brigade, under General Delamain, was allotted the attack on "V.P.," to be pushed in from the three sides: the 17th Brigade, under General Hoghton, with the 48th Pioneers in place of 103rd Mahrattas, was to carry out the "holding attack," while General Mellis was to command the mixed force of cavalry and infantry on the extreme right.

On the morning of Sunday, 21st November, these three columns separated; the 17th Brigade, with the 104th Battery (heavy), and a Field Battery, and first line transport were on the left, near the river, while the other two columns with their artillery moved due north until opposite that part of the enemy's line which was to be their objective—in the case of General Mellis's column (cavalry and 76th Punjabis) wide of the enemy's left flank. The approach march was to be made under cover of night so that the attack could be made at dawn, and now the various columns moved only a short distance in order to be on a direct line for their night marches.

The 17th Brigade, on the left, marched about two miles along the caravan road, and then halted from 9 till 3 p.m. It was during this halt that we got our first glimpse of the arch: owing to some atmospheric trick, mirage or a ground mist perhaps, it appeared quite suddenly where a minute before had nothing been visible but flat, bare desert. Though only eight miles distant, it seemed to be a tremendous way off, and yet gave one the impression of immense height—it looked like some huge mass of mountain, blue and shimmering in the haze above the glaring desert, and it seemed almost incredible that it could be a mere ruin.

Its size was, of course, exaggerated by the atmosphere, and the extreme flatness of the surrounding landscape to eyes unaccustomed to anything more lofty than a date palm, but one thing struck everyone who saw the arch that afternoon—its value to the enemy as an observation-post. From the top they must have been able to command a wide view of the desert in all directions, and must even then, we thought, be observing our preliminary deployment. Bets were exchanged as to whether our "heavies" would knock it endways before the day was out, and before, on the morrow, it would be used to direct the enemy's batteries from.

But Ctesiphon Arch still stands—the archaeologist will say "Of course," and perhaps feel outraged at such a Hunnish proposal for its demolition when there was no actual proof that the Turks were making use of it; others may consider that, in view of the casualties in the battle, too high a price was paid for its immunity.

The 17th Brigade moved on again at 3.30 and marched till 6, when another halt was called on the river bank and animals watered. So far, no opposition had been met with from the enemy, though some zealous gunners on our own side (rumour whispers of a gunboat) put two shells very near us—luckily without doing damage. Here we were told that we should march at 9 p.m. to within 2000 yards of the enemy's front line, where we should dig in during the night, and from there work forward slowly as and when our action was needed; the remainder of the force was now somewhere away on our right and would develop their attack at dawn. During this halt, water-bottles were filled and rations served out for the morrow.

The 17th Brigade moved off again at 9 p.m. and marched for two and a half hours, which brought them to near Bustan—the northern downstream end of the Ctesiphon loop; here a halt was made and final orders given out. There was to be no farther advance that night: the column would parade at 5.30 and march straight for the arch as soon as it grew light— for various reasons it was impossible for us to work up close during the night as originally intended. We were then cautioned against any deeds of violence in holy places: Sulman Pak, the tomb of Mahommed's barber, just behind the arch, was exceptionally sacred; likewise, certain mosques and tombs in and near Baghdad which we were not to interfere with. By the light of a brilliant moon we duly marked them on our maps—that we should have no need to worry about Baghdad never entered our heads!

We were now very near, almost uncomfortably near, the Turkish front line, which, according to our maps, was only about three miles away, and there was a brilliant moon; however, as at Kut, the *drabis* and *syces* seemed not at all anxious, and until thumped into silence did their best to create pandemonium—talking and coughing and hammering in iron picketing-pegs. But here again the Turk slept through it all or at least took no notice of it—perhaps, this time, there was method in his apparent madness.

CHAPTER 20

The End of the Year

It was a bitterly cold night with a freezing wind, and little sleep was to be had before it was time to get a move on: 5 a.m. (22nd) came round very soon, and by 6 a.m. we were off.

Marching north-west, we soon reached the top of the bend, and then turned towards the arch. It was still dark and very cold—all of those who had them were marching in greatcoats. About 7 a.m. the sun rose, though it was a very foggy morning, and one could see little in front; behind us the sky was a mass of golden mist and the air had the fresh feeling of an autumn morning at home.

Soon after sunrise we could hear our heavies booming away from behind us, though, as yet, there was no sound from our right—evidently things had not started on the flank yet. We continued marching for about an hour over open ground covered with barley stubble, making out very little of what was in front of us owing to the mist. But this suddenly lifted about 8 a.m. and we saw the whole show before us. The arch seemed to hit one in the face, it was so near and, in that flat landscape, so immense. It reared its huge brown bulk above the desert, standing, it appeared, near a large lake, with its arched roof showing up clearly against the blue sky, and the recesses of the facade clearly visible. Left and right of it could be seen the jagged outline of wire entanglement, and, running from the river to near its right side, the long ridge of a ruined canal.

Except for the wire there was no sign of enemy. As for our immediate surroundings, we found in front of us a deep *nullah* which was at once put into a state of defence; beyond it was ground studded with tamarisk bushes; and, beyond again, more broken ground, where all the cover had evidently been recently burned. Away on the right, two or three thousand yards distant, was some high ground over which we could see troops moving—evidently Delamain's column on its way to "V.P."

Range-finders were at once turned on to the arch, and the result was surprising. According to our maps, the ruin was over a mile behind their front-line trenches, and yet we were here within 2500 yards of the arch, and therefore should have been about 700 yards from the enemy's line—which we obviously were not. Our guns had ceased fire and there was absolutely no sound or sign of enemy or warfare; peace brooded over the scene, and men stood about on the sky-line eating bully sandwiches.

Orders came for the 17th Brigade to stand fast—rumours suggested that the position had been evacuated and Baghdad left to us; but about 9 a.m. we received orders to advance again, and, leaving our *nullah*, we proceeded. We had covered about 1000 yards and just entered the belt of broken ground where the cover had been burnt, when we found ourselves in it. From the canal banks on our left front machine-guns began to gibber at us, and shells came in with a *whoop* and *wump* from somewhere behind the arch, throwing up clouds of the blackened soil. The ground was luckily intersected in every direction by small ditches and covered with mounds—the ruins of the old city—and under this cover the brigade rapidly made itself inconspicuous. But ammunition and machine-gun mules, chargers, and those with them, everything and everybody who could not take advantage of the ground, were in for a bad time: the Turk had "laid low" and waited till we were near before he started in.

The 17th Brigade formed a firing-line in the ditches about 1000 yards from the arch and replied to the enemy's fire whenever a target presented itself; but by now there was a very bad mirage which considerably hampered operations, especially for our guns, which had to cease fire as they could see nothing with any degree of certainty.

In the meanwhile, things had gone well at "V.P." Though met by a heavy rifle fire the Gurkhas and 24th Punjabis (under Colonel Climo) had not stopped to ask any questions. The attack was carried out with remarkable dash, and neither bullets nor ground bare as a board could stop them before they were into the "V.P." trenches and among the enemy. The latter gave it up in the face of such rapid and determined tactics and were immediately seen streaming away towards the second line, on the flank of which the 18th Brigade were already hammering.

It was now that a hitch occurred which, in the end, was to cost us dear. The discomfiture of the garrison of "V.P." was interpreted as the

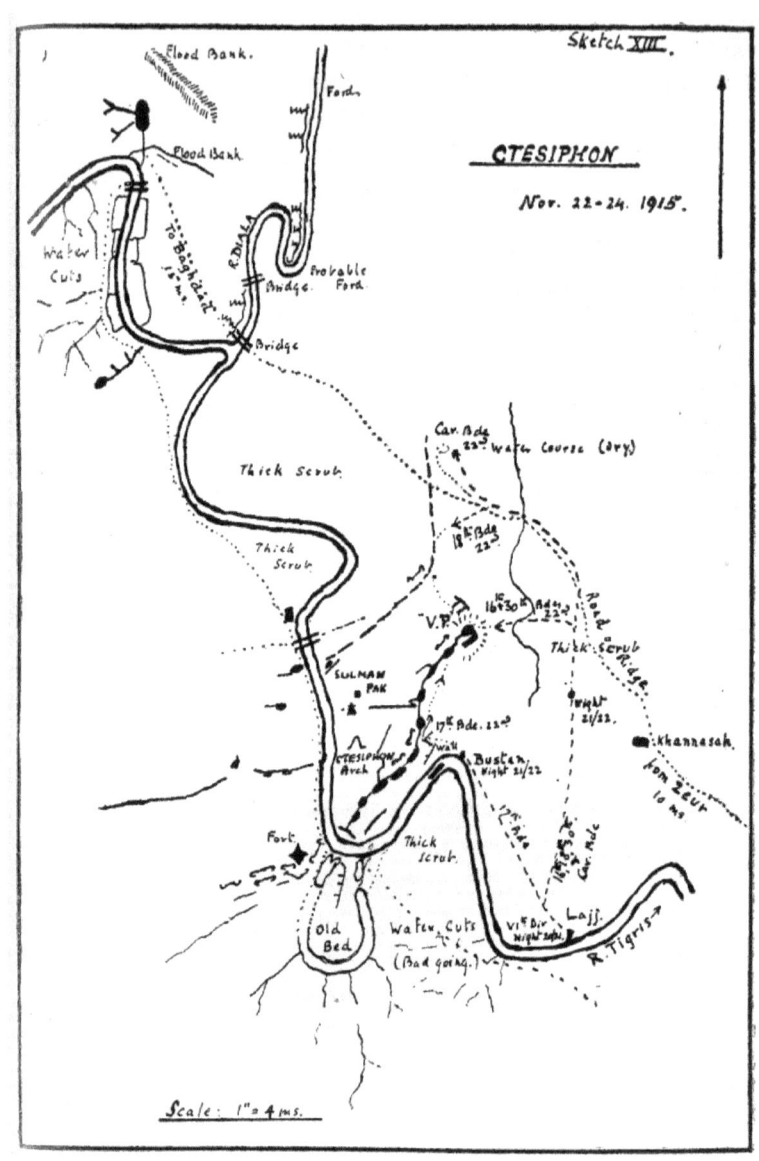

HRB sketch Ctesiphon

flight of the whole first line. Delamain's column, instead of turning southwards and rolling up the line as intended, carried straight on, with the exception of half the Dorsets, after a comparatively small number of fugitives from "V.P.," thus leaving the 17th Brigade lower down faced with a frontal attack against very strongly held positions, without any prospect of help from the flank.

It was soon realised that their task was hopeless, and orders were immediately sent to the 17th Brigade to move up to "V.P." in order to get round the flank of the first line and reinforce Delamain's column which, with the 18th Brigade, was by now up against the second line and in the thick of it.

The order arrived, "Advance at right angles to your present line of advance"—and someone realised the situation. The 17th Brigade, leaving, where possible, a few bunches and machine-gun sections to the last, to keep up a rapid fire, left their hastily scratched trenches and started to move northwards. It was a march straight across the enemy's front at a distance of 1000-1500 yards, over absolutely flat desert without a blade of cover. It was carried out with perfect steadiness, and a position south of "V.P." was reached; but the Turk saw his chance and covered the ground, with fire—rifle, machine-gun, and shrapnel—so that only the lucky got through. Why the enemy should not take such a splendid chance for a counterattack would have been rather a mystery, had not the enemy been the Turk.

A little more than half the brigade got through to the cover of a ditch 200 yards from the enemy's line and 1000 yards south of "V.P.," and here it was held up until a combined attack supported by the howitzer battery at last carried a series of trenches and a big redoubt.

That once gone, the left of the line was broken, though the river end (right) was not touched and its occupants effected their retirement during the night. However, the resistance of the first line was broken with heavy loss to the enemy, including 1300 prisoners.

The remainder of the 17th Brigade now joined the 16th, 30th, and 18th Brigades, which were engaged on the second line. They made some progress on the right, capturing two batteries of guns and a number of prisoners; but, though they established themselves in sections of the line, they were counter-attacked again and again by fresh troops, and at last had to be withdrawn slowly, and fighting all the way, to the first line, which was organised and consolidated. The captured guns changed hands repeatedly but had finally to be abandoned. The enemy was fully conscious of the importance of his left flank; here, in

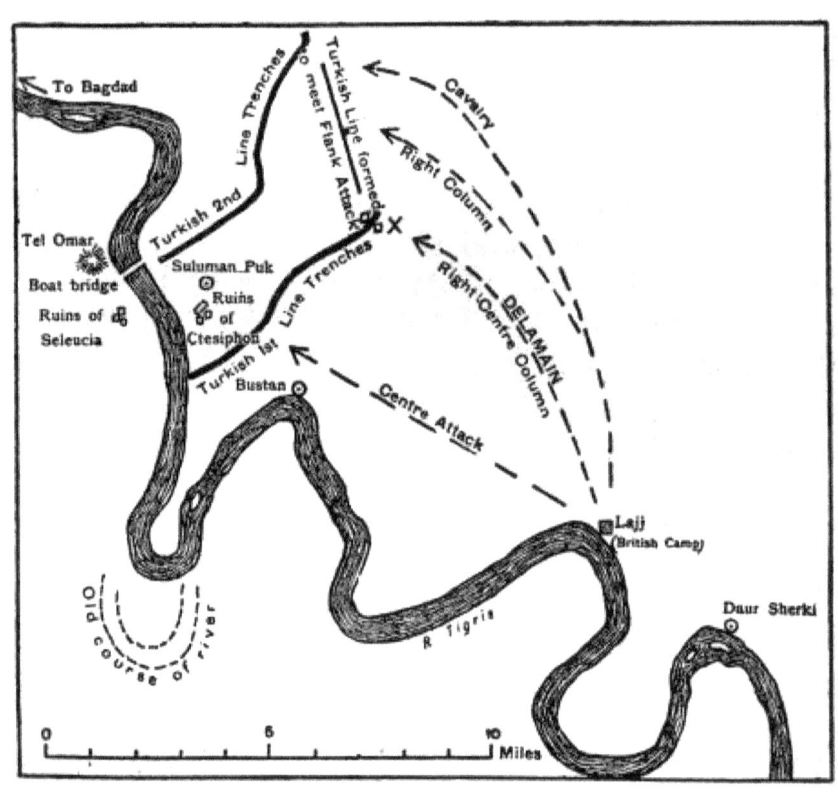

BATTLE OF CTESIPHON

the second line, it was found that his trenches were extended farther north and west than was expected, and the cavalry could make no progress with the intended turning movement.

By nightfall we were back in the Turkish first line, and ready for the counter-attacks which were to be expected.

But casualties had been terribly heavy—the 17th Brigade had lost nearly half its strength in the morning, the 16th and 30th Brigades had lost nearly as many in the heavy fighting of the afternoon and evening—all over the desert the wounded lay and had now to be collected.

No doubt personal experiences are apt to lose sight of real proportions, but, when all is said and done, that "looker on who sees most of the game" in a battle is a rare person these days, and one's truest impressions and memories are of one's own little corner of the field. This must serve as an apology and excuse for any purely personal experiences.

The confusion seen at Kut was repeated over again but on a bigger scale: walking-wounded wandered about looking in vain for collecting stations which could not be found: the more severely hit lay where they fell and waited until the search parties discovered them, though here and there, where the casualties had been thickest, they lay in groups. One such group, of about 50 British and Indian, had been wounded while lying in a shallow ditch south of "V.P.," about 100 yards from a Turkish redoubt, where the snipers had been many and accurate—so much so that scarcely a man who had attempted to return their fire had escaped.

The Turks had spotted that the ditch was full of men and had managed to flood it, with the consequence that the occupiers were faced with the alternative of getting out of the ditch and being shot or remaining in and being drowned—some of the most seriously wounded were, in fact, drowned before help reached them. The gradually rising water was icy cold, but there was no escape from it, for the slightest movement produced a storm of bullets, and a howitzer was also dropping shells just in rear; ammunition had run out; so there they had to stick for about three hours until the front line was cleared and they could be moved from the water by the few sound men that remained.

Then followed a long wait, wet through and very cold, till, at last, after dark, some stretchers were found and the wounded transported to a collecting station, 1000 yards south of "V.P.," where they were lowered into the deep Turkish trenches and first field dressings applied. Everything possible was done by the doctors, but they were short-

A British firing-line

handed and short of material.

That night all was quiet: the Turks had withdrawn from the river-end of the first line and gave no sign of the expected counter-attack, and the consolidation of our line went on unmolested. There was a certain amount of activity next morning (the 23rd), and, by the afternoon, it was plain that the Turks meant counter-attacking.

An order came for all men who could walk or ride to get back at once, and before long a crowd of limping and bandaged figures was making its way to the rear: Lajj was about ten miles distant, so they had a journey before them.

But the trenches were still full of badly wounded men who could not move themselves yet would be in the way in the coming fight: these cases were to be removed on transport carts. At last these carts arrived; the fight was getting nearer every minute, and shells were already bursting nearby, but there would still be just time to load up the carts and get them away. However, something happened: there was a sudden rattle and jingle, and before anyone knew what was up, the ponies had whipped round and the whole convoy of carts was off, wildly stampeding over the desert. The last hope of getting the wounded out was gone, and the field ambulances received urgent orders to retire. So, the wounded, with the doctor and the *padre*, remained and spent an exciting night.

At sunset, after a heavy bombardment, the enemy attacked 2000 yards to the left of "V.P." They came on in mass and were killed in mass. Twice during the night, they came on again and, though the line was forced back in sections, it held, and inflicted tremendous casualties on the attackers; towards morning the firing died down and the battle came to an end.

The enemy had been held about 300 yards from the centre, but in rear of "V.P." the Arabs had joined in, and there a collecting station was obliged to defend itself all through the night, the doctor and every available man, even men on stretchers, having to use rifles. They managed to keep the Arab away, but it was a close call.

In the counter-attacks of 23rd-24th the Turks, according to prisoners' evidence, lost the best part of another division. They had already lost one division, the 45th, with their front line, in the early part of the 22nd; they were now exhausted and fought out, and, on the morning of the 24th, the remnants were to be seen withdrawing towards Baghdad, leaving us in possession of the battlefield. It seemed that Ctesiphon was a great victory; but bought at a price.

The VIth Division had suffered about 4000 casualties in killed and wounded, and these had mainly fallen upon the infantry; the battalions had been weak before the battle and had lost 50 *per cent*, or more in the fighting. The losses in officers had been particularly heavy: most Indian regiments had only two or three British officers left, and the British regiments were little better off. Owing to the losses among the mules carrying reserve ammunition, this was short, and all further supplies had to be brought up from Lajj, ten miles away. Many wounded had yet to be collected and all had to be evacuated back to the river and put on board the ships. In view of the situation, pursuit of the retiring Turks was out of the question; and, indeed, in the light of after-events, it seems possible that this withdrawal on the part of the enemy was designed to tempt us farther up river. The ships could not advance farther owing to the accurate fire of concealed guns on the right bank.

General Townshend decided to evacuate his wounded and prisoners, to get up stores and reorganise the defence before taking further measures against the enemy.

It must have been about 9 a.m. on the 24th that the transport carts again put in an appearance and started to load up the wounded.

Now the transport cart—generally known as an "A.T." cart—is merely a framework of iron upon two iron-tyred wheels: there is not a spring in its whole make-up. It is drawn by two mules or ponies and driven by a "*drabi*"—Indian driver. The journey these carts had to make was about ten miles, in a straight line, to the river, and over rough desert, in places sun-baked plough, and everywhere intersected by dry ditches, with here and there deep *nullahs*.

The wounded were heaped into these carts, three or four in each—there was no other way—clinging on as best they could: they were all serious cases, fractured limbs, abdominal wounds, head wounds—there were no cushions or padding available. In some cases, dead bodies were used as cushions. Then the journey began. The carts bumped and clattered over the rough soil; the ponies were nervous and now and again broke into a jinking trot; the *nullahs* had to be rushed to get the carts up the farther edge. Before long, a chorus of groans went up from that convoy of carts, which changed to yells as the carts bumped and crashed into ditches; here and there men threw themselves off, unable to bear the torture any longer. The convoy lost its way and wandered over the desert, stopping constantly to pick up men who came crawling towards it—wounded whom the search parties had not found. At last, late in the afternoon, Lajj and the hospital ships were reached.

But arrangements had been made for 500 casualties; before the battle began there were already 500 sick and wounded (from the skirmish at Zeur) on board. Somehow or other the wounded had to be got away, so they were crowded on to other ships and barges, from which stores and animals had scarcely been unloaded; only the very worst cases were put on the *Mosul* and *Blosse Lynch*. Even here the arrangements were inadequate: the doctors, working superhumanly, were short-handed, food and hot drinks were scarce; there were no mattresses to lie on.

Early on the morning of the 25th, the ships, each with a barge on either side, left Lajj and started on their long trip to Basra, over 400 miles downstream. Aziziyeh was made that same afternoon, and, after a short stop there, most of the ships went on: but one of the paddles of the *Blosse Lynch* was broken and she had to lie up for some time for repairs to be made. That night it poured with rain—the first rain of the year—and the angle-awnings were little protection; the icy stream flowed over the decks and the wounded lying upon them, so that soon all were soaked through—there were no spare blankets and no means of drying the wet ones. Kut was at last reached on the evening of the 26th, and there all the wounded had to be transhipped on to "P" boats— the shallow-draught ships like the *Julnar, Blosse Lynch*, and *Mosul* being urgently needed upstream. The transhipping was a weary and painful business.

But upstream things had been happening. In the afternoon of the 25th, aeroplane reconnaissance reported large columns of enemy moving down both flanks—in particular there appeared a large body moving wide north of Ctesiphon, evidently in order to turn our right flank; enemy cavalry also soon put in an appearance in rear of our line. In view of his terribly reduced numbers and shortness of supplies General Townshend decided to abandon the position and to withdraw to the river at Lajj. This withdrawal was safely effected under cover of night, 25th-26th.

In spite of great shortage of machines and pilots (we had only started the action with six aeroplanes fit to fly, and three of these had been lost during the operations) the R.F.C. continued to carry out reconnaissances; these showed only too certainly that the enemy had been very heavily reinforced with fresh troops—probably outnumbering us four or five to one. Under these circumstances Lajj was untenable, and, on the night of 27th-28th the retreat was continued to Aziziyeh. Here a halt was called. The river, it must be remembered, is very winding in these reaches, and the ships had to cover more than twice the distance that the troops marched by land: time had to be allowed for the ships to catch up. Besides, they were in great difficulties owing to shallow water and shoals. On the 28th the *Shaitan* went aground and could not be refloated, though her guns and stores were salved during the 29th by H.M.S. *Firefly* and *Shushan*, under heavy rifle and, eventually, gun fire.

But Aziziyeh was not capable of any prolonged defence, and, after burning all stores and kit that were not removable, the march was continued. The Turks were now pressing on and, in spite of hard marching, were soon to catch up with our columns, worn out as they were with ten days' incessant marching and fighting, short of sleep, often short of water, and sniped from behind every bush by lurking Arabs, and hampered by 15,000 prisoners. On 29th November enemy cavalry had appeared and been driven back by the 6th Cavalry Brigade with heavy loss; but, on the 30th, General Townshend was obliged to halt again, owing to several ships being in difficulties. The force bivouacked at Um-el-Tubal. Early next morning it was found that the Turks were within 2000 yards; the surprise was mutual, as the enemy had marched up in the night and had evidently no idea he was so close.

As soon as it was light a furious battle began, the Turks doing all they could to get round our inland flank and pin us to the river. It looked as if they would succeed, until a successful counter-attack by the Cavalry Brigade on the right flank gave General Townshend an opportunity of breaking off the engagement. The order was given to retire by echelons of brigades from the right, and gradually each brigade edged away from the fight, the guns supporting the withdrawal with rapid fire at a range of under 3000 yards and inflicting very heavy casualties on the enemy. At last the force got clear, and, with the 17th Brigade as rear-guard, the march was continued.

But H.M.S. *Firefly* had been put out of action by a shell in her boiler and was stranded under close-range rifle fire. H.M.S. *Comet* (Captain Nunn, S.N.O.) took her in tow, but, in trying to turn, both ships ran aground. The *Firefly* floated off, but the *Comet* was wedged fast, and now the Turks brought up field guns and opened fire at a range of under 100 yards—both ships were hit over and over again and were soon on fire. But, through a perfect storm of shellfire, rifles, and machine-guns, Lieutenant Tudway brought the *Sumana* alongside and took off the crews of the two ships; their guns were put out of action and they were then abandoned.

The enemy had suffered very severely and did not come for a second helping. On the evening of 2nd December, after a 36-mile march, dead-beat and parched with thirst, the column was in sight of Kut, and the next morning the town was entered. It was a retreat which has few parallels.

But to go back to the 26th and the convoy of wounded being transhipped at Kut. The work was finished late that night; the wounded were put aboard "P" boats, barges, and tugs—anything, in fact, that was available and could not be used farther upstream—and on the morning of the 27th the ships started downstream. In five days at most it was expected Basra would be reached, and a quick journey was most urgently necessary. Most of the ships, fresh from carrying stores and transport, were in a very insanitary condition, the wounded were terribly crowded together; doctors, dressings, medicines, and food were scarce—even the very worst cases could only be dressed every two days, and, even so, the doctors and assistant surgeons worked incessantly, never seeming to rest or eat or sleep.

But our luck was out. The evening of the 27th, just before the first of the ships reached Sheikh Saad, two natives paddled out from the bank signalling frantically for it to heave to. Taken on board, they explained that a large force of Arabs, 2000 or 3000, were lying up for the convoy round the next bend. A hasty council of war decided that it was useless in the uncertain state of the channel to trust to getting past under cover of dark: the only thing was to return to Kut. So back again they went, reaching Kut on the 28th.

By the next morning more ships had been collected, and the monitor—H.M.S. *Butterfly*—was available as escort, so another start was made. But again, our luck was out. Just before the danger-zone was reached, a terrific wind sprang up and blew the monitor, which was leading the convoy, hard aground and up against the steep bank; in no time all the other ships, forced to stop, had suffered the same fate. It was just such a chance that the Arabs had been waiting for, and they took it. From 1 p.m. till evening they kept the ships under a hot fire. A small escort of *sepoys*, under General Kemball, was landed and managed to keep them at a distance; but rifle ammunition soon grew scarce, and things looked bad.

The ships were right against the bank, and all on board knew what would happen if the Arabs made a rush and got on board. Kits and valises and rolls of blankets had been piled against the port rails, but such a parapet was scarcely bullet-proof, and many on the ships and barges were wounded over again or killed. Owing to her closeness to the bank the monitor could not use her 4-inch guns. But at last, just before sunset, the wind dropped and, somehow or other, H.M.S. *Butterfly* managed to get off, and, standing out in midstream, opened fire with 4-inch shrapnel, which was effective in driving back the Arabs.

The immediate danger was over; but again, it was found impossible to pass Sheikh Saad by night, so once more the weary convoy made its way back to Kut.

A long wait then ensued—so long, that it seemed unlikely that Kut would ever be left behind; but probably it was the least serious cases that suffered most, for to the others there comes often enough a blessed torpor when nothing on this earth matters very much, and chances for or against cannot be reckoned. Already many of the worst cases had died. But at last, on 2nd December, the ships left again, and this time got through, a strong escort of half a battalion and two mountain guns ensuring their safety; though, even so, their troubles were not ended. Time and again the ships stuck on mud banks long weary hours and could not be moved; all food, except bully and biscuit, ran out on some ships, as did the supply of filtered water. Dysentery raged, but the men had to be left where they lay crowded together; there were scarcely any sweepers. The situation rapidly became too horrible for description.

Amara, after a night hard aground, was reached on the 4th December. Here it was intended to evacuate all the worst cases; but hospital accommodation was found to be hopelessly inadequate, so that only those requiring an immediate operation could be put ashore. The remainder continued the voyage more hopefully now as, on these reaches, there was less danger of running aground. However, on 6th December, just above Kurna, the engines of the leading ship broke down, and a long wait ensued before the rest could pass. The ship itself had to wait for repairs, and could then only proceed at half speed, so that Basra was yet a day's journey distant.

At last that awful pilgrimage came to an end, and Basra was reached the next evening. By midnight the hospital ship *Varela* was loaded up with the worst cases, while the others were sent to the Basra hospitals. It must be owned that, considering the utter lack of preparation, the heavy casualties, shortness of personnel and material, together with the difficulties and disorganisation of an unforeseen retreat, it was wonderful that the wounded (and prisoners) were ever got away down the river. How far that lack of preparation and the consequent appalling

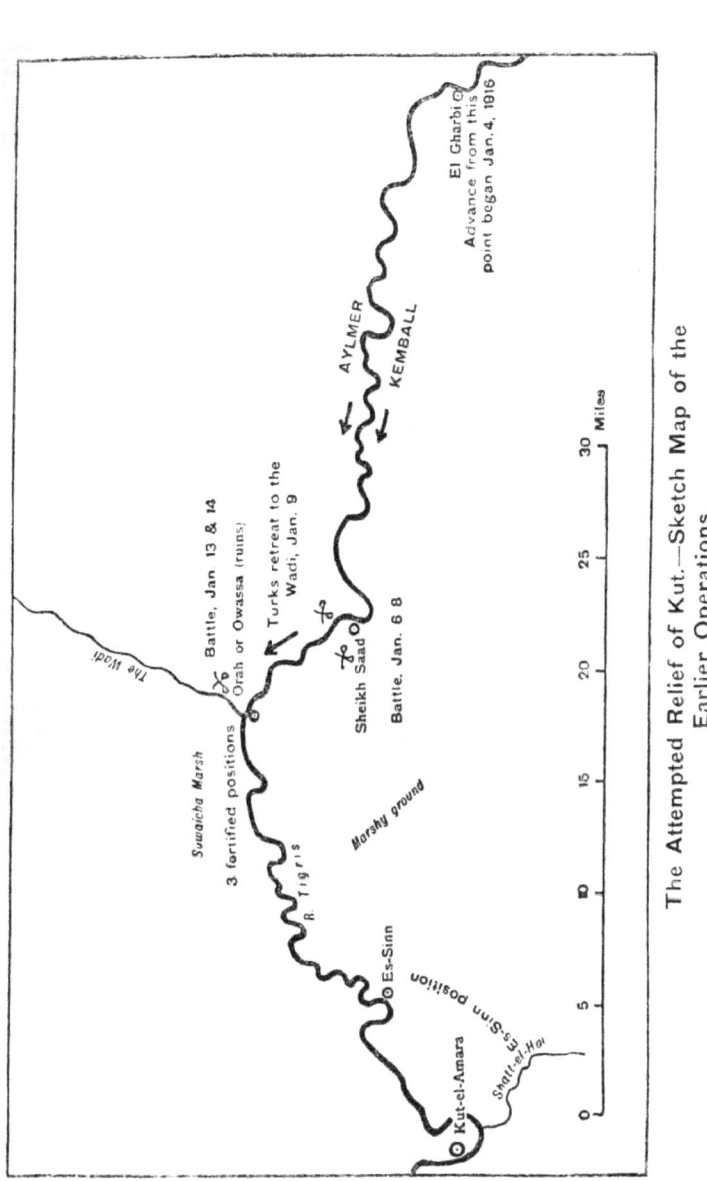

The Attempted Relief of Kut.—Sketch Map of the Earlier Operations.

waste of life and suffering were necessary or unavoidable has been discussed elsewhere, and a commission has pronounced its verdict.

There can be little disgrace attached to a genuine blunder: however gross, it must be forgiven—in time. But it is remarkable that the state of these wounded was well known to all responsible in Basra. While the ships were still in midstream, before they came alongside, a sickening smell tainted the air; before the wounded disembarked they were seen lying in filth of every kind, crowded and huddled together upon the iron decks. In hospital, and on board the hospital ship, their wounds were found to be in the most advanced stages of septic poisoning; in several cases men with comparatively slight wounds were dying from huge bed-sores.

That was their state, and it was obvious to any bystander. And yet the report was cabled to India:

> General condition of wounded very satisfactory. Medical arrangements, under circumstances of considerable difficulty, worked splendidly.

For whoever was responsible for that deliberate lie there can be no forgiveness.

The wounded arrived at Basra on 7th December, sixteen days since the Battle of Ctesiphon. On the same day the Turkish forces closed round Kut, and the remainder of the VIth Division was besieged.

So, the first year in Mesopotamia was finished. The splendid story of that five months' defence has been written elsewhere, a great chronicle of grit and pluck and sufferings patiently borne that will long remain famous. In spite of every effort by the relieving force the siege could not be raised, and General Townshend and his force were obliged to surrender on 29th April 1916.

The majority were taken, or more properly driven, by forced marches up the Tigris and into the interior of Asia Minor, where those who survived the march were distributed among prison camps.

What the conditions of that march were, what their treatment was in the camps, can best be told in figures. Out of the 12,000 British and Indian soldiers and followers taken at the fall of Kut over 70 *per cent*, had died in captivity before the armistice with Turkey was signed.

Few of the original force now remain. Once more history will show that it needed a disaster to fully awaken Great Britain and induce her rulers to be strong. But if it is this disaster that brought a great army into Mesopotamia to drive the Turk northward, to reclaim a wilderness, and to rebuild a great civilization after many years of anarchy and desolation; if here a new country and a new people are to be made by Great Britain and to remain—then disaster and sacrifice were perhaps not in vain.

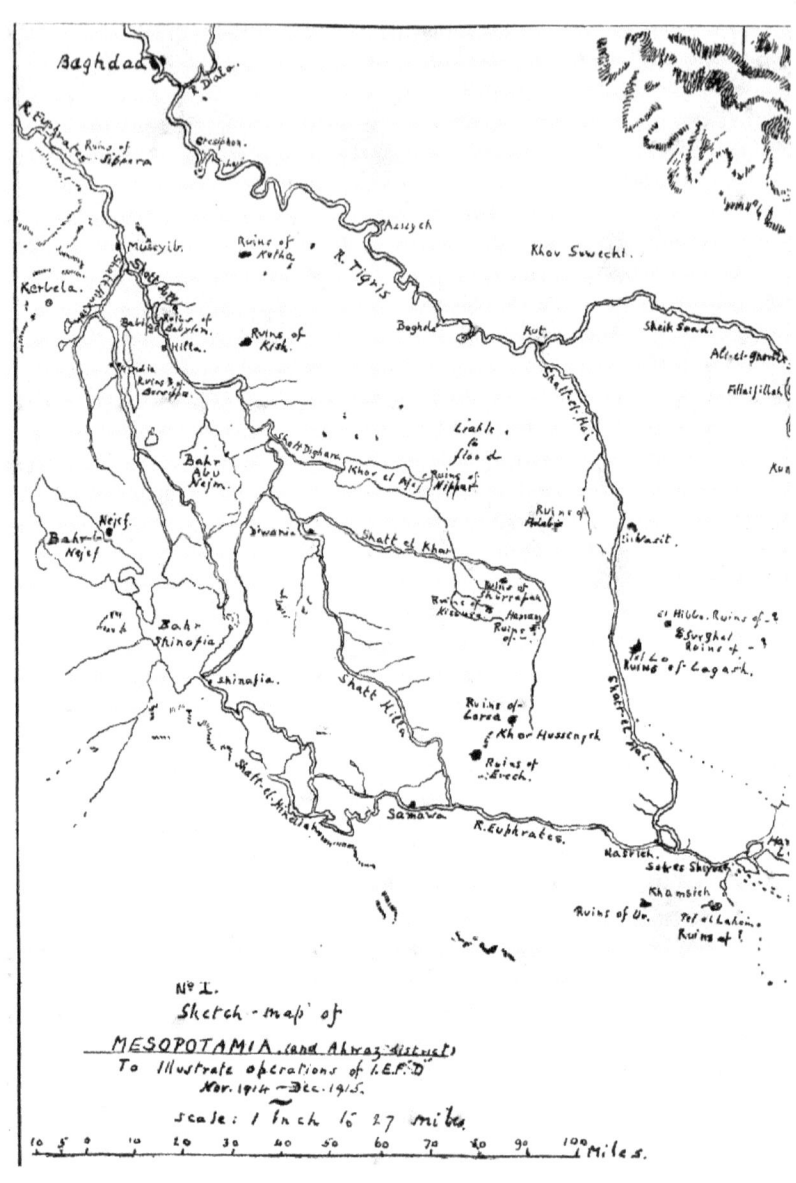

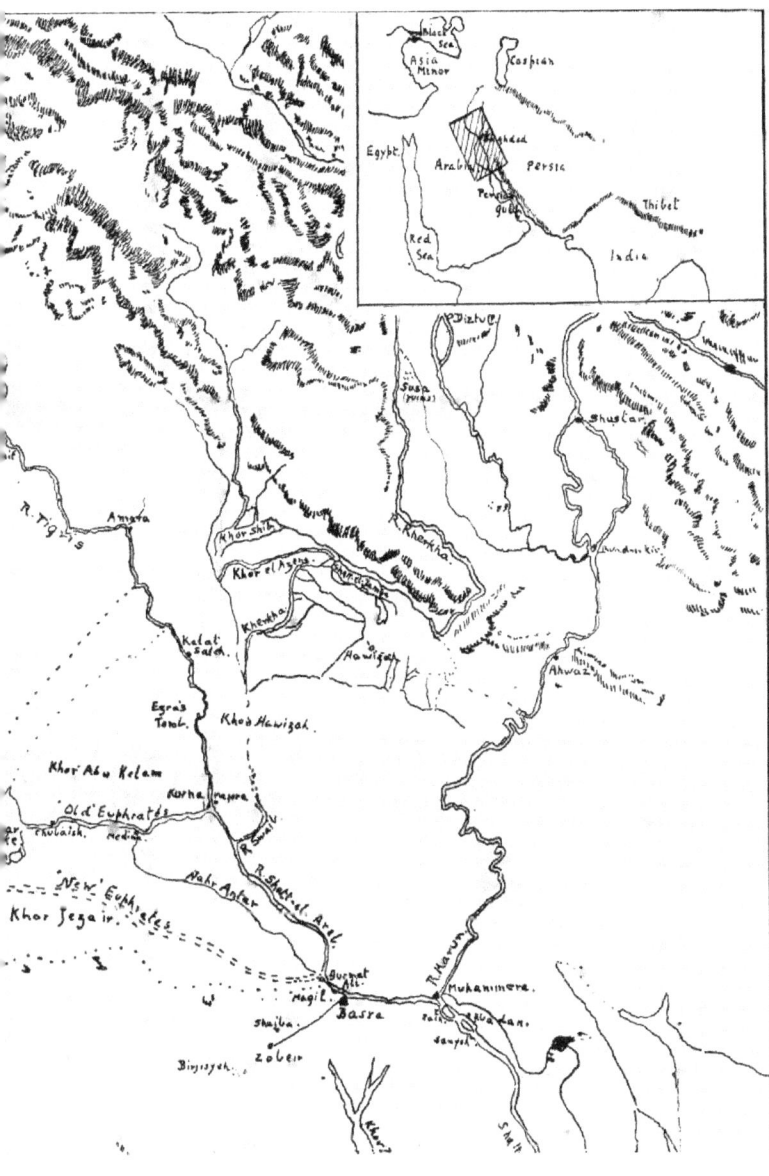

MESOPOTAMIA

MESOPOTAMIA

I.E.F. "D."

November 1914.

VIth DIVISION.

LIEUT.-GENERAL SIR A. A. BARRETT, K.C.I.E.

16th (Poona) Brigade.
Brigadier-General DELAMAIN, C.B.

2nd Dorset Regiment.	104th Rifles.
20th Punjabis.	117th Mahrattas.

17th (Ahmednagar) Brigade.
Brigadier-General DOBBIE, C.B.

1/ Oxf. & Bucks Lt. Infty.
22nd Punjabis.
103rd Mahratta Light Infantry.
119th Infantry.

18th (Belgaum) Brigade.
Major-General C. I. FRY, C.B.

2nd Norfolk Regiment.	110th Mahrattas.
7th Rajputs.	120th Infantry.

Divisional Troops.

10th Brigade R.F.A. [63rd, 76th, 82nd Batteries and VIth Divisional Ammunition Column].
1st Mountain Artillery Brigade [23rd and 30th Mountain Batteries].
33rd Q.V.O. Cavalry.
48th Pioneers.
17th and 22nd Companies, Sappers and Miners.
Sirmoor Imperial Service Sappers.
34th Divisional Signal Company.
Wireless Section Royal Engineers.
Searchlight Section (Calcutta Port Defence Volunteers).
Transport and Medical Units.

I.E.F. "D."

April 1915.

General Sir JOHN NIXON, K.C.B

VIth DIVISION.	XIIth DIVISION.
Maj.-Gen. C. TOWNSEND, C.B.	Maj.-Gen. G. GORRINGE, C.B.
16th Bde.—Brig.-Gen. Delamain, C.B.	12th Bde.—Maj.-Gen. Davison.
17th Bde.—Brig.-Gen. Dobbie, C.B.	30th Bde.—Maj.-Gen. Melliss, V.C.
18th Bde.—Maj.-Gen. Fry, C.B.	33rd Bde.—Brig.-Gen. Lean.
34th Divisional Signal Coy.	12th Divisional Signal Coy.

Army Troops.

6th Cavalry Brigade*—Brigadier-General H. Kennedy.

    7th Hariana Lancers.   23rd Cavalry.
    16th Cavalry.   (33rd Cavalry.)
    "S" Battery R.H.A.

* All regiments much under strength.

Xth Brigade R.F.A.

63rd, 76th, and 82nd Batteries R.F.A.; 6th Divisional Ammunition Column.

1st Mountain Artillery Brigade.

23rd and 30th Mountain Batteries.

1st Heavy Artillery Brigade.

86th Battery R.G.A.
104th Battery R.G.A.
1/4 Hants Howitzer Battery R.F.A. (T.).

Rangoon Port Defence Volunteer Battery.

Maxim Battery (machine guns mounted on transport carts).
48th Pioneers.
12th, 17th, and 22nd Companies Sappers and Miners.
Sirmoor Imperial Service Sappers.
Wireless Section Royal Engineers.
Searchlight Section.

Transport and Medical Units.

Lionel Muirhead's Letter to Henry Birch Reynardson
&
Book Reviews at Time of Original Publication

Haseley Court Wallingford
Jan: 11: 1920

My dear Henry,
As today there is out of doors every appearance of a repitition of Noah's flood, ere the deluge becomes univer-sal I sit by the fire to tell you how heartily I have enjoyed reading your graphic account of Mesopotamia 1914-15. Twice have I read it through with thorough enjoyment from co-ver to cover my only regret being that you could not have been present at the capture of Baghdad itself which would have been a fitting crown on all your exertions instead of the painful & depressing miseries which Fate ordained. I was specially interest-

-ed by the peep you give of the Marsh Arabs & their extraordinary existence in a state of perpetual amphibious warfare 'pour passer le temps' & largely for the fun of the thing as I suppose their ancestors from far back in the stone age have always done. The discomforts of your expedition must have been at times almost intolerable & the pluck & determination of the troops in the midst of floods & heat & sandstorms & the deceptions of the mirage was most marvellous: the delight of killing the Turk I suppose wd aid largely to discount such trials day after day, but still recollecting how unendurable was the Sun's heat du-

-ring June July & August which I passed at Orfa in semi-luxury I marvel at the endurance of the officers & men both on land & river. — I spent these 3 months largely under a deep old arch with a cruise of water, a narghile & a Gibbon & recall the fascination of his account of the taking of Ctesiphon by Omar (Cap. LI) & the destruction of the magnificent carpet of the throne room &c., thankful that I could, in peace & shade, be a spectator of the centuries of turmoil, whilst you spent these months in the making of history, a very different matter, & with no prospect of loot from the palace of Khosru to hearten you! I salute you accordingly.

Clearly can I recall the disgust that the perpetual blue sky inspired, but the early mornings & sunsets were glorious & the splendour of the stars at night. Who can describe adequately — though you have done uncommonly well in some passages which brought the enchantment of the vision all back to me in a moment; with the feeling too that one almost must bow down in worship of the Sun, the Moon & the host of heaven for their power & loveliness. The fate of the old "Comet" touched me nearly, but she did her duty nobly, & I suppose that the fate of a vessel so named ought quite properly to end in a blaze.

I cannot attempt to touch on all the things in your book which interested & delighted me — how fortunate that you have come home to chronicle them — but must content myself by thanking you for a most interesting volume, & also for transporting me in spirit, by the magic of the pen, to happy days spent 50 years ago.

Yours most sincerely

Lionel Muirhead.

Mesopotamia, 1914-1915.
By HENRY BIRCH REYNARDSON.
(Captain, 1st Oxford and Bucks Light Infantry).

Demy 8*vo.* *Price* **9s.** *net.*

This is not a story of the complete Mesopotamia campaign, but only of the first phase. Captain Reynardson was a subaltern in India when the war broke out, and this record of the early days when in India the Army went about its usual routine of military duties in a feverish state of anticipation, has a freshness and interest even yet. The first year's campaign is the story of one who went through it and saw everything with the keen eye of a soldier; but while the book is invaluable as a record of a portion of the campaign, it is above all highly distinguished by its vivid pictures of that wonderfully picturesque country. In fact, by these pen pictures alone, the book has a claim to be denominated literature. The style is sensitive and quick, and the impression left after a perusal of the volume is of having been in the company of an exceptionally intelligent and interesting guide.

Mesopotamia, 1914-1915. By Captain H. Birch Reynardson. (Melrose. 9s. net.)—The author served in the 17th (Ahmednagar) Brigade of the Sixth (Poona) Division, which opened the Tigris campaign in November, 1914. He recounts the operations up to the battle of Ctesiphon, partly from personal experience and partly from the accounts of fellow-officers. The details are interesting, and some of the rough sketch-maps of actions and the photographs are useful. In describing the important action at Birjisiyeh, April 12th-14th, 1915, in which a large Turkish force advancing to recapture Basra was beaten and dispersed, the author repeats the rumour that, after the British attack had been checked for hours, the order for retreat was given. "Whether or not the order was given, it never reached the Dorsets, for, just as things were looking at their worst, the regiment, led by Major Utterson, jumped up and assaulted the Turkish position." The other troops did the same, and the Turks fled in great disorder. It was a good instance of the old maxim, dear to Marshal Foch, that a battle is never lost till it is won.

LIBRARY

IN MESOPOTAMIA.

THE STORY of our campaign in this quarter of the globe will for a very long time to come have a romantic attraction for readers of war literature, for our men, of course, fought upon classic ground, and in addition, there was enough romance, which included both tragedy and comedy, to invest the whole campaign with an atmosphere of adventure that makes an excellent story to read, though those who took part in it may have another point of view to regard it from. Capt. H. Birch Reynardson, of the 1st Oxfordshire and Buckinghamshire Light Infantry, in his book entitled *Mesopotamia*, 1914-15 (A. Melrose; price, 9s. net), deals with the early part of the campaign, up to and including the battle of Ctesiphon, his regiment reaching the Persian Gulf in November, 1914, after Basra had been occupied, though he gives a *précis* of the early fighting which gave us the command of that place. The author evidently comes of a sporting family (indeed, the name of Birch Reynardson will be remembered by coaching men as the author of a very readable book), for in the intervals, when there was nothing to do but to await the good pleasure of the enemy, he filled up his spare time with shooting and fishing, and these parts of his book will have an undoubted interest for *Field* readers. The brave old 43rd, however, as everybody knows, is a regiment with a splendid military record, and the 1st Battalion added to its laurels in this much criticised campaign, the difficulties it had to contend against being vividly brought out in this well-written account. The author, in addition, was a man fortunately endowed with a sense of humour, which no doubt enabled him to bear philosophically with all kinds of misfortunes, and when the floods started, there is little doubt that great calls were made on everyone's powers of endurance. Capt. Birch Reynardson, moreover, was a keen observer, and we get many excellent word-pictures of the country and its inhabitants, and both were undoubtedly worth studying if only in the cause of self-preservation. The actual fighting is also well described, and the chapters which deal with our aquatic adventures are very readable indeed. Though he has no criticism to level at the arrangements made by his superiors the author here and there throws a little light on the glaring neglect which characterised the Indian Government during so many months of that at first ill-fated campaign, and in one instance there is a grim humour in the story. Every regiment had been promised four machine-guns instead of two, as it was known that the Turks were well supplied with this useful weapon, so extra gun teams had been carefully trained, and extra mules drawn by the 43rd, and by-and-by the long-delayed guns arrived. The rest may be related in the author's own words: "One look was enough—the much-advertised machine-guns were strange and uncouth monsters, mounted on pram wheels, and looking more like mangles than anything else; they told us that you fed them through a hopper—gently—and that they had been quite the thing in the early eighties! We shed tears and left them. Later, after a long search and many inquiries through the force, one man was at last discovered who knew how to work them. He was an old white-haired Sepoy—a reservist—who remembered in his youth how they had instructed him in the ways of such guns. So he and a few old friends and the strange weapons were told off for duty on the 'L. of C.'—and that was the result of asking India for more machine-guns." Of course, much of the ground covered by the author has been already written about, though to many readers the earlier stages of the fighting here described will not be too well known; but no one will fail to succumb to the pleasant, captivating manner in which the author tells his story, for he does it in such a natural way that it is easy to imagine the scenes described, and no higher compliment can be paid a writer. It should be added that there are numerous capital photographs of scenery, several diagrams, and a map of the district fought over.

NEAR EAST BOOKSHELF.

MESOPOTAMIA, 19.4.1915.*

Captain Birch-Reynardson tells the story of the Mesopotamia campaign from December, 1914, to December, 1915, with a brief account of the events of the month before the arrival of his regiment. Thus the book forms a self-contained narrative of a definite period of the campaign, during which we had firmly established ourselves at Busreh and its hinterland, had conceived the fatal plan of advancing with totally inadequate forces on Baghdad, and had suffered the horrors of the retreat following on the Pyrrhic victory of Ctesiphon. The story is told strictly from the point of view of the regimental officer. We seldom hear of the Staff and never of higher powers. This concentration on one point of view gives the book a very special value, which is still further enhanced by the entire exclusion of any personal matter concerning the writer from beginning to end. Indeed, Sherlock Holmes himself could hardly guess from the book that the author had been very badly wounded at Ctesiphon, had endured all the agonies of lying on that field and the subsequent ghastly transport to the sea, or that he had prepared this book during a gradual and painful convalescence. Seldom has it been our good fortune to read a war book so thoroughly selfless and so thoroughly imbued with the fine spirit which was the proud tradition of our Army before the war, and which we all hope to see continued in its successor.

It would not be fair to say that the book could not have been a better one. The arrangement is at times somewhat confusing—due, no doubt, to want of practice with the pen. The sketch maps are not so helpful as they should be, mainly because of the minute and indistinct lettering of place names. But, having said this much by way of criticism, we have nothing but praise for the book. Not only does it give a most vivid impression of the surroundings and appalling conditions in which our troops managed to live, and even to get some enjoyment; but it brings the actual fighting clearly before us. The mud, "the rich, adhesive article that must be slept in to be really appreciated," the "trench-warfare among marshes in a temperature of 120 degrees—the trenches crowded and full of dysentery cases," the hopelessly inadequate transport, and generally the innumerable miseries endured by the force without any of the mitigations, which were then so strangely neglected but were not denied to their more fortunate successors, are all presented with startling vividness and a good deal of grim humour. But the author never dwells morbidly on the painful side, preferring to give some of his space to the valiant efforts at sport, and to telling us of the marvellously beautiful effects of light on the dreary landscape of the Garden of Eden in the short intervals between day and night.

He brings out well the real meaning of the decision to advance on Baghdad; a decision which involved the abandonment of a policy of defence for one of offence; and one wishes that those who took this step so lightly and with such terrible consequences had had some of the clarity of thought displayed by this plain regimental officer.

His account of the battle of Ctesiphon, and of the sufferings of the wounded after it, is written with studious avoidance of sensationalism or personal feeling. But his plain, straightforward account produces a sense of tragedy and anger that more skilful and detailed narratives have not surpassed.

We shall leave this fascinating book with one quotation:—"After the war we must look forward to a British Mesopotamia—must, because for three years we have shown the people what it is to live under honest administration, and taught them to rely on justice, and have begun to make the desert blossom as the rose; and to surrender the people and the country again into the hands from which we rescued them would be an act of national cowardice, a deliberate and cynical refusal to fulfil our obligations."

C. S.-W.

ALSO FROM LEONAUR
AVAILABLE IN SOFTCOVER OR HARDCOVER WITH DUST JACKET

THE FALL OF THE MOGHUL EMPIRE OF HINDUSTAN by H. G. Keene—By the beginning of the nineteenth century, as British and Indian armies under Lake and Wellesley dominated the scene, a little over half a century of conflict brought the Moghul Empire to its knees.

LADY SALE'S AFGHANISTAN by Florentia Sale—An Indomitable Victorian Lady's Account of the Retreat from Kabul During the First Afghan War.

THE CAMPAIGN OF MAGENTA AND SOLFERINO 1859 by Harold Carmichael Wylly—The Decisive Conflict for the Unification of Italy.

FRENCH'S CAVALRY CAMPAIGN by J. G. Maydon—A Special Correspondent's View of British Army Mounted Troops During the Boer War.

CAVALRY AT WATERLOO by Sir Evelyn Wood—British Mounted Troops During the Campaign of 1815.

THE SUBALTERN by George Robert Gleig—The Experiences of an Officer of the 85th Light Infantry During the Peninsular War.

NAPOLEON AT BAY, 1814 by F. Loraine Petre—The Campaigns to the Fall of the First Empire.

NAPOLEON AND THE CAMPAIGN OF 1806 by Colonel Vachée—The Napoleonic Method of Organisation and Command to the Battles of Jena & Auerstädt.

THE COMPLETE ADVENTURES IN THE CONNAUGHT RANGERS by William Grattan—The 88th Regiment during the Napoleonic Wars by a Serving Officer.

BUGLER AND OFFICER OF THE RIFLES by William Green & Harry Smith—With the 95th (Rifles) during the Peninsular & Waterloo Campaigns of the Napoleonic Wars.

NAPOLEONIC WAR STORIES by Sir Arthur Quiller-Couch—Tales of soldiers, spies, battles & sieges from the Peninsular & Waterloo campaingns.

CAPTAIN OF THE 95TH (RIFLES) by Jonathan Leach—An officer of Wellington's sharpshooters during the Peninsular, South of France and Waterloo campaigns of the Napoleonic wars.

RIFLEMAN COSTELLO by Edward Costello—The adventures of a soldier of the 95th (Rifles) in the Peninsular & Waterloo Campaigns of the Napoleonic wars.

AVAILABLE ONLINE AT www.leonaur.com
AND FROM ALL GOOD BOOK STORES

ALSO FROM LEONAUR
AVAILABLE IN SOFTCOVER OR HARDCOVER WITH DUST JACKET

WINGED WARFARE *by William A. Bishop*—The Experiences of a Canadian 'Ace' of the R.F.C. During the First World War.

THE STORY OF THE LAFAYETTE ESCADRILLE *by George Thenault*—A famous fighter squadron in the First World War by its commander..

R.F.C.H.Q. *by Maurice Baring*—The command & organisation of the British Air Force during the First World War in Europe.

SIXTY SQUADRON R.A.F. *by A. J. L. Scott*—On the Western Front During the First World War.

THE STRUGGLE IN THE AIR *by Charles C. Turner*—The Air War Over Europe During the First World War.

WITH THE FLYING SQUADRON *by H. Rosher*—Letters of a Pilot of the Royal Naval Air Service During the First World War.

OVER THE WEST FRONT *by "Spin" & "Contact"* —Two Accounts of British Pilots During the First World War in Europe, Short Flights With the Cloud Cavalry by "Spin" and Cavalry of the Clouds by "Contact".

SKYFIGHTERS OF FRANCE *by Henry Farré*—An account of the French War in the Air during the First World War.

THE HIGH ACES *by Laurence la Tourette Driggs*—French, American, British, Italian & Belgian pilots of the First World War 1914-18.

PLANE TALES OF THE SKIES *by Wilfred Theodore Blake*—The experiences of pilots over the Western Front during the Great War.

IN THE CLOUDS ABOVE BAGHDAD *by J. E. Tennant*—Recollections of the R. F. C. in Mesopotamia during the First World War against the Turks.

THE SPIDER WEB *by P. I. X. (Theodore Douglas Hallam)*—Royal Navy Air Service Flying Boat Operations During the First World War by a Flight Commander

EAGLES OVER THE TRENCHES *by James R. McConnell & William B. Perry*—Two First Hand Accounts of the American Escadrille at War in the Air During World War 1-Flying For France: With the American Escadrille at Verdun and Our Pilots in the Air

KNIGHTS OF THE AIR *by Bennett A. Molter*—An American Pilot's View of the Aerial War of the French Squadrons During the First World War.

AVAILABLE ONLINE AT **www.leonaur.com**
AND FROM ALL GOOD BOOK STORES

ALSO FROM LEONAUR
AVAILABLE IN SOFTCOVER OR HARDCOVER WITH DUST JACKET

OFFICERS & GENTLEMEN *by Peter Hawker & William Graham*—Two Accounts of British Officers During the Peninsula War: Officer of Light Dragoons by Peter Hawker & Campaign in Portugal and Spain by William Graham .

THE WALCHEREN EXPEDITION *by Anonymous*—The Experiences of a British Officer of the 81st Regt. During the Campaign in the Low Countries of 1809.

LADIES OF WATERLOO *by Charlotte A. Eaton, Magdalene de Lancey & Juana Smith*—The Experiences of Three Women During the Campaign of 1815: Waterloo Days by Charlotte A. Eaton, A Week at Waterloo by Magdalene de Lancey & Juana's Story by Juana Smith.

JOURNAL OF AN OFFICER IN THE KING'S GERMAN LEGION *by John Frederick Hering*—Recollections of Campaigning During the Napoleonic Wars.

JOURNAL OF AN ARMY SURGEON IN THE PENINSULAR WAR *by Charles Boutflower*—The Recollections of a British Army Medical Man on Campaign During the Napoleonic Wars.

ON CAMPAIGN WITH MOORE AND WELLINGTON *by Anthony Hamilton*—The Experiences of a Soldier of the 43rd Regiment During the Peninsular War.

THE ROAD TO AUSTERLITZ *by R. G. Burton*—Napoleon's Campaign of 1805.

SOLDIERS OF NAPOLEON *by A. J. Doisy De Villargennes & Arthur Chuquet*—The Experiences of the Men of the French First Empire: Under the Eagles by A. J. Doisy De Villargennes & Voices of 1812 by Arthur Chuquet .

INVASION OF FRANCE, 1814 *by F. W. O. Maycock*—The Final Battles of the Napoleonic First Empire.

LEIPZIG—A CONFLICT OF TITANS *by Frederic Shoberl*—A Personal Experience of the 'Battle of the Nations' During the Napoleonic Wars, October 14th-19th, 1813.

SLASHERS *by Charles Cadell*—The Campaigns of the 28th Regiment of Foot During the Napoleonic Wars by a Serving Officer.

BATTLE IMPERIAL *by Charles William Vane*—The Campaigns in Germany & France for the Defeat of Napoleon 1813-1814.

SWIFT & BOLD *by Gibbes Rigaud*—The 60th Rifles During the Peninsula War.

AVAILABLE ONLINE AT **www.leonaur.com**
AND FROM ALL GOOD BOOK STORES

www.ingramcontent.com/pod-product-compliance
Lightning Source LLC
Chambersburg PA
CBHW031620160426
43196CB00006B/213